Urban Nongrowth

Earl Finkler
William J. Toner
Frank J. Popper

The Praeger Special Studies program—utilizing the most modern and efficient book production techniques and a selective worldwide distribution network—makes available to the academic, government, and business communities significant, timely research in U.S. and international economic, social, and political development.

Urban Nongrowth
City Planning
for People

PRAEGER SPECIAL STUDIES IN U.S. ECONOMIC, SOCIAL, AND POLITICAL ISSUES

Praeger Publishers   New York   Washington   London

Library of Congress Cataloging in Publication Data

Finkler, Earl.
  Urban nongrowth.

  (Praeger special studies in U.S. economic, social,
and political issues)
  Bibliography: p.
  Includes index.
  1. Cities and towns—Planning—United States.
I. Toner, William J., joint author. II. Popper,
Frank, joint author. III. Title.
HT167.F57   309.2'62'0973   75-23962
ISBN 0-275-02230-7

PRAEGER PUBLISHERS
200 Park Avenue, New York, N.Y. 10017, U.S.A.

Published in the United States of America in 1976
by Praeger Publishers, Inc.

789   038   98765432

To Bonnie Finkler, Leslie Toner, and Deborah Popper: our wives.

ACKNOWLEDGMENTS

This book is a joint product, completed in December 1975. Each of us participated in developing its ideas and reworking its drafts. Nonetheless, each of us also had primary responsibility for writing particular chapters: Earl Finkler for Chapters 1, 2, and 3; William J. Toner for Chapters 4, 5, and 8; and Frank J. Popper for Chapters 6 and 7. We are equally responsible for the book's facts, opinions, and conclusions, so the blame for errors can be shared, as well.

We would like to thank Frank S. Bangs, who wrote the legal portion of Chapter 2, and Susan Graves and Evelyn Varela, who typed the manuscript. We are also grateful to Pantheon Books, a division of Random House, Inc., for permission to reprint sections of Studs Terkel, Working: People Talk About What They Do All Day and How They Feel About What They Do © 1972, 1974 by Studs Terkel.

The magnitude of our intellectual and editorial debt to our wives is indicated, very inadequately, in the dedication.

CONTENTS

THE NONGROWTH MOVEMENT:
PERSISTENT PEOPLE, SPECIAL
PLACES, AND NEW MOODS

More and more Americans no longer view rapid or boundless growth as either desirable or inevitable. Heedless growth—in terms of population, geographic size, commercial or industrial development, or government bureaucracy—is increasingly coming to be viewed as a public problem.

This book will describe and analyze the nongrowth movement that has appeared in recent years, primarily at the local level but, also, in some regions and a few states, such as Hawaii and Alaska. Our use of the term "nongrowth" to describe the movement is not meant to imply that communities want to stop any and all future growth. It is meant, rather, that the rate, amount, location, and type of future growth have become items of open and legitimate public concern. Growth has become a variable, one that can be influenced by public policy in pursuit of a better quality of life. A number of managed or controlled growth options are being considered, including, in some cases, the temporary or permanent stopping of growth.[1]

The nongrowth movement has developed spontaneously in a wide variety of communities and geographic areas in the United States, mostly within the last five years. Communities pursuing nongrowth strategies can serve as laboratories, sites of experimentation and innovation, for other communities and higher levels of government facing larger, broader problems. While many of the most visible nongrowth efforts have been undertaken at the local level by citizens concerned with the direction which growth is taking in their home areas, the lessons from the movement have already started to filter up through the system. As nongrowth economist Herman Daly has observed, "Arguments for 'not doing it here' often lead to the recognition of reasons for 'not doing it at all.'"[2]

There is also a nongrowth movement at the world level, although it exists almost entirely in theory. We acknowledge that movement as necessary, vital, and educational. A number of people who read The

Limits to Growth world model report[3] in the early 1970s took the antigrowth message to heart and started to challenge various developments in their home communities. Thus, the various movements do have some links, but this book will focus on the local community level. The local level, presently the setting for the most action, is probably the least represented in overall monitoring, research, and analysis.

As the authors reviewed the local nongrowth movement in 1975, it was obvious that more and more people were getting involved in the action and that some breakthroughs had been made, especially in places like Ramapo, New York, and Petaluma, California. Voters were also being heard as they elected nongrowth or managed-growth candidates or ones who opposed expansion of public bureaucracies.

However, the local nongrowth movement and similar movements seem to be spawning heavy criticism and opposition on two basic fronts. One front is social equity (defined in this book as the redistribution of resources, such as housing, jobs, and public services). Those who restrict growth in their home community or elsewhere, the argument goes, will severely restrict opportunities for those who have less income or who live in poorer environments. The second front is economics. Local nongrowth and other nongrowth movements, it is contended, will cause massive unemployment and economic chaos.

These are serious charges, and they deserve attention. If the nongrowth movement does not develop answers and responses in these areas, it will never become part of the mainstream. It was first thought that these charges should be sorted into neat subheads, with answers provided for each of them. For example, an entire string of defenses could be assembled on the premise that rapid growth in the past has not, by itself, guaranteed social equity. On the economic front, continued population growth, community sprawl, and high consumption rates do not seem to result in automatic economic prosperity. However, it was felt that it would be more productive to delve into the local nongrowth experiences and the citizen attitudes underlying those experiences for answers to the social and economic criticisms.

COMMUNITY ACTIONS

While precise numbers of growth-challenging communities are difficult to assemble, it appears that the movement, itself, is a growing one. For example, in 1973, the Urban Land Institute assembled a list of 39 cities, counties, and townships that had enacted some kind of growth constraints. Another seven were listed as possibilities.[4]

A survey by the International City Management Association indicated in early 1974 that 258 cities had enacted some form of growth control. This was 23 percent of the 1,115 cities surveyed. Of the 258 growth-limitation cities, 170 were suburbs, 51 were independent cities, and 37 were central cities.[5]

In June 1975, another list was compiled as part of a research project funded by the National Science Foundation.[6] This list contained 138 cities, counties, and towns described as "growth control localities," with another 300 to 400 being considered. This active list included large communities, such as Los Angeles, Denver, Miami, Honolulu, and Minneapolis, as well as smaller communities, such as Belle Terre, New York; Eugene, Oregon; Gillette, Wyoming; and St. George, Vermont. It included communities in 29 states, although California clearly led in the number of communities, with a total of 36. Only a few of the communities listed had any kind of explicit or proposed population quotas or limits, such as Boca Raton, Florida; Petaluma and Santa Barbara, California; and Carson City, Nevada. Almost all were either implementing or considering much stiffer controls on land use and development, including urban limit lines, phased development, downzoning to lower densities, and interim moratoriums against all or some new development.

Neither a major comprehensive national overview survey of the movement nor detailed field research over time in a great number of individual communities have been undertaken. Probably, any number of communities and areas are challenging growth in some way, but they remain largely unknown. The whole thrust toward local identity and the danger of nationally financed legal challenges by builders and others sometimes inhibit a community from reporting its nongrowth strategies. The cool reception that nongrowth has received from most of the established professions—planning, law, architecture, economics, management, and so on—also tends to minimize detailed objective communication of developments through professional and municipal publications.

The mass media have been slow to discover more than the tip of the iceberg of the nongrowth movement. Coverage is spreading—from the New York Times out to the Associated Press and even the Reader's Digest—but each new media discovery is made at the same superficial level. Major court cases, such as Petaluma and Ramapo, get some exposure, especially if they occur on familiar media turf, such as California and New York. Major dramatic events, such as Colorado's rejection of the 1976 Winter Olympics, are reported, along with the election of antigrowth or controlled-growth politicians, such as Governor Richard Lamm of Colorado and Mayor Pete Wilson of San Diego. But the most prevalent media responses to nongrowth have been the quickie overview kind of article or the television news report. Typical headlines read: "To Grow or Not to Grow," "Growth Battle

Lines Up," "Don't Build Here," "New Battle in Suburbia," and "Grow
Slow." Few reporters are assigned (or have the training) to prepare
deeper reports on citizen attitudes underlying local nongrowth movements, how various growth-retarding strategies work in practice, the
real issues and feelings in the nongrowth-social equity debate, and the
almost total lack of comprehension of the movement on the part of the
courts.

Most of the national media coverage is prepared with a minimum
of field work, except where a reporter needs to personalize the issue,
for example, something like "family of construction worker starving
in Petaluma because of growth restriction." Sometimes a television
crew will fly over a nongrowth community in a helicopter to gain the
necessary visuals for their account.

Surprisingly, the professional studies of nongrowth have not done
much better in terms of field work. One major study of urban growth
management systems, funded by the National Science Foundation in
1973, provided extensive review and comment on systems in Boulder,
Ramapo, and elsewhere, but it was based on extensive literature
searches and very limited detailed field research.[7] One of the primary
researchers admitted that the report "would have been significantly
strengthened if we had the resources to do more [field research]."[8]

Despite the lack of exposure, analysis, and communication within
the nongrowth movement and between the movement and the rest of the
world, there does appear to be a general concentration of nongrowth
efforts near the East and West coasts, generally throughout the West,
in university towns, and in areas with a distinct and/or fragile environment. But often, there is a more common denominator—communities
and areas become interested in nongrowth strategies when experienc-
ing rapid population or economic growth, substantial increases in
construction, quantum jumps in the size of the local government, and
the anticipation of dramatic change that it is felt will result from all
such growth.

HIGH- AND LOW-GROWTH AREAS: THE TRENDS
AND PROBLEMS OF MIGRATION

Since nongrowth activities often originate in response to rapid
growth, it will be helpful to briefly note some of the present trends
and prospects for such growth across the nation. First, in the nation
as a whole, the population in January 1976 was about 215 million. Census Bureau projections for the year 2000 range from 251 million
(series F) to 300 million (series C). The series F projection is based
on an average of 1.8 births per woman, while the series C projections
are based on 2.8 births per woman. The figure on "expected" births

per woman in 1973 was about 2.1 children in the younger groupings, much closer to the series F level. The general trend has been toward lower expectations. Thus, the overall rate of growth, at least from net natural increase, might be a lot less than it has been in the past. In the fairly short period of 1950-70, the United States grew by over 51 million, more than it will grow in 30 years under the series F projections.

However, there will still be millions of new people to contend with, as well as many interstate migrants. Americans are a very mobile people. According to one study, a U.S. resident can expect 13 to 14 years with moves during the course of a lifetime. In England and Wales, the number of years with moves drops to eight, while in Japan it is just under five.[9]

Where are these ultramobile people in the United States coming from? Where are they going? The North and the East generally appear to be losing people to the South and the West. During the 1960s, California surpassed New York as the nation's largest state. Arizona and Florida were the fastest-growing states between 1970-75. But the big demographic news seems to be the flight from many big cities. The flight apparently does not stop at the nearest suburb. In the 1970s, entire metropolitan areas, not merely their central cities, are showing absolute population declines. Only one of the 25 largest Standard Metropolitan Statistical Areas (SMSAs) decreased in population during the 1960s. But by 1974, ten of the largest 25 were not growing.[10]

Where are the people heading? Outlying suburbs are still attractive, as are newer cities, such as Tucson, Houston, and San Diego. But a trend to watch is the revival of growth in the nonmetropolitan areas, even those that offer the least possibilities for commuting to work. Generally, one demographer noted that "the more remote kinds of places—those that as a group used to be regarded as 'nowhere'—have today become 'somewhere' in the minds of many migrants."[11] The nation's nonmetropolitan counties showed a net out-migration of 300,000 people per year during the 1960s, but they are now gaining 350,000 migrants per year.[12]

Demographic studies have also noted that certain types of people are more likely to make interstate or intercounty moves. As one demographer observed, the younger, better-educated people tend to make many more interstate and intercounty moves. Professional people and those in higher occupational categories also make more long-distance moves than laborers and people in lower occupational groups,[13] thus prompting one demographer to note:

> Persistent and severe out-migration is invariably selective, and gradually alters the composition and structure of local population. Specifically, such out-migration produces an increasingly disadvantaged population whose

needs mount as the municipality's capacity to meet them
erodes. Problems of dependency and poverty—not inherent problems of the affected municipality—come increasingly to be located in it.[14]

Thus, people who see limited migration as some sort of a major
barrier to social equity do well to review the present situation. They
should realize that intercounty and interstate migration might be primarily a luxury for the better-off. Communities that are receiving a
high rate of net in-migrants could also find that the new residents have
higher consumption patterns and higher expectations in terms of community services, as well as different life-styles. Reaction to this type
of in-migration might already be fueling local nongrowth efforts.
    Thus, it appears that growth pressures in various areas of the
country are part of a continuing manifestation of the frontier spirit—
make money or start off in some older central city or inner suburb
and then move on to a warmer climate, a new community, retire, or
build a second home in some area with fewer problems.
    Racial fears and tensions, crime, and fiscal problems in older,
larger cities are probably adding a "push" effect, in addition to the
"pull" effect of newer places in better climates, with less pollution
at present. One recent report notes a number of studies on the changing conditions that are spawning growth in the nonmetropolitan areas:

> A distillation of recent studies of the economic changes
> under way in nonmetropolitan America suggests some of
> the reasons for the new growth there: decentralization of
> employment, easier access to open space for recreation
> or residence, and the spread of retirement settlements
> beyond the traditional areas of Florida and the Southwest.
> All in all, these factors probably generate growth in dif-
> ferent ways in different parts of the nation. In some non-
> metropolitan areas, growth may be due mainly to the re-
> tention of native residents who no longer feel compelled
> by economic pressures to migrate—to be pushed away;
> in other areas, growth may be due to urbanites from out-
> side who are drawn there for a variety of reasons—being
> pulled to those areas.[15]

BEYOND DEMOGRAPHICS AND TECHNIQUES TO ATTITUDES

Demographics tell only part of the nongrowth tale. Migration patterns enlarge some areas and drain human and fiscal resources out of

others. But nongrowth attitudes are human responses, based on human perceptions and attitudes. Specific legal and political nongrowth tools and strategies are important, but they are based on a changing body of national and local opinion, which deserves detailed attention. The nongrowth movement has been characterized as an elitist effort, a white upper middle class concern, just as the women's movement was stereotyped a few years back. However, both movements are spreading beyond the social base of the pioneers.

The Florida experience shows the broadened wave of citizen support that nongrowth is gaining in contrast with the narrower base of the older environmentalist movement:

> In Florida, the 1972 vote on the bond issue for purchasing endangered areas was overwhelmingly favorable. Virtually every precinct in Dade County backed the bond issue, including those made up primarily of blacks (although the margin of victory was narrower in Cuban and Spanish neighborhoods).[16]

The experience in Florida was reflected in California, where a 1972 initiative to regulate growth and development along the coast received substantial support from a variety of political and social groups:

> the coastal initiative, Proposition 20, carried in most coastal and urbanized counties, drawing considerable support among working-class voters despite the opposition of many labor unions. It squeaked by in highly conservative Orange County (an unexpected victory) and was supported by blacks and Chicanos at about the 55 percent victory margin it received statewide.[17]

Nongrowthers and social equity advocates have appeared at public meetings to oppose certain types of development. In Tucson, in 1975, one young radical Chicano leader appeared at a public hearing to protest a rezoning for a distant new town being proposed by the Dow Chemical Company. Construction of the new town would divert more and more services and resources from the inner-city barrios, he contended. He acknowledged that some construction jobs would be gained by the development, but added that they were still a few years away, would be short-term, and would probably go to local Chicanos on a last-hired, first-fired basis.

The Rockefeller Brothers Fund report, The Use of Land, noted that although the nongrowth movement "has broadened considerably, in many areas it still has not shed its white middle-class image."[18]

But the report added that the development of new coalitions is
fairly widespread:

> A few issues have transcended economic and social bar-
> riers. The use of pesticides is one. Transportation is
> another. New roads have often been cut through poor
> neighborhoods, destroying decent housing and communi-
> ties without any plans for relocation or rejuvenation. Now,
> civil rights groups and environmental organizations are
> pushing the alternative of mass transportation in a com-
> bined effort to cut down pollution and to preserve neigh-
> borhoods.[19]

The nongrowth movement is also spreading to consumers on a
wider scale. Contrary to some popular beliefs, people are apparently
willing to give up some aspects of a high-consumption life-style to
avoid the prospect of continued general problems with the economy.
A Louis Harris poll reported in early December 1975 that the American people would opt by a margin of 77 to 8 percent for a change of
life-style that would include buying fewer products, not expanding their
standard of living, not working as many hours or weeks and winding
up with less income as an alternative to the pattern of higher inflation,
more shortages, and more recessions.[20] The same poll indicated a
substantial 61 to 23 percent majority thought it "morally wrong" for
the people of the United States, who comprise 6 percent of the world's
population, to consume an estimated 40 percent of the world's output
of energy and raw materials.

Local nongrowth advocates have often been accused of wanting to
ruin the American dream of bigger and better housing and second
homes, but the Harris poll found people ready for quite radical changes
in housing. By 73 percent to 19 percent, a majority would favor "pro-
hibiting the building of large houses with extra rooms that are seldom
used"; by 66 percent to 27 percent, a majority would support "doing
away with second houses where people go weekends and vacations";
and a significant 57 percent majority (34 percent against) would like
to see it "made much cheaper to live in multiple-unit apartments than
in single houses."[21]

Americans are apparently not willing to sacrifice the environment
in the name of rampant economic growth. In March 1975, as the recession continued, another Harris poll found Americans rating water and
air pollution as the nation's third and fourth greatest problems, re-
spectively, right behind inflation and unemployment but ahead of the
energy shortage. They also opposed proposals to sacrifice environmental cleanup for either emergency energy programs or programs
to boost the economy. Harris found three out of four Americans were

not convinced that a temporary slowdown of water and air pollution control programs would "get the economy going again" or "ease unemployment."[22]

In addition to the general attitudes that are skeptical off all-out growth, there are also indications of widespread grass-roots opposition and questioning of the local growth ethic. A Gallup survey, commissioned by Potomac Associates in April 1974, asked the following question of a nationwide sample:

> Speaking now of the general area where you live, some
> people say population and industrial growth in this area
> should be regulated in order to prevent more pollution
> and improve the quality of life. Others say this would
> mean fewer job opportunities and slower economic pro-
> gress. Do you yourself feel that population and indus-
> trial growth in this area where you live should be or
> should not be regulated?[23]

The answers showed a majority of Americans favored regulating population and economic growth in their home communities:

Should be	54 percent
Should not be	37 percent
Don't know	9 percent

Black Americans were predominantly in favor of regulation, but their percentage was only 42 percent, compared with 56 percent for whites. They also had a higher "don't know" response. On the basis of party affiliation, Independents (63 percent) were most in favor of regulating population and industrial growth, compared to only 54 percent for Democrats. A slight majority of Republicans (52 percent) were opposed to such regulation of growth. Business and professional people, along with people living in the West, were found to be more highly in favor of regulating local growth.

The same survey found considerable reluctance to have the federal government directly involved in the regulation of growth, such as through national land-use legislation. This result would correlate with the findings that people were more inclined to trust local and state government rather than the federal government. Some antifederal sentiment may have reflected the Watergate situation, which was peaking when the poll was taken, but subsequent polls have not reflected any great upsurge in confidence in the federal government.

The lack of confidence in not only big government, but in big business and big organizations in general, was rapidly becoming a primary social, planning, and political issue, as 1975 came to an end. Pollster Louis Harris told the U.S. Conference of Mayors, which met in Boston in the summer of 1975, that "confidence in government at all levels in this country has hit rock bottom," adding:

> I am compelled to report to you today that as a nation we
> have reached record peaks of demoralization: a full 67
> percent of the people feel that "what you think doesn't
> count much anymore," up from 37 percent who felt that
> way in 1966; the number who feel that "people in power
> are out to take advantage of you" has risen from 33 per-
> cent to 58 percent; the number who think "the people run-
> ning the country don't care what happens to you" has
> gone up from 33 percent to 63 percent in less than a dec-
> ade; most of all, most poignant—the number who say "I
> feel left out of things going on around me" has soared
> from 9 percent in 1966 to 41 percent today.[24]

The toll on confidence in institutions has been enormous, both in the private and public sectors.

Yet, Harris did find some focus for confidence in the local community:

> A substantial 42 percent of the citizens feel that local
> government affects them personally, 72 percent acknowl-
> edge that local government is closer to the people and
> ought to know their problems best, and 69 percent would
> opt for strengthening local government, if the right lead-
> ership asked for it. Most important of all: by 90 to 5 per-
> cent, an overwhelming majority still have the faith; they
> say that local government can be made to work well.[25]

Another Harris poll, in October 1975, found 40 percent of the people saying that local government was out of touch with the people it is supposed to lead or help. But a significantly higher proportion, 51 percent, thought the White House was out of touch, while an even greater percentage (54) thought Congress was out of touch. Major private companies were also viewed as out of touch by 50 percent of the respondents.[26]

A lot of the cynicism and disenchantment in the country is no doubt feeding the local nongrowth movement. But the citizen attitudes show some sophistication about simple progrowth solutions, as well as a positive concern for the quality of life. There is an identity with

the local community and the neighborhood that can serve as a foundation for new coalitions to work toward new positive community goals.
A number of local community attitude surveys and polls have shown
both highly negative citizen feelings toward continued rampant sprawl,
population growth, and bureaucratic expansion, as well as some equally strong new desires for both social equity and better local planning
done under the general ethic of scarcity and nongrowth.

For example, a random sample of the Tucson, Arizona, area population, taken in early 1974, showed that almost 70 percent of the respondents wanted policies established to slow down the population
growth rate.[27] The same respondents, however, backed several programs to increase social equity. "More public housing for low income
people" was ranked sixth from the top on a list of 45 programs and
services needing public support. Job-training programs for local residents was ranked 17th, but promotion of tourism ranked 45th. Almost 94 percent of the respondents wanted improved bus service,
while less than 40 percent favored more freeways.

In Orange County, California, one of the more rapidly growing
areas of the country, a questionnaire return of almost 1,600, completed
in early 1974, indicated that over 65 percent of the respondents thought
continued population growth would worsen the current lack of low-
and moderate-income housing.[28] Only 8 percent thought that continued
population growth would result in improvement of this housing problem. The percentages were roughly the same for the problem of unemployment.

There is a strong, revitalized spirit of innovation and citizen participation in most nongrowth communities. Growth-associated projects,
such as freeways, high-rise buildings, and even entire new towns,
bring out unprecedented numbers of citizens to public meetings. Some
local officials estimate that more people turn out on these issues than
they ever did in the days of more vague long-range planning efforts.
Citizens up and down Long Island, New York, for example, have appeared in great numbers at public hearings to protest rezonings for
higher-density residential units, shopping centers, and even new industries.

However, public meetings represent only the tip of the iceberg of
increased citizen participation in nongrowth. Citizens do not always
wait for planners or politicians to move into action but, rather, take
the initiative themselves. In 1972, voters in the San Francisco Bay
Area communities of Livermore and Pleasanton passed initiative measures on the ballot that prohibited the issuance of residential building
permits until problems of water, supply, sewage treatment, and school
capacity were solved. Citizens of Dade County, Florida, have petitioned
for, and have received, 12 neighborhood moratoriums on new development, ranging in size from 40 acres to 50 square miles. Citizens have

also made demands on their local governments for funds to further
their own nongrowth activities. This has taken place in places such as
Orange County, California, and Boulder, Colorado.

Citizens often appear to get involved in nongrowth in response to
problems from past growth or from traumatic new proposals—a new
freeway, which would cut out a view of a bay or a mountain, or a new
subdivision, which would chew up open space or prime agricultural
land. They respond to such threats with direct negative action—an
injunction, a moratorium, or a packed public protest meeting. But
the same citizens often advocate positive and innovative planning. Demands are made to open up the processes that make growth decisions,
to update existing information, and to try techniques that have worked
in other jurisdictions, often with improved local twists.

CONCLUSION

Local nongrowth involves more than planning or land-use devices,
such as urban limit lines, moratoriums, environmental impact statements, and impact zoning.[29] It is also more than economic measures,
such as pay-as-you-go public service policies or cost-benefit and cost-
revenue studies. It is really a state of mind that challenges the growth
ethic and some of the more negative aspects of the cowboy frontier
spirit. It is not aimed at stopping all kinds of growth everywhere for
all time. Rather, it seems to be aimed at creating some power shifts
in the processes that determine local population and geographic, economic, and bureaucratic growth. There is a demand for much more
citizen input into these processes and much more citizen control over
their outcomes. These matters have always been something of a
sacred cow in planning and government circles. But now citizens are
saying that they want the right to say "no" when the costs and benefits of a proposed expansion are not clear or when something doesn't
seem fair about the procedures. And they seem willing to live with
lower economic returns and to make some social equity contributions
to retain this right.

NOTES

1. See Earl Finkler and David L. Peterson, Nongrowth Planning
Strategies: The Developing Power of Towns, Cities, and Regions (New
York: Praeger, 1974), for more details on the origins and early devel-
opments in the nongrowth movement.

2. Herman E. Daly, "On Limiting Economic Growth" (Testimony before the 94th U.S. Congress, 1st Session, Joint Economic Committee, Hearings on Economic Growth, October 23, 1975), p. 5.

3. Donella Meadows et al., The Limits to Growth (New York: Universe Books, 1972).

4. "List of Areas With Growth Restraints," mimeographed (Washington, D.C.: The Urban Land Institute, March 1973).

5. "Managing the Environment at the Local Level," Urban Data Service Report (Washington, D.C.: International City Management Association, February 1974), p. 8.

6. "Constitutional Issues of Growth Management" (National Science Foundation research grant to University of North Carolina Center for Urban and Regional Studies, Chapel Hill, N.C., project deadline: May 1976). According to Kinney Harley, Executive Director, Florida Home Builders Association, as of 1973, there were 340 moratoriums of one type or another in Florida alone. See Kinney Harley's remarks in the unpublished transcript of the Conference on State Land Use Legislation (sponsored by the National Association of Home Builders), Washington, D.C., November 29-30, 1973, p. 126.

7. Michael E. Gleeson et al., Urban Growth Management Systems: An Evaluation of Policy Related Research, Planning Advisory Service Report nos. 309, 310 (Chicago: American Society of Planning Officials, 1975).

8. Letter from Michael E. Gleeson of the University of Minnesota School of Public Affairs, Minneapolis, Minn., to the author, dated August 6, 1975.

9. U.S. Department of Commerce, Bureau of the Census, Population of the United States, Trends and Prospects 1950-1990, Current Population Reports, Series P-23, no. 49 (Washington, D.C.: U.S. Government Printing Office, 1974), p. 131.

10. Peter A. Morrison, The Current Demographic Context of National Growth and Development, The Rand Paper Series (Santa Monica, Calif.: The Rand Corporation, September 1975), p. 3.

11. Ibid., p. 12.

12. Ibid., p. 9.

13. U.S. Department of Commerce, Bureau of the Census, op. cit., p. 137.

14. Morrison, op. cit., p. 8.

15. Ibid., p. 12.

16. The Rockefeller Brothers Fund, The Use of Land: A Citizen's Policy Guide to Urban Growth, ed. William Reilly (New York: Thomas Y. Crowell Company, 1973), p. 52.

17. Ibid., p. 52.

18. Ibid., p. 54.

19. Ibid.

20. Louis Harris, "Most Americans Willing to Curtail Lifestyle,"
Arizona Daily Star, December 4, 1975, p. 5.

21. Ibid.

22. Louis Harris, "Public Still Favors Pollution Controls," Arizona Daily Star, March 3, 1975, p. 3.

23. Gallup Survey, commissioned by Potomac Associates, quoted in William Watts and Lloyd A. Free, The State of the Nation, 1974 (Washington, D.C.: Potomac Associates, 1974), p. 174.

24. Louis Harris, "Sinking Confidence—Still Time for Change" (Paper delivered at U.S. Conference of Mayors, Boston, July 1975), in Western City, August 1975, p. 13.

25. Ibid., p. 25.

26. Louis Harris, "Leaders Called 'Out of Touch'," Arizona Daily Star, October 16, 1975, p. 5.

27. Arizona Institute for Research, Community Attitude Survey: A Report to the Comprehensive Planning Process (Tucson, Ariz.: City of Tucson Planning Department, July 1974).

28. Orange County Citizens Direction Finding Commission, Citizen Responses to Orange County's Population Growth (Santa Ana, Calif.: Orange County Planning Department, February 1974).

29. For a detailed discussion of types of growth management techniques, see Gleeson et al., op. cit., chap. 3, pp. 35-49.

2

LOCAL NONGROWTH AND
SOCIAL EQUITY

The poor and their advocates have been joined by unions, lenders, insurance companies, oil companies, and the like on some of these [nongrowth] issues. These influentials have been moved not out of some altruistic motive, but rather by the possibility of using a good sub-issue (helping the poor) in their fight against the environmentalists. The poor should not be misled. How do their new supporters feel about building public housing in the suburbs? Do they lobby in Washington for a guaranteed annual income?[1]

The nongrowth movement described and analyzed in this book has the potential to develop into a powerful and innovative American institution, one that will lead to increased local awareness, more diverse communities, and new relationships between citizens, planners, politicians, and developers. But the older environmental movement has been questioned and opposed a number of times for its real or imagined antipoor thrusts. The new, broader nongrowth movement has also received heavy criticism for being exclusive and elitist.

As one observer contends, the negative impacts of nongrowth might extend beyond the poor:

We are entering an era when growth controls will affect more than racial groups and the lowest-income persons. If communities are allowed to proceed unilaterally to restrict absorption of future predicted growth simply to preserve "the current order of things"—and it is done without any careful social and housing planning/consideration, . . . then the pressure will begin to reach upward into other levels of the income spectrum. Thus policies on growth, if mismanaged, could strike directly at a large portion of the American public . . . and indirectly on the

general economy, on the costs of housing and transportation, and on the life-styles of nearly all our
citizens.[2]

Such charges and concerns, although serious and deserving
attention, are often made in haste, from the perspective of a developer or other special interest; and, generally, on the basis of
little or no knowledge of the deep and diverse roots of the nongrowth
movement. Although this book could have been written to defend
nongrowth from various charges of exclusion and parochialism, it
was decided to take another approach; it will explain some of the
positive community benefits that many nongrowth advocates seek,
benefits which can apply to everyone—rich and poor alike. Following
the list of benefits, reasons will be given as to why nongrowth advocates should take a strong positive stance on social equity and
why social equity advocates should do the same with respect to
nongrowth. (The term "social equity" in this book is defined as
the redistribution of resources, such as jobs, housing, and public
services to help those who are less well-off.)
Throughout this chapter and the next, it will be noted that the
track record of past rapid, unchecked growth as a direct positive
social equity force is often not encouraging. For example, some of
the most rapidly growing areas of the country, such as Orange
County, California, and other newer suburban areas, remain almost
exclusively white. The final two sections of this chapter will delve
more deeply into key economic and legal assumptions that attempt
to connect nongrowth to exclusion, as well as other negative impacts.
Nongrowth has taken some rather cheap research "shots" from
judges and "experts," especially with respect to social equity.
This book will move beyond such criticism to chart realistic,
positive social equity responses on the part of nongrowth communities.
The next chapter presents the results of a special questionnaire sent
out by the authors to a variety of communities to gauge local thought
and performance on the issues of nongrowth and social equity. Finally,
recommendations will be made to help nongrowth communities
achieve positive social equity results. These recommendations will
be generally designed for immediate action and will also serve as
standards to help all observers judge the future social equity performance of nongrowth communities, as well as the performance of
higher-level governments that deal with these communities.

WHAT ARE NONGROWTH ADVOCATES
TRYING TO ACHIEVE?

There are a number of very good reasons why many people attempt to push their communities toward some form of nongrowth:

1. They want a feeling of local identity, local roots, and local stability for themselves and their children.
2. They want continued or improved access to nature, to quiet places, and to the great outdoors.
3. They want safe neighborhoods and a personal feeling that they have some control over their immediate environment.
4. They want local politicians and officials who are attentive to their individual needs and aspirations.
5. They want comfortable, decently priced housing.
6. They want clear, up-to-date information on where their community is going, and they want a chance to participate in future plans and decisions.

The Rockefeller Brothers Task Force report, The Use of the Land, verified, in 1973, that there was a "new mood" against unchecked future growth, but it also described some of the more positive goals of the movement, including those toward a more humane environment:

> This mood [against growth] defies easy generalization because it springs from a melange of concerns—many that are unselfish and legitimate, some that are selfish and not so legitimate. The mood is both optimistic and expansive in its expectations of the future, and pessimistic and untrusting about inevitable change. . . .
> The new mood reflects a burgeoning sophistication on the part of citizens about the overall, long-term economic impact of development. . . . But the new attitude toward growth is not exclusively motivated by economics. It appears to be part of a rising emphasis on humanism, on the preservation of natural and cultural characteristics that make for a humanly satisfying living environment.[3]

Richard Appelbaum, a sociology professor and community nongrowth activist from Santa Barbara, California, contends that most

of the minorities and the poor passively support growth control,
recognizing the costs of growth. He explained the passivity with
the following reasons:

1. Lack of institutionalized means. The middle class
   neighborhoods have improvement associations; the
   middle class (and upper class) people belong to a
   host of voluntary associations. In general, workers
   and poor and minorities do not.
2. Other priorities. Even where organizations
   exist (e.g., La Casa de la Raza, a highly progressive Chicano communtiy organization with broad-based
   support), they tend to pursue more immediate concerns: housing, police harassment, drug problems,
   farmworker support.
3. Nongrowth seems to be remote, theoretical,
   and middle class in style. Probably turns many
   non-middle class people away.
4. Poorer people (and minorities) tend to have
   a realistic sense of their inability to influence
   public policy, and so prefer not to waste their time
   (and lack the independent means which permit such
   waste).[4]

Thus, there appear to be a number of positive goals that now
motivate nongrowth advocates and which could motivate the poor
and minority groups if some blockages were removed and if more
of the positive nongrowth aspects were explained to them. But
before that happens, both sides might need some education in order
to see more clearly the benefits of cooperative action.

THE IMPORTANCE OF NONGROWTH
TO SOCIAL EQUITY
AND SOCIAL EQUITY TO NONGROWTH

The poor and minority groups could find nongrowth advocates
to be strong and powerful new allies in their fight for social equity.
The concerned, educated, and, usually, more affluent people involved in nongrowth often have the time, the contacts, and the power
to apply pressure on insensitive bureaucracies or local power structures. In addition, the poor could find that support of nongrowth
results in actual improvements in housing and employment

opportunities, more than they have been receiving through the trickle-down process associated with unchecked growth.

As nongrowth concerns proliferate, more and more communities will become concerned about meaningful local nongrowth strategies. Many will observe or learn that such strategies will have to contain some kind of social equity response to gain political support or legal approval. If the hundreds of nongrowth communities made some kind of social equity effort regarded as token, the sum total of such actions would result in major equity breakthroughs. For example, a host of minimum low-income housing quotas for new development in communities where no such quotas existed previously could result in a more balanced form of new housing construction.

Local nongrowth in suburbs or isolated rural communities can also have positive results for older inner cities. For example, if newer, more desirable communities in a metropolitan area all clamp down on zoning for new footloose industries, these industries might work harder and consider remodeling and other remedies in order to stay in inner cities. This would preserve more job opportunities that would be closer to those who need them. The same principle applies to residential and commercial development—strong nongrowth policies in the suburbs can result in more preservation and vitality in central cities.

Positive social equity statements from the nongrowth perspective could help introduce the movement to people in the civil rights, fair housing, and other movements, who might then be more inclined to seek grounds for common discussion. Such discussion could lead to joint political action on some issues. (A number of individual nongrowth advocates are said to be veterans of the civil rights movement. A positive local stance on social equity in conjunction with their nongrowth efforts would help salve their consciences.)

In addition, it is fairly certain that someone will be analyzing the typical nongrowth community for signs of exclusion, inattention, or hostility toward social equity concerns. This could take place in the legal arena or in the process of securing a federal grant, such as the funds from the Housing and Community Development Act. Ignoring social equity will not make it go away. But sincere and substantial community involvement at an early date will help keep consideration of the issue in the community's own ballpark. There will be considerably more community input and influence not only on minimum required efforts (in areas such as subsidized housing) but also on the maximum efforts that any reasonable person could expect from a community. The community's land-use powers, a primary tool for achieving goals through nongrowth, will

also be much safer from political or legal attack by a developer if
the community has an open and positive social equity program.

Redistribution efforts within a single local nongrowth community should gain much wider political acceptance. At this level, such
efforts can be aimed at neighbors (hopefully, with some visible results); there would be potential benefits to givers, as well as to
receivers. For example, environmentalists who back upgraded
community services in an inner-city area might, in turn, be able to
gain some minority group support for a major greenbelt acquisition
program at the urban fringe. Capital improvement planning and programs offer considerable potential for diverse interests to get involved and work out trade-offs that would be of mutual benefit.

Critics might object that many of the most serious social
equity problems cross jurisdictional lines and, thus, local action is
not always very relevant. This may be true, but a major force of the
nongrowth movement has been the local community. The emerging
principle of local self-sufficiency can be applied to social equity. It
thus seems important that a starting point in social equity be one's
own back yard. At the local community level, clearer assessments
of social equity problems can be made, appropriate responses tried,
and actual results seen.

Once some foothold in government activity is established at
the community level, nongrowth advocates can consider moving
some of their efforts out to neighboring areas. Not only can positive financial or related contributions be made toward social equity,
but information can be widely circulated that the community tried
this kind of social equity approach and that it worked, or seems to
have promise, or that it did not work.

At present, a lot of mistrust and misinformation exists between a number of nongrowth and social equity advocates. But there
is a lot to be gained by both groups if they switch from conflict to
cooperation. Increased social equity initiatives and improved performance by nongrowth communities are prime ways to further such
cooperation. However, some of the apparent conflicts, especially
those in the economic and legal areas, need further discussion and
increased factual analysis. Without such analysis of economic
issues, including housing costs and legal issues, discussions tend
to get bogged down in rhetoric, and major legal and other decisions
are made with a distorted view of the real world.

NONGROWTH TECHNIQUES
AND HOUSING COSTS

Most of the challenges to nongrowth in the area of social
equity have been legal, but close behind the specific legal point of
the spear is a long and sometimes winding shaft of economics. From
Petaluma, California, to Ramapo, New York, to Mount Laurel, New
Jersey, and in many other recent legal cases, there have been
assertions made that restricting land use to control growth inflates
the price of housing beyond the reach of all but the wealthy.

In the Mount Laurel case, the Supreme Court of New Jersey
invalidated part of the community's zoning ordinance in response
to what it stated was the key legal issue:

> Whether a developing municipality like Mount Laurel
> may validly, by a system of land use regulation, make
> it physically and economically impossible to provide
> low and moderate income housing in the municipality
> for the various categories of persons who need and
> want it.[5]

Direct legal limits on growth will be discussed later in this
chapter. Here the economic assumptions of such statements will be
addressed. Although sharing the basic goal of integrated communities, both in racial and economic terms, the authors are generally
amazed at the extremely thin base of economic analysis that has
underlined some of the major recent exclusionary court cases, such
as Petaluma and Mount Laurel. Judges make the decisions and
judges know the law, but they make it in a context of housing and
land economics that is rather weak and unfocused. They also have
an unsupported general faith in growth and new housing in new areas
to solve major social problems.

One of the leading housing and land-use attorneys in the country, Herbert Franklin, acknowledged in his recent book In-Zoning
that the impact of large-lot zoning on increasing housing costs is
"widely debated in the literature."[6] Franklin rightly notes that
higher service costs associated with lower densities may drive up
the costs of some large lots. On the other hand, he points out that
large-lot zoning can lower raw land prices on a square foot basis and,
thus, make it profitable for a developer to construct lower-priced
housing if a rezoning can be obtained.

According to Franklin, a shortage of land zoned for multifamily, townhouse, or mobile home development can drive up the

the price of land that is zoned for these residential uses. But he
adds that expensive multifamily housing can also be built on such
sites, especially if they are prezoned. In addition, he warns that
excessive prezoning of such land could mean the abdication of a
community's right to plan and influence its future development and
result in poorer families winding up miles from essential services
or in environmentally undesirable areas. Franklin concludes that
"all of these alleged 'exclusionary' requirements can serve
important public health, safety, and environmental needs, if appro-
priately limited."[7]

Franklin's book, one of the more recent and comprehensive
attempts to explore some of the middle ground between nongrowth
advocates and social equity advocates, notes that land-use controls
and court decisions, by themselves, build no housing. He points out
the prime importance of federal housing subsidies, such as those
provided by the Housing and Community Development Act, to the
local provision of additional lower-income housing.

Other recent studies have tended to support Franklin's contention that the issue of more low- and moderate-income housing is
much more complex than the striking down of parts of a local zoning
ordinance. One major study of development controls and housing
costs, funded by the National Science Foundation in 1973, involved
an exhaustive search of hundreds of sources and pieces of literature
on the subject. Yet, the resulting conclusions were disappointing:
"Despite a lengthy, thorough search, we uncovered only twelve research studies which met [our] criteria. . . . The policy relevance
of research on zoning and housing costs is both definitive and am-
biguous."[8]

The "definitive" policy relevance apparently relates to the
finding that the price of building lots and houses is dependent upon
"residential density and density-related uses." There are some
qualifiers to this conclusion, however, which make it something less
than definitive. The direct correlations found between zoning controls and housing costs were low. The same low correlation applied
to building codes and housing prices. One pair of studies concluded
that zoning had no distorting effects on the land prices or supply.[9]

The NSF researchers drew up a comprehensive list of development controls, including such devices as the following: (a) subdivision regulation; (b) staged growth-management techniques, such
as those used by Ramapo, New York; (c) flood control ordinances;
(d) development moratoriums; and (e) environmental protection
ordinances. Some of these are becoming more revelant to nongrowth
court cases and related debates on exclusion than traditional zoning
and building code controls. Yet,

despite the number of controls on this list, and their
potential for affecting housing costs, we were able to
find a rather small amount of empirical research on
only the first two development controls (zoning ordinances and building codes). This is not to say that no
other research exists, but it can be said without fear
of contradiction that the effects which these remaining
controls have on housing costs are inadequately researched.[10]

Some Answers on Controls and Housing Costs

It is not enough to say that such key factors in the nongrowth-
social equity debate have been inadequately researched. We attempted
to develop a few answers on exactly how much of the cost of a house
could possibly be attributed to the acquisition and improvement of
sites. The general answer was not as much as many people, or
judges, might think. Land-use controls do not build housing, and it
appears that even if the land was free in some cases, some of the
poorer and even middle class families could not even afford the
housing that was built on it.

Table 1.1 (from the report Building the American City) contains data that are fairly old, but it does illustrate certain points.
For one thing, it shows considerable differences in the distribution
of single-family housing costs by area of the nation. For example,
in California, land acquisition costs were 24 percent of the total
costs, while in the Midwest, such costs accounted for only 8 percent
of the costs. In Ohio, land acquisition costs were about twice as
high as site improvement costs, while in the Northeast, the improvement costs were higher than the land acquisition costs. Structure
costs constituted a majority of the housing cost in all places listed
except California, where they accounted for only about 42 percent
of such costs. Financing and mortgage points costs in Ohio almost
equaled site acquisition costs.

In a more recent survey made by the Department of Housing
and Urban Development (HUD), it was found that average site acquisition and improvement costs constituted 13.4 percent of the total
value of a single-family house in 1955.[11] In 1972, these same costs
had risen to 21.4 percent of the total house value.[12] A survey by
the National Association of Homebuilders, in 1970, showed that the
price of a "typical finished lot" increased from $2,851 in 1960 to
$6,217 in 1969.[13]

TABLE 1.1

Distribution of Costs for Single-Family Houses in Selected Developments, 1966-67

Item	Project				
	South	California	Midwest	Northeast	Ohio
Components of selling price (in dollars):					
Area of house, square feet	—	1,678	1,263	1,263	1,000
Selling price, average	24,350	25,000	24,990	21,990	20,155
House construction cost	15,020	10,450	14,650	11,200	11,111
Site costs:					
Acquisition	—	6,000	1,999	2,067	2,298
Site improvement	—	2,000	2,449	2,837	1,068
Selling price, less site costs	20,105	17,000	20,540	17,090	16,791
Price and cost per square foot:					
Selling price per square foot	—	14.90	19.75	17.31	20.16
House construction cost per square foot	—	6.24	11.60	8.86	11.11
Selling price, less site costs per square foot	—	10.20	16.22	13.51	16.79
Percent distribution of selling price:					
All components	100	100	100	100	100
Site costs:					
Acquisition	—	24.0	8.0	9.4	11.4
Site improvement	—	8.0	9.8	12.9	5.3
Subtotal	17.43	32.0	17.8	22.3	16.7
Structure	61.70	41.8	58.6	51.0	55.1
Supervision	—	0.7	7.9	7.2	1.2[a]
Marketing	3.57	4.0	3.3	4.7	5.0
Financing	6.22	4.8	2.0	2.3	4.0
Mortgage points	—	6.0	3.4	2.9	5.0
General overhead	9.11	4.7	7.0[b]	9.6[c]	4.1[d]
Profit	1.95	6.0	—	—	8.9[d]
Subtotal	20.86	26.2	23.6	26.7	28.2

[a]Includes overhead.
[b]Includes engineering, 1.2 percent, and mortgage processing and title closing, 0.9 percent.
[c]Includes engineering, 1.5 percent, and mortgage processing and title closing, 1.1 percent.
[d]Includes preliminary costs, closing costs, and contingency.
Source: Adapted from National Commission on Urban Problems, Building the American City (Washington, D.C.: U.S. Government Printing Office, 1968), p. 418.

Thus site costs are increasing. But a reduction or even removal of such costs would not give many more poor people access to single-family homes. According to the U. S. Census Bureau, the median price of new single-family homes sold in 1970 was $23,400. In January 1975, the median price had increased to $37,500.[14] Assuming that site acquisition and improvement costs account for even 30 percent of the final sale price for a house, a 30 percent reduction in the 1975 median sales price would leave a balance of $26,250. This house would still be beyond the reach of a family making $5,000, $8,000, or even $10,000 a year. Thus, housing for the poor needs more to get it going than a local abdication of land-use powers.

A 1975 housing study of one of the best home-building years on record (1973) concluded that even during that period, more and more moderate-income families were being priced out of the new housing market.[15] As one table from the report shows, a family with the U. S. median income of $12,051 for March 1973 could not afford a $25,000 house (see Table 1.2). The study also showed that virtually no nonfederally subsidized new homes were available for sale under $20,000. Only about 17 percent of the 361,000 unsubsidized, unsold homes either completed or under construction at the close of 1973 were priced under $25,000.

Some say that increased new housing production at least helps low- and moderate-income families by making more existing housing available through the filtering-down process. However, the poor condition of some of the existing stock, demolitions, and inflation resulted in a situation where the availability of existing homes for all families with under a $15,000 annual income declined when compared to 1972, according to the report. It predicted that the relative availability of homes for households in the $8,000-$12,000 income bracket in 1975 was likely to be much more limited than in previous years. Much of the rise in housing expense was attributed to inflation and the cost of utilities.

Conclusion

It appears that economic studies are far behind the current judicial wisdom in the matter of land-use controls and their effect on the price of housing. Much research remains to be done in this area. However, some elementary analysis reported previously shows that the provision of more and better housing for the poor and some of the middle class will require a lot more than the weakening of local land-use controls.

TABLE 1.2

Derivation of Total Housing Expenses and Income Required
for Purchase of Homes at Selected Prices and Terms, 1973

| Home Price | Percentage Downpayment[a] | Mortgage Amount | Monthly Housing Expenses | | | Required Minimum Annual Income[c] |
			Principal and Interest	Estimated Taxes, Insurance, Maintenance Repair, and Utilities	Total[b]	
$20,000	5	$19,000	$144.13	$ 82.00	$226.13	$10,854
22,000	5	20,900	158.54	89.00	247.54	11,882
25,000	10	22,500	170.68	99.00	269.68	12,945
27,000	10	24,750	187.73	108.00	295.73	14,195
30,000	10	27,000	204.81	120.00	324.81	15,591
35,000	20	28,000	212.40	144.00	356.40	17,107
35,000	25	26,250	199.12	144.00	343.12	16,470

[a]Terms of finance, besides downpayment, are an 8.5 percent interest extended over a 30 year term.

[b]Total of monthly housing expenses.

[c]This column indicates the required annual income to support the various mortgages, based on a 25 percent housing expense to income ratio. The amount in "Total" column is multiplied by 48 to produce the required annual income.

Source: Adapted from Warren E. Farb, "Availability of Homes for Middle-Income Families," HD 7287, U. S. A. 75-43E (Washington, D. C.: Congressional Research Service, Library of Congress, February 13, 1975).

Obviously, a community can have some influence on land and housing prices if it requires developers to contribute more in the way of sewers, sidewalks, project design, parks, and school sites. However, in some cases, such as strict energy conservation standards for housing, higher initial costs can be amortized within a few years (or so) based on cost savings in utility bills. Other initially higher costs but longer-term savings can result when improvements such as sidewalks, adequate paved streets, parks, and so forth are required of the developer at the start of a project rather than being added later by the public or special districts in an incremental, ad hoc manner. Comprehensive public information on all of the costs and revenues of a new development, before it is built, enables people to identify subsidies to builders, neighborhoods, or income groups. The public then has a chance to say whether or not it wants its tax dollars spent on those kinds of subsidies.

SUPPLY AND DEMAND—A LAW IN SEARCH OF AN ECONOMIC BASE

The simple response of some courts to local nongrowth has been that such community action constricts the supply of land available for housing and, thus, in the face of continued demand, raises the prices of existing housing and potential new housing sites.

This kind of reasoning was applied by the federal trial court judge in the Petaluma, California, case. The judge's decision in striking down the Petaluma quota of 500 new residential units per year was later reversed by a federal appeals court, but the economic basis of the original decision was not directly challenged in the appeal case and is still worthy of analysis.

In a report prepared for the trial court by an economic consultant for the construction industry, there was a new, slightly more sophisticated twist to the argument that local land-use controls prevent the poor from obtaining decent housing. The construction consultant conceded that Petaluma's quota alone would probably not have a significant effect on the San Francisco Bay Area housing market. But he then made the gross assumption that if Petaluma and all other regional "growth centers" were to jointly enact such policies, the area would experience a 25 percent decrease in housing production, resulting in a shortfall of 107,000 housing units in the decade 1970-80, with the following dire consequences:

The most obvious and most oppressive impact of the
housing production shortfall that would result from
the cumulative impact of the growth-stunting suburban ordinances would be the reduction in social mobility that would be caused by the decrease in housing
supply opportunity. The American society has always
been mobile both geographically and socially, and the
two go together.[16]

The consultant added that growth centers, such as Petaluma,
contain "the most desirable" land for development at any given
time. Finally, he concluded that older areas, such as central cities,
do have some land available for development but that such areas
rarely have large tracts available, and if they do, the price is usually
quite high.

It is time to pull back from generalized statements proclaiming
that local nongrowth per se is reducing social mobility or that regulations such as Petaluma's could "tear up the fabric of the Republic"
(as a construction industry consultant noted in a subsequent inter-
view).[17] If we are all talking about maximizing every possible opportunity for consumers and builders to have potential housing everywhere and anywhere, local nongrowth may signify some pullback in
the name of community identity, environmental concern, or local
planning responsibility. However, the preservation of small town
environment, open spaces, and low-density character were viewed
as legitimate public welfare concerns when the Petaluma system
was finally upheld by the federal appeals court.[18] But the court did
not delve very deeply into some of the basic land and housing economics of the case. Such issues will continue to be raised in subsequent nongrowth cases and deserve more detailed attention.

Land prices develop in a much more complex system than
some simple concept of supply and demand. We are really talking
about changing perceptions and builder performance in regard to
"desirable" locations for housing. There are plenty of sites for
housing for anticipated population growth in central cities or older
suburbs. In addition, not all communities are likely to enact strict
nongrowth policies at the same time. Places like Dayton, New
Orleans, Milwaukee, and even San Jose and Tucson would welcome
growth in certain vacant or bypassed areas within their city limits.

Builders and their economic consultants may have to rethink
their estimates of what is desirable and what is not in the case of
potential housing sites. In addition, smaller sites in older areas
may prove to be feasible for new construction in many cases if only
someone will take the time to innovate and to do objective investment calculations. Planners and city officials, working closely

with neighbors, can help by providing some flexible zoning and building code regulations. "Small is beautiful" should apply not only to
manufacturing technology, as British economist E. F. Schumacher
advocates, but also to residential building sites.[19]

One article, by Sylvan Kamm in a 1971 issue of Urban Land,
helped to explain the complexity of the land market and the danger
of using hard-and-fast supply-and-demand assumptions:

> The market for undeveloped land is very imperfect and
> there have been very few empirical studies of its oper-
> ation. As a result, efforts to explain price behavior have
> to depend largely upon observation and insight. . . .
>
> Nationally, there is far more land than could ever
> be required for urban purposes, and even within metro-
> politan areas the supply of undeveloped land is very
> large. . . . The land which enters the price equation is
> only that land which is, or expected to be, suitable for
> development. . . .
>
> Neither the interaction of supply and demand nor
> imperfections of the market are adequate to explain land
> price behavior. It is clear that land speculation is a
> significant factor in the inflation of land prices. This
> speculation is partly a consequence of the federal tax
> laws, which provide shelter for a large proportion of
> income derived from land investments, and partly a
> natural phenomenon of the market itself.[20]

Kamm's article echoes some of the concerns expressed earlier by Franklin with regard to a number of factors that can influence not only land price but the overall value of the land and
housing to its occupants. These factors include location, under
which Kamm notes that "highway construction has probably been
the most significant factor in expanding locational values during
the past two decades."[21]

Other factors listed included: (a) infrastructure and facilities, such as water and sewers; (b) public services, such as education; (c) police and fire; (d) physical characteristics, such as
water table and slope; and (e) legal constraints, such as zoning and
subdivision regulations. Kamm says that the latter are probably
the most important in determining the suitability of land for development, but offers neither information nor analysis in the way of proof.
Finally, Kamm lists market factors, including willing sellers and
buyers, and mechanisms for bringing them together and for financing the transaction.[22]

What about actual buildable vacant land in central cities? Surprisingly, there is not a lot of comprehensive information on this vital topic. However, one author reviewed information from studies and sources, such as the National Commission on Urban Problems, and also personally contacted planning officials in 86 large cities. His conclusion in 1971 was that

> there is a significant amount of land in the large
> American city that is not devoted to any functional
> use, i.e., vacant urban land. In cities over 100,000
> there are approximately 1.5 million acres of vacant
> land, with this land comprising between one-fifth and
> one-fourth of the land area of the large city. Intercity
> variations in the amount of vacant land are consid-
> erable, as are inter-regional variations.
>
> There are several types of vacant land in the
> urban center, one of which consists of vacant land
> that is considered as unbuildable, mainly due to physi-
> cal constraints.
>
> The types that remain can be considered as build-
> able. Buildable vacant land in 86 cities over 100,000
> amounts to over one million acres or between three-
> fourths and four-fifths of total vacant land in the city.
> There is considerable variation in the amount of va-
> cant land that is considered buildable, with the amount
> ranging from about 25 percent to 100 percent.[23]

The estimate of 1 million acres of buildable vacant land in 86 of the 130 cities over 100,000 is equal to about three-fourths of the total area of the state of Delaware and about 20 percent of the area of New Jersey. At a relatively modest density of 20 people per acre, this much land could accommodate 20 million people, or more than the anticipated population growth in the United States—from 213 million in 1975 to about 231 million in 1985.

The figures just quoted may be conservative. Many central cities and mature suburbs have vacant developable land. Some local officials classified land as unbuildable because it fell short of the minimum lot sizes prescribed by local zoning ordinances. Given an aggressive and innovative central city infill program, smaller lots might be utilized. Public land banking and higher taxes on vacant land could help retard speculation. A number of renovations and scattered clearance efforts might also provide more space for development. Development of air rights and underground space could also add more dimensions to central city land.

HOUSING AND SOCIAL EQUITY—WHAT NOW?

The present authors have tried to let nongrowth communities off the hook when blame is passed around for the lack of decent housing for the poor. But who should be on the hook, and what should be done? If emasculating local land-use powers will not provide the answer, what will?

No simple solutions spring forth. The housing market is not some classic free national, state, or even regional mechanism, where all potential consumers have the information, access, and desire to optimize their housing situation. It is much more fragmented and complex. Lot and housing prices vary considerably in different areas of the country. Uncontrolled growth for growth's sake will probably not clear up this nation's housing problems, as housing attorney Charles Haar noted in 1974:

> The annual rate of dwelling unit construction for six-
> teen years after World War II was double the rate at
> which new families were formed. Yet the decision to
> let private enterprise satisfy the housing shortage with-
> out providing a public policy framework for urban
> growth has affected significantly the nation's geographic
> segregation of residences and the unequal satisfaction
> of housing demand by Americans. In spite of the high
> rate of dwelling unit construction by private enterprise,
> more than 12 percent of American families cannot now
> afford decent housing; at least 10 percent of the nation's
> existing units are in substandard condition.[24]

A number of social equity advocates have a general faith in the growth ethic, as opposed to anything more restrained. If growth has not helped housing very much so far, they might reason, perhaps it has at least helped income redistribution. But the record here is not encouraging either.

Economist Paul Samuelson has noted that

> when we look at the crude statistics of income and
> wealth, we find that the last few decades have not
> much changed the proportions of total income going
> to the lowest and the highest fifths of the population
> and to the fifths in-between. The total of the social
> pie has grown. But the sharing of the separate pieces
> is much the same as in 1950.[25]

"The rich get richer faster since they start from a higher base," said Lewis Mandell of the University of Michigan Survey Research Center.[26] Mandell noted the results of some sample surveys which indicated that the top 10 percent of the people in the nation get 29 percent of the income and own 56 percent of the weatlh, while the bottom 10 percent get 1 percent of the income and owe more than they own.

John T. Dunlop, the U.S. Secretary of Labor, said in May 1975 that the unemployment rate of 16- to 19-year-old blacks nearly doubled between 1954 and 1973, while there was no significant change in the rate for white teenagers in the same age group.[27] In 1954, the unemployment rate for the blacks in the age group was 16.5 percent, while whites in the same age group had a rate of 12.1 percent. In 1973, the rate for blacks rose to 30.2 percent, while the white rate went up only very slightly—to 12.6 percent.[28]

Given such continuing or growing inequalities in basic wealth and income, it seems as though social equity efforts that focus exclusively on housing costs and local land-use controls may be rather myopic, as one author noted:

> Economists have long held that public provision of commodities below cost to households is less efficient in improving family welfare than unrestricted transfers of income. . . .
> Many federal programs subsidize costs of construction, in general, instead of low-income or badly housed families. If such programs are to be justified, the desire to redistribute income cannot be the central motivation.[29]

However, another author defended incrementalism in public housing policies, even though he acknowledged the deeper roots of the problem:

> While agreeing with the radical critique that the solution to housing problems is ultimately bound up with more fundamental issues such as the maldistribution of wealth and income, I would still argue that—pending a political millennium—some government action is better than none, even if the treatment is merely palliative, the relief stopgap, and the results insufficient.[30]

The present authors do not defend incrementalism and do not always agree that "some government action is better than none," as later chapters on bureaucratic nongrowth will show. We suggest that both nongrowth and progrowth advocates push toward some kind of "political millenium" if that is what it will take to improve social equity. But it is not enough to report that one is working only on something as general or global as a political millennium. Nongrowth advocates should find out the housing, land cost, and social equity facts in their community and participate in effective, immediate action to improve the situation for those less well off. Immediate pressure should be put on local political leaders to fully participate in federal housing programs and to require quotas for low- and moderate-income housing in all substantial new residential developments. As mentioned earlier, Franklin's recent book In- Zoning is one of the best sources of ideas for a local inclusionary zoning and land-use program. Nongrowth advocates should read this book, pass it on to their officials and fellow citizens, and take the lead in mounting effectively community action based on some of Franklin's suggestions.

But there is even more to nongrowth than specific equity housing efforts and some sort of ultimate push for a political millennium. Nongrowth assumes that economic growth and present patterns of business and consumption are not automatically relevant or good for all communities. Citizens are starting to ask a lot more questions and to demand more environmental safeguards before they endorse or accept major new industries. It is being suggested that local economic development efforts deal first with the needs of the resident unemployed and underemployed. There are demands to consider the value of trees, wildlife, and amenities such as peace and quiet, as well as any specific dollar benefits from a particular development. There is still a strong belief in the private market and a really free enterprise system, but no longer as much blind faith in automatic benefits from economic growth. Citizens want to know more about their local economy, how it functions, and what new industries will cost. Later chapters of this book will delve more deeply into nongrowth economics, but it is assumed here that the spirit of more citizen involvement in the local economy and the challenging of traditional economic assumptions could be extended to develop economic initiatives to benefit social equity.

Hazel Henderson has charted some new socially responsive economic directions that appear very relevant for nongrowthers:

> The issue now confronting environmental groups is
> how to pick their way through our existing economic
> system so as to find points of leverage and intervention

where they may advance environmental goals that
parallel, rather than conflict with, the goals of
labor, the poor, and those who suffer discrimination. In some areas, we see that it is possible
to change government policies so that funds flow
into such areas as mass transit and health care,
which can help graft new, less destructive sectors
onto our economy and which can also provide new
jobs.

Environmentalists and less-affluent Americans might join in development of "grass-roots
capitalism" in community-based human service
areas, such as entrepreneurial day-care operations
run by local women who share "pieces of the action";
community cable TV franchises; or small health
clinics using para-professionals.[31]

NONGROWTH AND THE LAW*

Overview

Nongrowth is spawning new perspectives on social equity and
the field of economics. At the same time, it is continuing to pull
on the tiller of the law.[32] The local nongrowth movement is sending
all kinds of new problems and dilemmas to the courts. Can small
towns try to stay small? Can a community limit sprawl, but not
population? Does every local zoning ordinance have to allow apartments and higher-density units? If so, how many? What is a region,
and what is a "fair share" of low- and moderate-income housing
for each community within that region? Even after a court determines what is fair, who is going to make sure that the housing actually gets built? Where does prudent planning end and unjust taking
of private property begin? Does all zoning interfere with the free
market and the presumed constitutional right to travel? Is some
interference all right? Do land-use controls of any kind deserve to

---

* This section was written by Frank S. Bangs, former editor
of Land Use Law and Zoning Digest, published by the American
Society of Planning Officials in Chicago. He is now a zoning and
planning attorney with the City Attorney's office in Tucson, Arizona.

be considered as legal obstacles to the right to travel? The questions are many, but the definite answers to date are few.

The theme of this chapter is that nongrowth and social equity goals can be in harmony and that the two movements should work together on this joint agenda. Those who advocate such joint action might initially think the courts would be sympathetic. First, environmental legislation severely limiting the development of land has been increasingly upheld by the courts in the face of challenges based on the constitutional protection of property rights. Second, the courts, in general, have moved ahead in some areas of equal opportunity in housing and employment.

These roughly concurrent case law trends should argue well for local nongrowth politics that discourage environmentally and fiscally disruptive urban sprawl and, perhaps, other forms of growth, while, at the same time, emphasizing a focus of government resources in older, developed areas (or directly on the needs of lower-income people). A community might follow this joint agenda by purchasing land to preserve greenbelts and provide future sites for lower-income housing. It could also shift the full cost of services to fringe developments through user charges, subdivision exactions, and development taxes, while upgrading the quality of inner-city services. The same type of exactions might be gained from high-rise redevelopers in some cases and be used to assist lower-income or residential and commercial areas that might be nearby. Quotas of lower-income or family units could be required in most housing developments. Some communities might elect to require lower-income housing as part of new shopping centers, and even some quality industrial park development. Local communities might allow firms the benefit of industrial rezonings only if significant local hiring or cooperation with local manpower programs is promised in return.

Many of these public interventions would appear to cover areas of nongrowth and areas of social equity and meet the goals of supporters of both objectives. The courts might be expected to approve such comprehensive thrusts. However, heavy reliance on the courts, particularly the federal courts, to reconcile social equity and nongrowth goals may be misplaced. Even though the Constitution emphasizes "equal protection of the law," the courts have not yet interpreted that expression to include a more equitable distribution of economic wealth. Constitutional guarantees of equal protection have long been overshadowed by "due process" considerations, especially the courts' high regard for property rights with regard to unlawful "takings" and other issues.

Those readers who grew up in the 1960s may find it difficult to conceive of federal judges not in the vanguard of social change.

But the Warren court of that period is now the Burger court, and we may expect the Supreme Court to lapse into its traditional role as the brake rather than the engine of society. Several recent Supreme Court and lower federal court decisions show evidence of a retrenching in the area of exclusionary zoning. The Burger court does not appear to be setting a strong federal tone on the growth of equal protection coverage. So far, it has rejected the claim that there is any constitutionally guaranteed "right to housing," no matter how necessary such housing is to survival.

A few state supreme courts have been more "activist" than the federal courts in the housing areas, although some, especially in Pennsylvania and New Jersey, appear to be acting on the basis of a rather blind faith in the growth ethic and the housing filtering process to solve serious problems, such as the lack of lower-income housing.

Diverse trends in judicial decisions should not necessarily be regarded with dismay. The fragmentation of the federal system has produced a new array of local nongrowth communities acting as laboratories. It may also be producing an array of judicial experiments, with significant differences between federal and some state court interpretations of local nongrowth strategies.

The federal system provides a variety of entry points for those who seek to change our society and its laws. If federal courts withdraw from an active role in legal change, then some state courts may pick up the baton. But there are institutional limits on the role that the courts will play in this process. Ultimately, as the appeals court decision in Petaluma began to note, the legislatures, particularly at the state level, may be forced to look at controversial subjects, such as nongrowth and social equity, at the same time and to develop some meaningful responses.

The exit of judges from the nongrowth-social equity arena can be viewed as a two-edged sword—it can remove the courts from an active role in social change, but it can also open up the path for more meaningful, less inhibited legislative initiatives.

Specific Judicial Responses

Assuming that legislatures, particularly at the local levels, enact nongrowth and social equity measures, how are the courts likely to respond? What limits have recent cases placed on such legislation? Because few communities have consciously integrated nongrowth and social equity objectives, there are correspondingly few cases in which the courts address the effect of one goal on the other. Nevertheless, cases flowing from the wave of environmental laws and the litigation against exclusionary zoning do afford some clues. In the following discussions of this case law, the decisions are grouped with respect to basic growth control objectives: where should growth be allowed to take place and at what densities; and assuming that development is environmentally sound at a given location, when should it take place with respect to the fiscally responsible provision of urban services? Decisions concerning social equity and jurisdiction of the courts are then discussed.

"Where" and "How Much" Techniques

Environmental Controls. With the growing awareness of the dangers of environmental degradation has come a multitude of environmental legislation from all levels of government. Many of these laws, particularly those enacted at the state and local level, have dramatic effects on land development. Environmental performance standards can severely limit development. Often, such laws relegate land to open space purposes. Had local governments sought to accomplish the same results with their conventional zoning powers, they would have been shot down by the courts for using the police power to accomplish purely aesthetic objectives or to obtain private property for essentially public use, which is in violation of the Fifth Amendment's prohibition against uncompensated confiscation.

But when local controls on development in environmentally sensitive areas, like floodplains and wetlands, are specifically authorized by state enabling legislation, the courts have shown a willingness to uphold them in the face of legal challenges based on the constitutional protection afforded property rights.

Wetland protection cases: In Just v. Marinette County,[33] in Wisconsin, a state-authorized local wetland protection ordinance was upheld against the argument that its prohibition of fill invalidly removed all development value from the plaintiff's property. The court said that land ownership does not necessarily include an inherent right to alter the natural state of the land when to do so would threaten the health, safety, and welfare of the other citizens of the state. Wetland protection legislation has also been approved recently in Connecticut.

Floodplain ordinance cases: Regulation of development in flood-prone areas had not fared well with the courts until the federal carrot of flood insurance prompted most states to adopt floodplain-zoning enabling legislation. Only a few decisions reflect this added muscle of state enabling legislation, but Turnpike Realty Company v. Town of Dedham,[34] where a floodplain ordinance

was upheld despite the argument that it amounted to an unconstitutional taking of property, may be a harbinger of future judicial
attitudes toward such laws.

Conventional Local Development Controls. Downzoning cases:
Crude downzoning to prevent large second-home developments in
environmentally sensitive areas is permissible, at least in the short
run, according to the federal court decision in Steel Hill v. Town of
Sanbornton.[35] In the face of a downzoning that dramatically reduced
property values, the California Supreme Court recently held in the
Cerritos case[36] that the property owner was not entitled to bring
an action in inverse condemnation to recover the lost development
value—his remedy was a conventional action to determine the consti-
tutionality of the downzoning itself. It remains to be seen whether
the downzoning will ultimately be upheld.

Fiscal and Exclusionary Zoning. When downzoning and similar conventional zoning techniques are used to accomplish purely fiscal or
exclusionary ends without reference to environmental dangers, then
the federal courts and some state courts, notably in New Jersey and
Pennsylvania, will be more likely to strike down such regulations.

"When" Techniques

Having determined that no serious physical environmental
limitations on growth exist, it may still be inefficient or fiscally
impossible to allow growth to occur haphazardly or out of sequence.
Some communities have begun to address this dimension of land
development control.

Ramapo, New York. New subdivision was not permitted unless the
prospective subdivision achieved a sufficiently high score, based
on proximity to existing public services. The control was tied to
a series of capital plans for the provision of services covering a
period of almost 20 years, and it was upheld in court.

Petaluma, California. This community placed annual limits on the
number of residential building permits as part of a total plan to
slow growth and redirect it within the community. A federal trial
court decision striking down the Petaluma plan on the grounds that
it violated the federal constitutional right to travel was reversed
by a federal appeals court, which found the plan within the confines
of the reasonable exercise of the police power. In February 1976,
the U. S. Supreme Court declined to hear the case. Thus, the appeals
court decision and the Petaluma plan stand as legally valid.

Boulder, Colorado. This plan for the phased extension of public
services (in this case, sewers) suffered a setback when the court
held in the Robinson case[37] that the city had become a "public
utility" with respect to a particular landowner who had brought the
case and, therefore, had lost the discretion to withhold the public
service. The decision was under appeal at the end of 1975. It should
be noted that the court did not find the use of utility extension to
effect growth policies unconstitutional per se. The issues raised
in the Robinson case are novel, and the courts will be navigating
uncharted waters as more cases reflect increasing municipal use
of such controls.

Can a Locality Promote Social Equity
Through Land Development Controls?

Local Actions

Active. The idea is that the community itself distributes the resource
(jobs, housing, better services) to the economically disadvantaged.
When local government takes affirmative action to help moderate
potentially negative side effects of growth limits (higher land and
housing costs, restricted job opportunities), the courts might be
less likely to hold those growth-limiting actions invalid. This concept has met with some favorable court responses.

    1. Ramapo: the New York Court of Appeals was able to dis-
count arguments that the Ramapo regulations were exclusionary,
in part because the township had established a public housing agency
and had actually constructed some subsidized housing units, despite
court suits by its own citizens.

    2. Mount Laurel: the court indicated that there was at least
a "moral obligation in a municipality to establish a local housing
agency pursuant to state law to provide housing for its resident
poor."

Passive. The idea is that public actions should encourage private
distribution of the resource (housing, jobs, and so forth). These
run the gamut from incentives to mandatory requirements (such
as a certain percentage of lower-income housing in planned-develop-
ment or large subdivisions). With respect to land-use controls, few
cases involving such techniques have come down. The Virginia
Supreme Court in DeGroff v. Board of Supervisors[38] invalidated
a Fairfax County provision that established a mandatory 15 percent

lower-income housing in planned developments on the grounds that
since it was "socioeconomic zoning," it was beyond the scope of
zoning powers delegated to localities by state enabling legislation.
Similar requirements in Montgomery County, Maryland, and Los
Angeles have not been attacked, and the DeGroff outcome will probably be confined to Virginia.

Beyond Local Boundaries—Regional Problems

Exclusionary zoning cases, particularly in Pennsylvania, repeatedly emphasize that communities cannot unilaterally ignore
pressures for housing generated and felt throughout the entire metropolitan areas. There are pronouncements that localities must accept
their share of regional growth, but few courts have tackled the following questions:
1. What is the region?
2. Assuming the region can be defined, must each community
determine what its fair share is, without regional planning for housing
distribution?
3. Assuming that a fair share can be determined, what must
a community do to make its share a reality?
The New Jersey courts, in the Mount Laurel decision,[39] and
more definitively in the forthcoming Madison Township case, have
been defining the limits of the regional and municipal obligations with
respect to lower-income housing. But there has been a strong judicial sentiment in favor of legislative resolutions of these questions
(see court's discussion of the desirability of legislative solutions
in the Ramapo case).[40] That state or regional level solutions will
be favored by the courts may be indicated by the judicial approval
of the Massachusetts "Anti-Snob Zoning Law," in Board of Appeals
of Hanover v. Housing Appeals Commission.[41]

Will the Courts Address These Issues, and To What Extent Should They Get Involved?

Federal/State Court Dichotomy

Several recent decisions of the federal courts—the Ybarra
case[42] and Warth v. Seldin[43]—indicate a growing reluctance on the
part of the federal judiciary to decide exclusionary land-use controls cases, particularly where economic, not racial, discrimination
appears to be involved. On the other hand, at least one state court
(New Jersey, in the Mount Laurel case) has said that the general

welfare, for which land-use controls are, in part, exercised, included the opportunity for decent, affordable housing.

Growing Recognition of Limits of Courts

Nevertheless, there is, even at the frontiers of judicial discussion of these issues (as in the Mount Laurel case), a growing recognition of the limits of courts to solve the problems implicit in the nongrowth-social equity issue.

There are limits on what courts can do in a competent manner. The courts may be able to deal with cases of overt racism, but they may have great difficulty understanding and dealing with cases involving income discrimination. Population ceilings that do not limit anything other than total numbers will, perhaps, be beyond the comprehension of the courts, at least in the near future. There is a question whether the facts in such cases can even be proved in an adversary context. Some courts may try to stretch and jury-rig available legal standards to cover these new situations, but the record is likely to be uneven and result in little overall direction.

In any event, it seems clear that the courts will probably have a difficult, if not impossible, task if they attempt to come in directly and develop and administer local zoning ordinances and housing programs. In the Chicago metropolitan area, the federal court has ordered that public housing be built in a pattern to encourage more integration, but enforcing the edict with Mayor Daley's administration has proven to be extremely difficult. School desegregation and municipal bankruptcy cases may offer some leads, but the reader can judge for himself or herself how effective the courts have been in these areas. Even the activist courts may find themselves interfering in local affairs and producing the wrong results. As noted earlier in this chapter, the courts' knowledge of housing markets and housing economics has not been substantial. If they want to get more directly involved and overturn local land-use powers on a broad scale, they will have to quickly educate themselves on how much land costs influence housing availability and how much zoning and other controls influence land costs. Other factors, such as access, environmental constraints, speculation, tax laws, and materials shortages will also have to be considered.

CONCLUSION

Those who would like to see a single general-standard equity approach required of all nongrowth communities are likely to be

disappointed if they focus their strategy on the courts. They are
also likely to be disappointed if they expect the courts to take over
the bulk of local land-use powers and affirmative housing programs.

The accomplishments on these fronts will probably be diverse.
The equity responses will be different in different nongrowth communities. Local legislative bodies will have to take the initiative and do
the best they can. States are encouraged to stimulate and assist
such local action. If they want to get more involved and attempt to
require and to assist regional approaches and real fair-share housing
allocations, the present authors wish them luck. There may be some
states that will have the sensitivity and the vision to succeed.

It would appear to be the role of the courts to first learn what
is going on and then try to keep social equity considerations on the
table in local communities by dealing with the more blatant attempts
to put a nongrowth cover on purely racial, and in some cases, income
exclusion. This will help to keep everyone a little more honest and
moral. The courts could also stimulate major equity progress by
looking favorably on attempts to make more direct economic transfers to the poor. This could, for example, include attempts to require local hiring and training of the poor before an industrial rezoning is approved. It could also include the quotas for low- and
moderate-income housing in not only residential developments but
also some major nonresidential developments, such as shopping
centers. Special community considerations of inner-city or poverty
area tax policies and municipal services should also be encouraged.

Attempts to transfer economic resources from one community to another should also be approved and encouraged. The whole
Minnesota tax-sharing approach can serve as one example. The
courts might also have to look favorably on transfer payments from
a community that wishes to retain a more distinct identity. A fee
in lieu of each low- or moderate-income unit derived from a fair-
share plan might be possible, for example. This fee could assist
the development or upgrading of housing and neighborhoods in
neighboring communities. Some communities might wish to provide
special parks, employment opportunities, or even educational facilities for the residents of other neighboring communities, but might
balk at providing more lower-income housing. The courts may again
have to decide if this is better than nothing.

Obviously, as this chapter has noted, nongrowth needs a social
equity component in action as well as theory. The courts can assist
in this goal, but they cannot do it alone. They probably cannot even
be among the leaders. But they do have a role, and the role may be
enlarged somewhat as more judges become more enlightened.

NOTES

1. Michael A. Agelasto, II, "Equity Considerations in Controlled Growth Policies," Management and Control of Growth, 3 vols. (Washington, D.C.: The Urban Land Institute, 1975), 1: 433.

2. Randall Scott, "Exclusion: Proposals and Prescriptions," ibid., p. 519.

3. The Rockefeller Brothers Fund, The Use of Land: A Citizen's Policy Guide to Urban Growth, ed. William Reilly (New York: Thomas Y. Crowell Company, 1973), p. 33.

4. Personal communication from Richard Appelbaum, Department of Sociology, University of California-Santa Barbara, Santa Barbara, Calif., September 10, 1975.

5. Southern Burlington County NAACP v. Township of Mount Laurel, 336 a. 2d 713 (N.J. 1975).

6. Herbert M. Franklin, David Falk, and Arthur J. Levin, In-Zoning: A Guide for Policy-Makers on Inclusionary Land Use Programs (Washington, D.C.: The Potomac Institute, 1974), p. 99.

7. Ibid., p. 6.

8. Edward M. Bergman, A Policy Guide to Evaluations of Policy Related Research on Development Controls and Housing Costs (Chapel Hill: University of North Carolina Center for Urban and Regional Studies, 1974), pp. 8, 17.

9. Steven Maser, William Riker, and Richard Rosett, "Municipal Zoning in Monroe County: A Preliminary Report," and idem., "The Effects of Zoning and Externalities on the Prices of Land in Monroe County, New York" (Rochester, N.Y.: University of Rochester, April 1974).

10. Bergman, op. cit., p. 22.

11. U.S. Department of Housing and Urban Development, 1972 HUD Statistical Yearbook (Washington, D.C.: U.S. Government Printing Office, 1972), p. 217.

12. Ibid.

13. Sylvan Kamm, "Inflation, Curbing Inflation in Residential Land Prices," Urban Land, September 1971, p. 6.

14. U.S. Department of Commerce, Bureau of the Census, Statistical Abstract of the United States: 1974, 95th ed. (Washington, D.C.: Government Printing Office, 1974), p. 697.

15. Warren E. Farb, "Availability of Homes for Middle-Income Families" (Washington, D.C.: Congressional Research Service, Library of Congress, February 13, 1975).

16. Claude Gruen, "The Economics of Petaluma: Unconstitutional Socio-Economic Impacts," in Management and Control of

Growth, ed. Randall W. Scott (Washington, D.C.: The Urban Land Institute, 1975), 2: 180.

17. Herbert G. Lawson, "Civil Libertarians Join Developers to Oppose Cities' Growth Curbs," Wall Street Journal, January 31, 1975, p. 1.

18. Construction Industry Association of Sonoma County v. City of Petaluma, 375 F. Supp. 574 (N.D.), rev'd., no. 74-2100 (9th Cir., decided August 13, 1975), 522 F. 2d 897.

19. E.F. Schumacher, Small is Beautiful—Economics as if People Mattered (New York: Harper and Row, 1973).

20. Kamm, op. cit., p. 6.

21. Ibid., p. 7.

22. Ibid., p. 8.

23. Ray M. Northan, "Vacant Land in the American City," Land Economics 47, no. 4 (November 1971): 355.

24. Charles M. Haar and Demetrius S. Iatridis, Housing the Poor in Suburbia (Cambridge, Mass.: Ballinger Publishing Company, 1974), p. 12.

25. Paul A. Samuelson, "Inequality," Newsweek, December 17, 1973, p. 84.

26. Lewis Mandel, Business Week, August 5, 1972, pp. 54-56.

27. "Black Youths' Jobless Rate Soared; Whites Stood Still," Arizona Daily Star, May 30, 1975, p. 7.

28. Ibid.

29. Henry J. Aaron, Shelter and Subsidies (Washington, D.C.: The Brookings Institution, 1972), pp. 10-11.

30. Arthur P. Solomon, Housing the Urban Poor (Cambridge, Mass., The MIT Press, 1974), p. 33.

31. Hazel Henderson, "Redefining Economic Growth," in Environmental Quality and Social Justice in Urban America, ed. James Noel Smith (Washington, D.C.: The Conservation Foundation, 1974), pp. 132-33.

32. For a full discussion of legal issues in growth management, see Michael E. Gleeson et al., Urban Growth Management Systems: An Evaluation of Policy Related Research, Planning Advisory Service Report nos. 309, 310 (Chicago: American Society of Planning Officials, 1975), pp. 57-95.

33. Just v. Marinette Co., 56 Wisc. 2d 7, 201 N.W. 2d 761 (1972).

34. Turnpike Realty v. Town of Dedham, 284 N.E. 2d 891 (Mass. 1972).

35. Steel Hill Development, Inc. v. Town of Sanbornton, 496 F. 2d 956 (1st Cir., 1972) aff'g 338 F. Supp. 301 (D. N.H., 1972).

36. Construction Industry Association of Sonoma County v. City of Petaluma, 375 F. Supp. 574 (N.D. Cal. 1974), rev'd, no. 74-2100 (9th Cir., decided August 13, 1975), 522 F. 2d 897.

37. Robinson v. City of Boulder, action no. 72-2033-1 (D. Colo., decided May 20, 1974).

38. Board of Supervisors of Fairfax County v. DeGroff Enterprises, 214 Va 235, 197 S.E. 2d 600 (1973).

39. Southern Burlington County NAACP v. Township of Mount Laurel, 336 a. 2d 713 (N.J. 1975).

40. Golden v. Planning Board of the Town of Ramapo, 30 N.Y. 2d 359, 285 N.E. 2d 291 (1972), app. dis. 409 U.S. 1003.

41. Board of Appeals of Hanover v. Housing Appeals Committee, 294 N.E. 2d 393 (Mass. 1973).

42. Ybarra v. The City of the Town of Los Altos Hills, 503 F. 2d 250 (9th Cir. 1974).

43. Warth v. Seldin, 95 S. Ct. 2197 (1975).

3

THE LOCAL RESPONSE ON
NONGROWTH AND SOCIAL EQUITY

The nongrowth movement, as described in this book, springs primarily from local communities (regions). However, much of the research and analysis of the exclusionary potential and practice of local nongrowth has been done at a distance from those planners and citizens actually on the scene. For example, when the famous Mount Laurel exclusionary zoning case was decided by the New Jersey Supreme Court, in March 1975, there were volumes of comments by noted legal and land-use experts but only very rare articles that named or quoted any of the Mount Laurel officials. (One well-written exception was an article by Ed McCahill, entled, ''In Mount Laurel, Issues Are Not Black and White.''[1] McCahill was the first outsider to discover that the mayor of Mount Laurel was a Puerto Rican and that he lived in an $18,000 house in the supposed exclusionary suburb.)

As theories and strategies for combined nongrowth and social equity were considered, it became clear that there was a need to check them out with practicing planners to see if they were really realistic and feasible or merely wispy gleams in the eyes of the authors. So, early in 1975, the present authors sent out a questionnaire on nongrowth and social equity to 30 cities, counties, and regions that were known to have had some experiences with nongrowth (at least in the discussion stage).

Neither Dayton, Ohio, nor New Orleans, two cities that were contacted and responded, has problems with population growth. But Dayton is the key central city in the innovative Miami Valley region (known for its lower-income housing allocation plan), and New Orleans has considerable local discussion and debate over historic preservation, opposition to freeways and new traffic bridges, and other issues that often arise in growth struggles.

A total of 14 responses were received by August 1975. While
the total is rather small, the geographic and size range of the
responding communities made the responses interesting. The one
questionnaire sent to Canada for an outside perspective resulted in
a return from the city of Toronto. Other respondents included the
city of Los Angeles; Dade County, Florida; Boulder, Colorado; and
the regional council of governments (COG) around San Francisco.
Names of the actual respondents in each area are not given here,
but the questionnaires were usually returned by planners active in
the community. The findings from the questionnaire effort do not
have any statistical significance, but they do show a variety of local
responses to some of the key nongrowth-social equity questions
raised in the previous chapter.

Each of the major questions in the questionnaire is listed on
the following pages. The edited responses to each question are presented, with an overview and comments.

EXISTING CONDITIONS IN RESPONDING JURISDICTIONS

The emphasis in the questionnaire was on more subjective
information and comments. However, two questions attempted to
frame the responses in a more objective context, that is, it attempted
to elicit background information on the jurisdiction and its present
situation with regard to minorities, the poor, and subsidized housing.
The two questions follow:

A. Please give some indication of the per cent of minorities and poverty-level residents in your jurisdiction. How
have these percentages changed in the past 10 years or so?
Are the minorities and the poor concentrated in certain
areas of your jurisdiction or are they more spread out?
Can most people employed in your jurisdiction afford to
live there?

B. How many housing units in your jurisdiction are supported by a public subsidy of some type? Please note
the distinction between elderly housing as opposed to
housing for low- and moderate-income families.

The answers received were often incomplete, described different
indicators, or related to different time periods. Thus, no comprehensive quantitative comparison among the 14 respondents was

TABLE 3.1

Questionnaire Respondents: Population and Percentage
of Minority Population, 1970

Jurisdiction	1970 Population	Minority Group(s) as Percent of Population[a]
Boulder, Colorado	66,870	7-10 (1975)
Petaluma, California	30,000	Less than 1
Eugene, Oregon	80,000	2.5
Amherst, Massachusetts	26,331	5
Lakewood, Colorado	92,787	Black less than 1; Spanish, 2
New Orleans, Louisiana	593,471	50
Los Angeles, California	2,816,061	Black, 17.2; Spanish, 18; other, 4.1 (1970)
Pinellas County, Florida	522,329	Black, 9.6
Dade County, Florida	1,267,792	15.5 (1970)
Mid-Willamette Valley Council of Governments, Oregon	186,658	1.5
Association of Bay Area Governments, San Francisco, California	4,600,000	Black, 8
Ada Council of Governments (Boise area), Idaho	112,230	Black, less than 1; Spanish language, 1.5 (1970)
Dayton, Ohio	243,601	Black, 33 (1975)
Toronto, Ontario, Canada	712,786[b]	n.a.[c]

[a]Year is included if given by respondent.
[b]1971 population.
[c]No answer.
Source: Compiled by the author.

possible. The population of the responding jurisdiction for 1970, along with the percentage of minority population listed by the respondents, is noted in Table 3.1.

Certain growth-sensitive communities have experienced racial change over the past ten years. Boulder, one of the more antigrowth communities in the country, reported that its percentage of minorities had about tripled from 1960, when it was about 2-3 percent. Amherst, another growth-sensitive community, reported a doubling of the minority percentage in the past ten years. Los Angeles, which had an overall gain of over 300,000 people during 1960-70, reported a 1970 black population of about 17.2 percent of the total, up only 1-2 percent from 1960. The white population in 1970 was reported down about three to five points from its 1960 percentage, with many reported as "moved to Orange County" (to the south). Dayton was estimated to be about one-third black in 1975, and the population of New Orleans was estimated to be about 50 percent minority (mostly black), with no specific year given.

Some interesting responses were provided to the question of whether people employed in the jurisdiction could afford to live there. The Boulder answer was "No, if they had to go out tomorrow and buy a house. Fortunately, most were already in units before the big run-ups occurred."

The estimate from Amherst was that about 60-70 percent of those employed there could afford housing in the community. "New Orleans is the poorest major city in the country. If they can't live here may God help them," came one rather pessimistic response. The answer from Los Angeles was what one might expect, "People can generally afford housing if they drive."

There was a definite "no" to the question from Pinellas County, where the respondent noted that the average single-family house sold for $36,000 and that 70 percent of the population was making less than $10,000 a year. On the other hand, the Boise area COG reported that everyone who worked there could afford housing, both in the city and in the surrounding county. The Toronto response reported that 30 percent of the households in the metropolitan area paid more than 25 percent of their income for housing.

With regard to possible minority concentrations, there were only a few answers, but both Boulder and Amherst reported that minorities were more spread out rather than concentrated, which in Boulder may be partially the result of its scattered public housing. Los Angeles has lower density concentrations of its minorities than many other major cities, according to the respondent. The person reported that the black concentration in Los Angeles occupied about 20 square miles, "which is a big area." Of the 349 blacks reported living in Salem, Oregon, 227 were listed as being in a state institution.

Precise reports on housing units supported by some form of
public subsidy were also rather infrequent. But again, growth-
sensitive communities, such as Boulder, Amherst, and Eugene,
reported substantial subsidized housing. In Boulder, it was estimated
that there were over 500 such units, about one-half available for
general occupancy. In Amherst, some 350 family units and 110
elderly units were reported. Eugene had over 2,200 units of subsidized
housing in 1973, of which about 700 were for the elderly. Los Angeles
reported over 8,000 conventional public housing units and over 3,600
Section 23 (leased housing units) units. Lakewood reported 96 units
of Section 236 housing. The Section 236 program involves federal
interest subsidies to lower rents in multifamily housing. Dayton
reported "several thousand units—more than our regional share,"
with apparent reference to the Miami Valley COG regional housing
allocation plan. Toronto reported over 13,000 assisted units out of a
total stock of 224,000 units in the city. Pinellas County and the Boise
area COG did not answer. Dade County, Florida, reported over 8,400
units in management, with about 44 percent of these being for the
elderly.

THE PLANNERS' RESPONSE

Following are the remaining, more subjective questions (and
the responses from local planners) on the topic of nongrowth and
social equity:

Question 1. Exact and universal definitions of nongrowth
or controlled growth strategies are difficult to apply, but
would you say that your community or region is actively
considering, developing or implementing strategies, policies or tools to reduce or more directly control the
amount, type and/or rate of growth below base or pro-
jected trends? Such growth could relate to population,
sprawl, or various sectors in the economy.

Comment

The word "nongrowth" often prompts confusion and emotional
reactions by some planners, as well as by some builders, politicians,
and, even, environmentalists. At the start of this book, the concept
of nongrowth was defined as clearly as possible. But with a questionnaire of this type, it was important to define the "nongrowth"
part of the nongrowth-social equity issue. It was also important to

determine whether some form of nongrowth was at issue in the community to give a better perspective on the social equity responses.

When asked if some kind of approach of nongrowth activity was taking place, none of the communities answered with an outright no. But several, including Lakewood, Colorado, emphasized that public influence on the amount and rate of population growth was not a topic the planners were putting on the table in their jurisdiction. While the Dayton response came from a community facing a kind of natural population decline, it did indicate some concern about slowing the growth of wasteful consumption. It is interesting to note that the Los Angeles response included an overview of some nongrowth activity at the state level, while the Toronto answer went even further and commented on activities of the government of Canada.

While the responses show a rather general concern over growth, especially the growth of wasteful sprawl, the range of descriptions shows the diversity of local and regional nongrowth situations.

Boulder, Colorado. Yes. The city has utilized traditional land-use techniques in a coordinated manner to achieve growth management of development. A spin-off from having it together was to discourage some developers, who then sought easier areas, thus reducing the rate of development in the community. There is now an attempt to consolidate the techniques into an umbrella process called "growth management system." The effort is too incomplete at this point to judge whether it is feasible.

Petaluma, California. The city of Petaluma has adopted a five-year plan called the "Environmental Design Plan," of which the Residential Development Control System is a part. This system limits growth to 500 residential units per year.

Eugene, Oregon. Here, in Eugene, the 1990 Metro Area General Plan (adopted, 1972) sets forth an urban service area within which urban development should occur. The five-year major update of the plan is coming up beginning next year, and an evaluation should provide some insight as to the impacts the service area has had, or not had, on the development-related problems of the metropolitan area.

Amherst, Massachusetts. Yes. The Select Committee on Goals published a report in January 1973. We are presently attempting to get a new zoning by-law adopted that is consistent with established goals.

Lakewood, Colorado. Yes, but it is the management of growth that we are concerned with, not the control of growth. We are attempting

to do this through the development of an activity center land-use
pattern.

New Orleans, Louisiana. New Orleans, the latecomer it is, is promoting growth at any cost within the city boundaries (parish); it has
great hopes of creating a suburban sprawl on the swamplands of New
Orleans East in an effort to increase its tax base. Faced with the
choice of promoting its older, unique inner-city neighborhoods or
recreating the "success" story of Jefferson, it promotes suburbs in
the swamps.

Los Angeles, California: Limited Efforts.
        1. State—Water Resources Department provides money based
on Series E population projections. Capacity that is excess is not
funded.
        2. County of Los Angeles—reduced 1990 population projections
in 1974, but it does not mean much. They are just reacting to a lower
birth rate.
        3. City of Los Angeles—downzoning program has been formu-
lated, but implementation strategy (either a rollback citywide at
once or on a community-by-community basis) not decided yet. In
theory, future development has been phased to the provision of adequate public facilities, but many roads are still overcapacity, as
are a few schools. Air quality alone should stop growth, but of
course will not.

Clearwater, Pinellas County, Florida. Outside pressures from
regional groups prompted new growth control methods and the
redirection of old methods toward a less rapid population growth
policy. The lack of water for drinking within the county borders
forced the purchase of water from fields outside the county. There
is a critical need for region and statewide planning for the water
needs of the region. This will call for regionwide population redistribution and timing of growth with the ability of the area to supply
water. We hope to include other facilities in this plan when it is
finally implemented.
        The current managed-growth program consists of the following:
        1. an official land-use map, with force of law backed by a
council of countywide officials (there are 24 municipalities in tiny
Pinellas)
        2. environmental zoning requirements in drainage, setback,
and tree removal
        3. site plan review for large developments, which considers
the ability of available facilities to handle a new development's impact.

4. strict control over sewage treatment facilities to handle a new development's impact

5. strict control over sewage treatment facilities other than publicly owned sewage plants (that is, package plants, septic tanks)

Dade County, Florida. Dade County is now in the process of developing the mass transit program. It is assumed that station points will be the sites of intensive development, which will lessen the impact on suburban areas. In addition, an environmental impact statement is now being considered at the county level—although growth limits are not suggested, controlled growth is now underway.

Mid-Willamette Valley COG, Salem, Oregon. Yes. The city and the two counties have adopted policies and ordinances to control the extent of growth and to phase growth, based on availability of certain services.

Association of Bay Area Governments (ABAG), San Francisco, California. Amount-rate reflected primarily in residential areas. This is true for several cities, and is exemplified as follows: (a) Petaluma plan; (b) city of Livermore is placing land into an urban transition zone from a mixed-uses zoning, which has effect of delaying development; (c) city of Santa Clara (in southern Bay) and cities in East Bay have much land zoned industrial, but it is not being rapidly utilized; (d) large cities (Oakland, San Francisco) are downzoning neighborhoods, which prevents breakup of large, old units into one-bedroom/studio units and retains family accessibility and existing density (the only "plus" in the list).

Ada COG, Boise, Idaho. This area is extremely concerned about sprawl and the subsequent withdrawal of irrigated and other productive land from agricultural use. Most people seem to say they would rather not see a great population growth or a significant change in the life-style that such growth would create, but, as of yet, there is no official or public commitment to policies or a strategy that would limit or control population growth or sprawl.

Dayton, Ohio. Yes. Planners and citizens are talking about the need to stop waste, check suburban sprawl, stop highways—go to mass transit. The economy is in a state of dynamic instability and will naturally bring about a nongrowth/slow-growth economy. Conservation, restoration of the existing housing stock, is not accepted policy by public officials.

Toronto, Ontario, Canada (Combined answer to Questions 1, 2, and 3). To various degrees, all levels of government are actively considering the implications of growth.

1. The Government of Canada has initiated studies, inquiries, and policy development processes in such areas as population growth, conservation of natural resources, and redistribution of wealth on both national and international scales. Specific proposals were put forward by Prime Minister Pierre Trudeau at the recent Commonwealth Conference in Jamaica. A national debate is underway to determine a new immigration policy for Canada. A national energy policy may emerge also, and it could have substnatial effects on redistribution of population (migration) and wealth between the provinces. The Ministry of State for Urban Affairs was established to initiate and coordinate policies and research in urban affairs, many of them related to the issues of your concern.

2. The Government of Ontario is developing an overall regional planning strategy. Ontario is now divided into five planning regions, and the Central Ontario Region (Toronto) is one of them. The impending provincial election may have a decisive influence on the growth strategy to be followed in Ontario. A Royal Commission is now reviewing all aspects of the Metropolitan Toronto government, and it is likely to affect many aspects of Toronto. A new Metropolitan Official Plan is being developed also.

3. In the City of Toronto, a Reform Council was elected in 1972, and re-elected in 1974. During these years, in response to public concern about the impact of continued redevelopment and change, the city has undertaken an extensive view of its plans and policies. A new housing policy was adopted, and the newly created Housing Department started its implementation. The main goal is quite ambitious: "The provision of all residents of decent housing in a suitable living environment at a price they can afford," and "the equitable distribution of the housing stock of the City in particular to meet the needs of identified target income groups." Alderman John Sewall has stated that the only reason for the City permitting substantial residential development in any area is if it will make a major contribution to housing to the poor who need it most. However, there are indications that Alderman Sewall's opinion may not represent the view of the majority, either in the council or in the community.

Question 2. Have you yourself or someone in your department evaluated or anticipated any exclusionary or negative impacts on minorities, the poor, women, etc. as a result of the strategies, policies and tools listed above? Be specific.

Comment

Given the high degree of involvement in some kind of nongrowth activity reported by the respondents in the answers to question one, it would follow that some thinking had been done about possible exclusionary or negative impacts on minorities and the poor. When the questionnaire was sent to some planners and fair-housing professionals for preliminary comments, it was noted that women should be listed with the other groups. This was done, but no respondent really raised any specific concerns for women as a result of some kind of nongrowth actions.

The tone of the answers varied, but no jurisdiction wrote off nongrowth as being undesirable because of exclusion. Some respondents, such as Boulder and the Mid-Willamette Valley COG, came out more on the offensive, noting that previous uncontrolled growth patterns had not provided much in the way of low- and moderate-income housing. Further, the Boulder response noted the city's willingness to reduce or suspend service fees for water and sewer hookups when these would impede low-income housing construction.

The excerpt from the San Francisco area housing report included a number of the prevailing regional cautions about individual community nongrowth activities, including a concern for the price of land and pressure on existing lower-income housing. But the report also saw a possible plus from nongrowth: "As people become aware that the supply of good housing is limited, they may become more strongly motivated to invest in its preservation."

The Mid-Willamette Valley COG has taken a rather different approach to the problem of land price inflation than that noted by the San Francisco area report. It said that the asking price of land in many cases has increased because of the imposition of an urban limit line, but it also stated the impossibility of determining how much, if any, of the increase was due to the line.

The response from Boise, Idaho, made the interesting point that sprawl puts some of the lowest-income people the greatest distance from needed medical, social, and recreational services.

Some of the answers to this question show a fairly high level of awareness and sophistication in weighing possible exclusionary aspects of some form of nongrowth policy. The local answers appear to be more diverse and thoughtful than the more simple approaches often taken by legal and planning experts, who attack nongrowth for being little or nothing more than pure exclusion.

Boulder, Colorado. Yes. From the beginning of the effort in 1967 to project the city into the growth-shaping business, this has been a major concern of the staff, legislative body, and various citizen groups. A "white paper" written by the City Manager and adopted, by the Council set forth the city's willingness to supplement funds or suspend fees whenever they were an impediment to low-income housing. The middle-income families were probably the ones who were most adversely affected. Filtering down of units does not occur in Boulder, so the idea of benefiting low income this way was unrealistic.

Petaluma, California. We were concerned about possible exclusionary effects of the growth control system when it was first formulated. For that reason, we have incorporated provisions for low- to moderate-income housing into the system.

Eugene, Oregon. We have talked about this during staff discussions, especially as it related to the cost of housing, but no formal evaluations have been made or even proposed. I suspect that something of this nature will be included in the major update of the 1990 General Plan. The Bureau of Governmental Research at the University of Oregon is currently in the process of applying for National Science Foundation money to conduct an evaluation of the urban service area.

Amherst, Massachusetts. We are in the process of developing such data, [by] comparing [the] existing zoning by-law with [the] proposed [new zoning by-law].

Lakewood, Colorado. (Response included in answer to Question 3.)

New Orleans, Louisiana. No.

Los Angeles, California. I am doing our housing element. Our environmental impact review will briefly discuss the effects of certain housing activities on the poor, minorities, and others. The housing element is only an indirect tool for growth equity factors though. Our element still starts with the basic assumption that we are "destined" to receive a certain 1990 population and must accommodate it.

Clearwater, Pinellas County, Florida. Lack of low-income housing for large families and the elderly is a serious problem in Pinellas County. It was not caused by the above growth control policies but by a misjudgment of the need for moderately high-income housing by developers. Land values are very high here due to high costs of improving the land for development and (principally) lack of land.

Although the demand for low-cost housing is greater, while we are overbuilt in high-cost condominium-type housing, prices have not come down due to banks' ability to wait out economic slump until population growth picks up again.

Dade County, Florida. The plan does not really directly address this issue. During the hearings on the plan before the Planning Advisory Board or even before the County Commission, I cannot recall this being raised as an important issue by those in attendance at the hearings. The issue of slow growth or nongrowth was raised by the developers, realtors, and, generally, those who favored unlimited, unbridled growth, not those concerned about exclusionary zoning or development.

Some of the developers who testified did mention the question of housing exclusion as an impact of the Comprehensive Plan's limiting where growth can occur. They used the argument that low- and moderate-income housing could be built in the hinterland (where land is cheaper) and that if this development were limited, it would limit the opportunity for low- and moderate-income housing in the county. Personally, this was the first time I had heard the developers or builders speaking of a need for low- and moderate-income housing and the need to provide it.

Mid-Willamette Valley COG, Salem, Oregon. The implications and possible results of an urban growth boundary were considered by staff, planning commission members, the governing bodies who adopted the policies and boundary, and by many others in the community. It was also raised by members of the real estate and development industry and the state housing office. The main criticism was that the boundary would increase the cost of the land by decreasing the supply, thus making it impossible to build low- and moderate-cost housing. We found that in many cases, the asking price of land had increased because of setting the boundary. But it was impossible to determine what, if any, amount of increase in assessed value of land was directly related to the boundary. Since the boundary was adopted, there have been so many other factors which have increased the cost of housing throughout the country that it is hard to believe that the urban growth boundary has had much effect on the cost of housing, so far. We also found here, as in other parts of the country, that developers were not building low-cost housing for low-income people without substantial subsidies. Even many of the moderate-cost housing projects were subsidized.

ABAG, San Francisco, California. Please see enclosed pages from ABAG Regional Housing Plan. There is no intensive documentation to our knowledge. We hope to do such a piece . . . Money, you know.*

Growth Controls and Housing Conservation

In their efforts to manage, to control, and, in some
instances, to limit urban development—its pace, pattern, and type—many Bay Area communities are currently reacting to problems generated in earlier
periods by rapid and unplanned growth. Zoning
ordinances and other development controls were
designed and implemented in such a way as to accommodate rather than control development. . . . As a
result, many localities experienced the conversion of
prime grazing and agricultural land to urban development, and the loss of potential recreation resources as
well. Moreover, inefficient development patterns have
generated excess costs in public facilities and basic
utilities, which are ultimately passed on to the full community. In older, more centrally located urban centers,
the amenities of existing neighborhoods were threatened
by pressures for increased densities. All this has occurred without producing the housing needed by low-
and moderate-income people.

In order to preserve irreplaceable resources,
many local governments are now seeking to devise
much stronger planning approaches and legal mechanisms to guide, limit, and even stop the growth of their
urban areas and the increase of their resident population. From the point of view of each individual community, such efforts not only appear justified but laudable.
However, from a regional perspective, there could be
serious negative consequences resulting from the aggregate of many separate local efforts to limit or stop
growth. For example, such controls tend to artificially
inflate the price of land available for development of
existing housing. This could mean that, under normal
market conditions, only high-priced development could
occur and only high-income people could live in those
parts of the region where such controls were in effect.
The pressures on existing lower-income housing would
grow, causing prices to rise here also, with no

———————

*Since the reference cited is rather brief, the excerpt from
the housing plan is presented.

commensurate increase in amenity. . . .

Growth controls would also place additional pressures on the existing housing stock, both for owners and for renters. The Bay Area now contains a large supply of good new and older housing, which will be at a premium as the rate of increase slows down. This may prompt many residential property owners to make substantial investments in housing conservation. On the other hand, as vacancy rates drop, and people lose the opportunity to move to housing that better suits their needs, overcrowding may increase in some areas. Any housing, and certainly that which is over-utilized, requires constant maintenance and occasional repairs in order to continue to serve as adequate shelter. . . .

The normal aging and wearing process would be aggravated by over-utilization, and presently standard housing could deteriorate rapidly unless strong and aggressive programs were instituted to provide the necessary incentives for preserving the existing stock. Today's housing conservation programs are admittedly inadequate to maintain our growing stock of older housing, and they will become increasingly so as we depend more on older housing to fill the region's housing needs.

It is also possible that growth controls will have the effect, in some sections of the region, of generating substantial investment in housing conservation and restoration of whole neighborhoods. As people become aware that the supply of good housing is limited, they may become more strongly motivated to invest in its preservation. Where this occurs, however, it is likely to result in the conversion of lower income housing into upper income housing unless there are adequate public controls and financial supports.[2]

Ada COG, Boise, Idaho. My worry is the negative impact on women, the poor, and so forth, of not controlling urban sprawl. Due to Federal Housing Administration policies of independent decision-making, it is the low income who are out there in the sprawl—at the greatest distances from hospitals, schools, social services, and recreational facilities. No one has threatened (yet) to challenge this kind of "exclusionary" policy in the courts.

Dayton, Ohio. The surplus of housing here (declining city population: 242,917 in 1973 to 197,238 estimated in 1975) leaves lots of inexpensive housing for everyone—low income, especially.

Unemployment was 8.7 percent in March 1975—blacks and women will definitely be the worst hit. Job creation is considered the number one priority. The regular economy needs manpower planning (and needs it to be done now) by all governments.

Toronto, Ontario, Canada. (Included in Question 1.)

Question 3. Assuming that someone has documented or anticipated exclusionary or negative impacts from non-growth or related policies, please note some of your suggestions or those of others with regard to minimizing or reducing such impacts or taking clear and positive steps in the other directions.

Comment

Tne range of responses and some of the innovations considered or suggested show something of the potential of nongrowth to provide breakthroughs on social equity not previously considered in rapid growth situations. The Mid-Willamette Valley COG response shows a number of attempts by the planning staff to deal head-on with possible land inflation associated with their urban limit line around the city of Salem. However, the response opens with the contention that the urban limit line is not exclusionary because of the ample supply of land. The answer provides some interesting observations on the low marketability of existing small lots, although it is noted that there is a demand for lower-cost older housing, much of which is on small 5,000- or 6,000-square-foot lots.

The Los Angeles response raises the importance of proper capital improvement program planning to emphasize the priority needs of poverty and minority areas.

The Boulder answer, as usual, contains a number of ideas, including the pressure on a shopping center developer to include low-income residential units in the development. Obviously, many answers, and even many problems, are missing from the following responses. But if any given locality or region considered all the techniques mentioned and implemented even a few, it would seem to be making substantial movement toward a socially responsible non-growth policy.

Boulder, Colorado. I cannot speak for the current administration. Previously we used a 15 percent requirement of low-income units as part of all new development proposing to annex or be developed as planned unit developments (PUDs). We aggressively sought subsidized housing programs and used staff to assist in the design to assure proper location and development. The city donated the only site of land it owned outside of its park program for 36 units. We permitted, on approval of the site plan and the assurance of the use of the units, a shopping center developer to capture the residential density from his business site if he would develop the units as integral to the center and provide a portion for low income. This approach theoretically provided free land costs and lowered the unit costs—no developer developed a shopping center under the previous administration, so we don't know if this works.

Petaluma, California. Please refer to the low- to moderate-income housing provisions in the city resolution.*
     In our case, we have tried to provide incentives for low-income housing; however, in past years we have not had great success in getting low-income housing.

Eugene, Oregon. No answer.

Amherst, Massachusetts. Allowing lifting minimum-site size requirement if developer includes 20 percent low-/moderate-income housing in residential PUD.

Lakewood, Colorado. Through the Lakewood Housing Authority, the city is attempting to deal with the lack of housing opportunity for low- and moderate-income families. Our "activity center" concept is expected to have some impact on that.

New Orleans, Louisiana. (Respondent answered previous question "no," implying that the issue was not on the table in New Orleans. No answer was provided to Question 3.)

Los Angeles, California.
     1. Los Angeles has a 15 percent low- and moderate-income housing ordinance. Housing element will have an allocation model in it, breaking down new units citywide.
     2. Our Housing and Community Development Act funding is intentionally not emphasizing poverty areas but the areas surrounding the poverty areas ("fringe" areas) to stem the tide of poverty. I do not like this and have said so. (The mayor did not listen.)
     3. Capital Improvement Program (CIP) may be tied to needy areas on a priority basis for the first time if my program in the

---

*The resolution establishes a goal that 8 to 12 percent of the yearly quota of building permits be provided in low- and moderate-income housing.

housing element stays. Believe it or not, our CIP has no real priority
other than political influence.

    4. Density bonus is proposed in new housing element.

    5. Land bank, although lacking details, is also in element.

Clearwater, Pinellas County, Florida. Negotiations with developers
prior to issuing of site plan approval has, at times, included moderate-
income housing demand. Low-income housing, however, is handled
in accordance to federal government money grants and occasional
developer-built, county-purchased units. These are not adequate.

Dade County, Florida.

    1. Dade County has initiated a program requiring large-scale
private developments to set aside a portion exclusively for low-
income housing. I do not believe an ordinance enforcing this has
been adopted yet. If the proportion has been established, I do not
know it.

    2. Section Three of the Affirmative Action Plan requires the
contractors to make every effort to employ at least 20 percent of
the work force from the neighborhood when working in urban renewal
areas.

    3. The Dade County Housing and Urban Development Department
offers no density bonuses. The policy is not to exceed a density of 70
people per acre—no matter where the project is built. With our
requirements for bedroom breakdown, this translates into approximately 10 to 11 units per acre.

Mid-Willamette Valley COG, Salem, Oregon. I believe it is the general consensus in the community that the urban growth boundary is
not exclusionary in relation to type of development, income levels,
employment, or other factors. There is more than enough land within
the boundary to take care of any foreseeable growth. There is evidence that the boundary has, and will continue to have, positive effects
on the community by restricting development on some of the best
agricultural land in the county and in the state.

    The community is actually working on programs to provide
low- and moderate-cost housing throughout the urban community.
We have also considered changes in the zoning and subdivision
ordinances to reduce standards and requirements for development.
However, the type of changes suggested would only reduce the cost
of a house by about $900. This amount is felt to have a minimum
effect on a person's decision to purchase or not to purchase a home.
Also, the type of changes may reduce the desirability and salability
of the land. For example, the minimum lot size allowed in the zoning

ordinance is 6,000 square feet. Most subdivisions contain lot sizes
of 7,000 to 10,000 square feet. One 6,000 square foot lot subdivision
was approved two years ago. Even though the 6,000 square foot lot
subdivision is in an area where lower-cost homes have been built,
the lots have not sold. The developer is now trying to get approval
to enlarge the lots to make them more salable. This subdivision is
on level land and is in the general area that developers and real
estate people most criticized with respect to the location of the urban
growth boundary. They contend that only on the level land east of
Salem can they build low- and moderate-cost housing and that the
boundary is too restrictive in this area. However, we have also found
that developers are not building low-cost housing in this area. Some
are putting in one-half acre lot subdivisions with $60,000 homes. It
appears that there is not a market right now for lower-standard subdivisions and lots in the Salem area. There is a demand, however,
for the older lower-cost homes, many of which are on 5,000 or 6,000
square foot lots.

Both Salem and Marion counties have adopted a "minisubdivi-
sion" ordinance. The intent is to reduce standards or to give vari-
ances for subdivision requirements to encourage and make possible
the development of by-passed, odd-shaped parcels for single-family
houses.

The three local housing authorities have various programs for
housing for low-income residents. There are also private agencies
active in this field. The state housing office and the legislature have
supported housing programs and legislation.

The Urban Renewal Agency is now making a study on the feasi-
bility of using floors above commercial establishments for housing
in the downtown area. They specifically want to find out why such
use has not occurred, what restrictions prevent or discourage such
use, and what is the market for such housing.

ABAG, San Francisco, California. A number of housing and employment quotas for low-income residents are needed, along with other
strategies, but, most importantly, a monitoring device to determine
what is happening as a result of any one of these. Also, pressure on
the Department of Housing and Urban Development (HUD) to reduce
701 grants to communities making use of such monies to develop
"growth management" tools that do not reflect an "equity impact
monitor."

Ada COG, Boise, Idaho. (No answer.)

Dayton, Ohio. We need a new system for the rational management of
human resources as a routine function of the economy. In a highly

interdependent society, nothing short of semiintelligent 15- to 25-year
contingency plans for full employment can be very meaningful. Band-
aids can no longer stop the flow of blood.

Toronto, Ontario, Canada. (Included in Question 1.)

> Question 4. Can any one planner such as yourself take
> strong positions both against some kinds of growth and,
> at the same time, for greater redistribution of resources
> such as housing, job opportunities, etc. and still keep
> his or her job or influence in the community?

Comment

Several respondents answered that they could safely take stands
both against certain types of growth and for a better distribution of
resources to the poor. But the general mood in the answers seems
to be not one of rash advocacy but, rather, one of pragmatism, with
some evidence of cynicism, especially in the answers from New
Orleans, Los Angeles, Boise, Eugene, and Dayton. The respondent
from Pinellas County, Florida, indicated that strong positions would
probably get the planner fired. On the other hand, the Boise response
raises some interesting thoughts on the effect of "advocating any one
side of a controversial issue," especially in a smaller, more rural
area. The respondent indicated that such action could result in a
permanent loss of the planner's credibility with one set of politicians,
even on future issues that are totally unrelated.

Based on this group of answers, there generally appears to be
room for the planner to take some stands against growth and, at the
same time, for social equity, but considerable attention should be
given to local political conditions. Survival in a job may be important, especially during a recession. But the Mid-Willamette Valley
COG respondent, for one, rejected "survivalism." "There is no
point in surviving if you cannot be effective." This response also
stated that the planner must understand the forces affecting community decisions and even "occasionally work to create counterforces."

Boulder, Colorado. Yes. The total picture has to be carefully drawn
to understand the interrelationships. Consistency of interpretation
is essential. Situations on individual developments vary, and you
cannot sell one out just to get it approved. By understanding the
adverse aspects and fears, you take steps and adopt strategies to
assure or to minimize these problems; then, you work to achieve

the goal. Just cramming things down peoples throats will cause
major problems. In some communities, obviously, you will not
succeed.

Petaluma, California. In recent years, the city has been taking strides
toward the provision of low-income housing through the establishment
of a Housing Authority. The growth control system has been over-
whelmingly supported by the city's residents, and at the same time,
there is a widespread recognition that low-income housing is needed,
especially for the elderly. Therefore, it has not been difficult for
the professional planners to take a stand on both of these issues.

Eugene, Oregon. I think the emphasis in the department has been
geared to equal treatment of both positions. However, in examining
the results of taking those positions, I think that we have fared better
in influencing the physical growth problems. This, of course, can be
attributed to our "role" as a planning department and the resources
available to us. Except for housing, which is a responsibility of our
department, we have not actually done much in the social areas.

Amherst, Massachusetts. Yes, at least in this town, but one must
retain some flexibility to deal with sometimes quickly shifting
political sands.

Lakewood, Colorado. There are fairly strong feelings both for and
against growth, so I am unsure of the answers.

New Orleans, Louisiana. Yes—as long as the "strong position" is
not vocal, visible, or embarrassing to the administration.

Los Angeles, California. In Lost Angeles planning, we could probably
recommend both equally. The Council would probably have reserva-
tions.

Clearwater, Pinellas County, Florida. One who persisted in pursuing
such action would probably be fired.

Dade County, Florida. The question is not whether one can take
strong stands on these issues but whether such strong stands would
produce any changes of policy. The Planning Department itself took
a strong stand in support of its recommendations in the Comprehensive Plan to channel or direct growth in the county. I support this
position and see no need to take an independent stand on this issue.
As far as a greater distribution of housing and other resources in

the county, I would support it—but taking a strong stand myself, or
even the department taking a strong stand, may not necessarily bring
the desired results. Housing opportunity and job opportunities are no
longer local issues, but relate to the region, state, and federal governmental level. Federal and state economic policy strongly influence
these issues, and what strong standards are, or are not, taken locally
may be irrelevant.

Mid-Willamette Valley COG, Salem, Oregon. First, I reject the idea
of "survival" as a criterion for deciding the position a planner should
take. There is no point in surviving if you cannot be effective. The
planner must be a combination catalyst, interventionist, and activist.
But he must also be a "politician" and be able to gauge the mood of
a community. He must understand the forces active in community
decisions. And he must occasionally work to create counterforces.

ABAG, San Francisco, California. Yes. (Respondent enclosed a number of newspaper clippings regarding a staff report opposing a
proposed new town, in part because of environmental constraints and
in part because of the lack of low- and moderate-income housing and
employment opportunities.)

Ada COG, Boise, Idaho. In our community, a planner has to weigh
carefully the long-term effect of "advocating" any one side of a
controversial issue. Once one has "lost credibility" with one set of
politicians, all subsequent advice is considered biased—even on totally
unrelated issues. The most comfortable situation (the same with
planners as with politicians) is being able to advise obeying the law
and having the support of the local attorney.

Dayton, Ohio. Dayton's poor have received full support from public
officials, planners, and so forth in terms of federal funds. We have
spent several millions, with little to show. If we gave 26,000 families
$5,000, it would cost $130 million. We do not have the resources to
prop up the unjust economic system. Systematic change is clearly
required.

Toronto, Ontario, Canada. I do not know any planner who has been
muzzled for taking a strong standpoint against growth or for advocating redistribution from the rich to the poor. In the city of Toronto,
planners are advocating fair-share housing plans and other actions
to help low-income people (with full support from many aldermen).
However, it should be stressed that only a few planners, if any,
among those who advocate help to the poor support a nongrowth

policy; "managed growth" seems the popular expression for greater control over growth.

> Question 5. Some nongrowth or controlled growth advo-
> cates say that there is a lot of positive potention for their
> movement to assist the poor and minorities, since slowing
> growth can raise the issue of redistribution for immediate
> public view and debate. Have any citizens or groups in
> your area shown any awareness of more positive connec-
> tions between nongrowth or controlled growth and
> increased social equity? This could involve alliances
> between environmentalists and minority group repre-
> sentatives to oppose a sprawling suburban development
> designed for wealthy occupants for example. It might
> also involve alliances based on tradeoffs, i.e., the
> minorities or poor will support a bond issue to purchase
> a green belt if the environmentalists will back bonds for
> community centers or sewer improvements in the inner
> city areas.

Comment

While the respondents had rather varying degrees of enthusiasm for the idea of nongrowth leading to positive social equity efforts, there were very few reports of citizen or political alliances along these lines. Boulder, Colorado, reported city staff awareness of the positive connections between the two movements, and Los Angeles reported that the Sierra Club had "realized this several years ago." Dade County, Florida, made the point that such alliances could be possible if both factions could see their common interests. The Lakewood, Colorado, response asserted that the basic assumption of the question is wrong, and the Toronto response suggested improved planning and less waste as ways of helping the poor, without threatening those higher up the scale with the ideas of non-growth and redistribution.

Several responses provide interesting thoughts about how non-growth and nongrowth-social equity alliances might come about and who would be likely to get together in their areas. For example, the Boise, Idaho, response noted potential alliances of retired people, farmers, and public employees, in addition to environmentalists. Both Boulder and Dayton noted improved employment opportunities for local residents as key elements in the nongrowth-social equity strategy. "Concentrate and drive for yardage up the middle," the Dayton response urged. Finally, the Eugene response described

joint nongrowth and social equity efforts as a "shuck and jive act,
two steps forward for Mother Nature and five steps backward for the
poor."

Boulder, Colorado. Yes—staff awareness. After studying who was
gaining from the type of employment and housing expansion from
1952 on, it was obvious low income was not necessarily benefiting or
sharing proportionately. The city did acknowledge that slow growth
would put pressure on housing and that direct efforts were needed
to overcome this. The market place was not, and will not, take care
of the problem. Sensitivity to the type of employment that is attracted
is another way of questioning if it is growth for growth's sake or is,
indeed, intended to provide added employment opportunities for locals.

Petaluma, California. No trade-offs of the type mentioned here have
been utilized in Petaluma. It is not likely that trade-offs of this
nature will be necessary in the future because the local residents
perceive the problem as being one of assisting elderly people in
finding their share of housing and not that of providing housing for
minorities, and so forth. Thus, they feel that they must provide this
housing for the elderly, and trade-offs do not enter into the situation.

Eugene, Oregon. I am extremely pessimistic about the possibilities
of such an alliance. I know few, if any, "environmentalists" who have
the kind of concern you describe. I do not believe for one that the
trade-offs will ever be in favor of the minorities and the poor. We
will always be vying for a share of what now amounts to an increasingly limited pie with richer, more powerful, and politically sophisticated and influential environmentalists. Using growth control to
raise the issues of poverty, racism, and so forth is a shuck and jive
act, two steps forward for Mother Nature and five steps backward
for the poor.

Amherst, Massachusetts. Few have really thought through the implications of the first question. Redistribution is rarely an explicit
issue. It is usually buried in rent control or zoning issues, for
example. Linking of issues (open space/housing bonds) is also rare.
What happens is that support is given to a proposal (for example, a
new zoning by-law) by different interest groups and individuals for
reasons related to their interests. It makes for strange bedfellows,
but it can happen.

Lakewood, Colorado. No. The assumption is wrong to begin with.
The market will be the major reflection of any artificial nongrowth

situation. With the pressures (economic, migration, and so forth) still there for growth (but controlled by government action), the demand and supply of the market will result in increased costs of housing and many services. The kind of consensus needed to combine social equity with nongrowth is contradictory in suburban America.

New Orleans, Louisiana. It has not happened because both groups are not quite mature enough. Both groups are still playing power games, such as "fight the bridge" and "MauMau the honky bureau-crat." I can see this happening within 10 years . . . if it is not too late.

Los Angeles, California. The Sierra Club realized this several years ago. No real strong advocate for twin concepts of nongrowth-equity have been heard because a regional nongrowth debate (as opposed to a homeowner's association wanting to keep out a new apartment) has not occurred in Los Angeles. There have been no union comments or civil rights that I have heard of speaking on topic. Why?

Clearwater, Pinellas County, Florida. Nothing has been done in this area. Citizen action is almost negligible here.

Dade County, Florida. I know of no such alliances. Such alliances may be possible but would be dependent on the awareness of the environmentalist faction and the social equity faction of realizing they may have some interests in common. I would recommend you contact members of these environmental or social equity groups for more information on this.

Mid-Willamette Valley COG, Salem, Oregon. I cannot think of an example where this has occurred. I suppose it could happen in the future but I would not guess under what circumstances. Salem has a small minority race population. Low-income people are not con-centrated in area. Concentration would encourage group action.

ABAG, San Francisco, California. Overall, there is very low aware-ness that such a question should be examined. However, we look for much participation in upcoming central area revitalization confer-ence funded by HUD through ABAG as part of the Citizen Alliance Program.

Ada COG, Boise, Idaho. No alliances are apparent at this time. Potential alliances for no- or slow-growth would be environmental-ists, retired folks, and farmers and public employees, I suppose. The low income and minorities are not nearly as organized.

<u>Dayton, Ohio</u>. The employment system is the key. Beware of fragmenting focus. Concentrate and drive for yardage up the middle.

<u>Toronto, Ontario, Canada</u>. There are a few individuals and groups, mostly academics who have shown awareness of the connection between controlled growth and increased social equity. However, this aspect of the problem seems to be the weak point in the drive for any slow-growth policy. Increasing numbers of people . . . seem to worry that further growth will deteriorate the environment or threaten current stability. Few of them seem to accept the proposition that slower growth will, or can, achieve more social equity. Although growth has not achieved greater equity either, at least it may have provided many with hope for fulfilling their expectations. As slow growth may threaten the expectations of many, they are hesitant to endorse a strong growth policy, particularly when it affects their income or job security and, consequently, their living standard. For these reasons, there are doubts about the approach suggested or implied in your questionnaire that nongrowth has a lot of positive potential to assist the poor. It is more likely that changes in quality could be more successful than control of quantity. Reduction in waste, improved quality of products, and better management of family budget are some of the tools that could be used successfully to help the poor without threatening expectations with a nongrowth policy. This seems to be the approach acceptable to many. In Toronto, for example, encouraging the development of significant amounts of new housing (with substantial numbers subsidized) within walking distance of major employment concentrations will probably have many beneficial effects besides providing housing and jobs to the poor. It would reduce the need for transportation, which would improve the environment and could make possible (redistribution) transfer of funds from transportation to social services.

Promoting similar approaches seems more appropriate than stopping growth in the present conditions and redistributing wasteful products and habits.

> <u>Question 6</u>. Please use this space to throw back any general opinions, comments, references to literature or other communities, etc. relative to the issue of nongrowth and social equity, assuming that nongrowth does not mean an immediate end to all population and economic growth, but rather some specific moves toward a harder local line against any and all growth or with a goal of reducing future growth below past rates.
>
> Is there anything <u>you</u> would like to see covered in a book of this type?

Comment

This general wrap-up question did not generate any lengthy or highly innovative responses, but some of the comments show future directions in the nongrowth-social equity analysis and debate.

The Los Angeles response noted possible negative psychological effects of nongrowth and redistribution on middle- and upper-class people. The Mid-Willamette Valley COG response from Oregon suggested greater attention on positive community benefits of controlled growth, especially in terms of more equitable provision of services and the creation of more desirable inner cities. The Dade County, Florida, response cited an innovative book on zoning and social equity that had recently been published, showing perhaps how quickly concerned local planners in growth-sensitive communities can pick up good new social equity and related material. The Eugene response cited some interesting "prerequisites for growth control."

Boulder, Colorado (No answer.)

Petaluma, California. We would just like to clarify that the Petaluma Growth Control System applies only to residential development and includes a growth rate in excess of five percent per year. This is approximately three times the growth rate of the Bay Area region as a whole. We would like to make it clear that our system is aimed at balancing growth in the various areas of the city and among the various housing types, while maintaining a level of growth to which the city can easily gear the provision of public facilities.

Eugene, Oregon. Some prerequisites to growth control:
1. full employment in a strong, diverse economy ;
2. racial and economic integration ;
3. adequate stock of safe and decent housing at affordable costs (subsidies may be the only way this can happen—preferably an income supplement);
4. general provision for public open space.

Amherst, Massachusetts. Is the concept of transfer of development rights of any value in a slow-growth situation? What are its advantages?

Lakewood, Colorado. These are my views as a planner and do not necessarily represent the views of the city.

New Orleans, Louisiana. As long as a growth policy is economically beneficial to those persons in power, there will always be growth.

Los Angeles, California.
    1. Dispell the contention that only a "growing economy" can enable the poor to improve their living standard. The gap between rich and poor has increased in absolute dollars between 1950 and 1970 (and will probably continue to do so). Our growth ethic has not brought about greater equality in income but has seemed to widen it. Will nongrowth reduce this gap? (It should.)
    2. Psychological effect on middle and upper class to nongrowth. Nongrowth carried to its logical conclusion of redistribution of wealth will bother many people.

Clearwater, Pinellas County, Florida. Manatee and Collier counties have instituted good managed-growth programs. Each of these has rather large minority populations.

Dade County, Florida. Are you familiar with the recent book by Herbert M. Franklin, David Falk, and Arthur Levin on In-Zoning: A Guide for Policy-Makers on Inclusionary Land Use Programs, published by the Potomac Institute in December 1974? This would seem to be must reading in relation to your research.
    Research should be conducted in Boca Raton, which actually took a step to limit its rate of population increase, as well as in Petaluma, California. Dade County is in neither camp as a result of adoption of the Comprehensive Plan. The question of social equity as related to slow or nongrowth has not been strongly raised here, because the latter has not been a strong issue, except for those groups that are more directly concerned with construction and building here.

Mid-Willamette Valley COG, Salem, Oregon. One of the benefits we talk about in controlled growth programs is how the community benefits. This is hard to document—at least, we have not done it. Some of the studies that have been made here speak to various aspects of community benefits, but I would like to see more definite background information and documentation to support the concept. I think this is part of social equity—how controlled growth can affect farmers, rural residents, and inner-city residents who have already paid for services and still pay for expansion of services. A theme we used in our public information program on the boundary was: How do we make the area inside a desirable and attractive place to live?

ABAG, San Francisco, California. (No answer.)

Ada COG, Boise, Idaho. In Ada County, it appears that the small, rural, conservative communities are more willing to discuss and adopt (and enforce) policies to at least control sprawl. Kuna (population 1,000) has recently adopted a comprehensive plan with an urban services growth area and is preparing zoning and other ordinances to follow it up. However, their policies will accommodate whatever growth occurs.

In conclusion, I would say that, at present, the issue of growth control is not related to social equity (here, in the public discussion of the issue) but to issues of private property rights, rising taxes, and the "eating up of agricultural land."

Dayton, Ohio. Capitalism is not working well anymore, and the complete collapse of the ideology in Viet Nam and the exploiter role in the Third World are all too obvious. We need to redesign the economic system along more mature, loving, and balanced value lines. The United States cannot grow in its spirit and self-image otherwise.

Toronto, Ontario, Canada. (Included in Question 5.)

SYNOPSIS

Reading through the answers to the questionnaires can be both exciting and frustrating. The 14 communities and regions involved appear to have some broad common concerns about wasteful growth and some general appreciation of social equity, but it would be extremely difficult to group then under a single standard and make firm universal moral, legal, political, or economic judgments.

The present authors find this array of distinct communities to be stimulating, since individual communities are seen as laboratories, experimenting with a variety of approaches to such problems as unchecked growth and social inequities. In an age of cynicism and mistrust in big government and large impersonal institutions, it is encouraging to see communities getting together and thinking about their individual problems and considering new or innovative responses. Obviously, the people who responded to the questionnaire do not necessarily speak for any group of local citizens or leaders, but the tone of many of the responses does indicate that there is some involvement, innovation, and down-to-earth thinking going on in the community or region.

The responses should be regarded as raw material; they were neither heavily edited nor was any attempt made to synthesize them. They stand by themselves as starting points for future discussion, thinking, and, perhaps, even inspiration on the part of the reader. These are real people in real local government situations, and they addressed growth and equity problems that will continue to emerge in a wide variety of communities. The reader should use the responses not as models for some response in his or her local community but as a starting point in the development of new and better ideas.

TRANSITION—THOUGHTS ON THE
NONGROWTH-SOCIAL EQUITY FRONTIER

The past two chapters have dealt with a topic where the evidence is real, but fragmented and changing in a diverse number of communities. Innovations and power shifts involved in local nongrowth could be forces behind new local breakthroughs in social equity.

Cooperative local nongrowth and social equity efforts could mean a better life for all people involved—rich and poor. A strong positive social equity effort can help keep nongrowth communities out of lengthy and costly court battles. It can also help environmentalists and other nongrowthers gain political strength on key decisions. To the extent that redistribution takes place locally in a nongrowth community, the givers can be more certain of its limits, effects, and efficiency.

Involvement in nongrowth would give the poor some powerful and knowledgeable new allies. It could also provide them with more local housing and job opportunities than they have been receiving through the trickle-down process associated with random, uncontrolled community growth.

But if this kind of open cooperation is such a good idea, why has so little been done about it? Why have not more of the hundreds of nongrowth communities developed explicit social equity redistribution concepts and goals in their plans? Why have the courts generally missed the point entirely? Why have social equity advocates forged more coalitions with builders than with environmentalists? Why did most of the planners who answered the questionnaire mention theories and experiments rather than substantial accomplishments in nongrowth and social equity?

The answer seems to lie in ignorance, misunderstanding, and fear. Until recently, local communities have been ignorant of some of the real powers they possess. Without power, there cannot be much responsibility. As long as local communities regarded themselves as essentially powerless in the areas of growth and social equity, they could pass on such responsibilities to a higher level of government.

But now, some local nongrowth pioneers have shown that communities can have much more clout, even if they only use more primitive land-use tools to shut off or delay development. Such powers probably will not remain primitive or misunderstood for long. But as local power increases, so does local responsibility.

As land-use controls are improved and exercised to gain more local power, they must come to grips with the local private economy— often a prime factor in local growth and a major resource in terms of social equity. The poor need more money, not just some token or indirect housing subsidy. The local public economy can also be helpful in both nongrowth and social equity efforts.

The disadvantaged have also not always been aware of some of the real powers their local communities possess. Many are generally ignorant of the details and developments in the nongrowth movement. Often, what they have heard about nongrowth has come from proponents of growth and development who use social equity as a smokescreen to conceal their real motivation of maximizing profits.

The poor and their advocates are often suspicious of the local nongrowth movement. Few attempts have been made to show them how such nongrowth might benefit them, and there are only a limited number of local experiments to serve as models. Thus, they often see their own salvation in increased development and rapid growth.

Fear is a major obstacle to nongrowth-social equity coalitions and breakthroughs. Some nongrowthers may acknowledge the need for some redistribution but fear that it may be ineffective, unending, and uncontrolled. Social equity advocates, on the other hand, fear an unknown, such as nongrowth, in comparison with a known, such as uncontrolled growth, which claims to trickle down benefits.

Almost everyone may fear to bring up two such controversial issues at the same time. Both nongrowth and social equity involve some major power shifts. During the process of debate and battle, some local people with vision are going to get caught in the middle. But local leaders and professionals alike are going to have to take some stands eventually. More citizens want it that way, and the failure and inattention of higher governments demand it.

RECOMMENDATIONS

The following recommendations are being made to stimulate
effective and responsible local action, in terms of both nongrowth
and social equity, and to serve as future guidelines for evaluating
the local nongrowth movement and its contributions to social equity.

The Local Community Level Should Be Emphasized and Supported in Both Nongrowth and Social Equity Strategies

This is a time of increased self-awareness for not only women,
gays, blacks, and the elderly, but small towns, hilly towns, hillbilly
towns, college towns, artist towns, and fishing towns. Few smaller
communities aspire to become another Los Angeles or, even, a San
Jose. People and communities are fighting for the right and the
power to be different, and to remain different.

Obviously cities are not as powerful as the federal government
or as their state governments. But the federal government shows no
signs of taking a leadership role regarding the problems of growth
or the maldistribution of resources. The failure of past federal
social equity programs almost parallels the failure of the federal
government to move on a real national growth policy. States, such
as New York, California, Colorado, and Arizona, have generally been
far behind local communities, such as Ramapo, Petaluma, Boulder,
and Tucson, in terms of innovation and planning in the areas of growth
management and social equity. The federal government and a majority of the states have failed to pass elementary land-use legislation.
Both levels of government will probably tend to remain fairly conservative, since they are isolated from local experience and rarely
are prone to innovation. Regional government, with a few exceptions,
has emerged slowly, with little in the way of power or innovation.
There is little reason to expect much change at that level.

A number of local communities lack dollars and have highly
restricted or antiquated legal powers. But the future seems to look
the brightest for local action. More and more people seem to favor
local approaches to problems. Urbanization has a dynamic history
in the United States, with suburbs, local nongrowth, massive ghettos,
and major city riots all emerging within the past 40 years. It appears
as though city and neighborhood powers will increase during the
coming 40 years, since information moves faster and people are less
docile and more identity conscious—also, energy shortages will
change all the rules.

Local communities are dynamic. A wide range of people are getting involved in local growth issues. Symbolic and real local actions can start to show the way. Federal and state governments should respond to this local potential in the following ways:

1. The federal government and state governments can assist the local efforts and experiments by collecting and disseminating information on these activities and their results. The dissemination should be widespread and rapid. Innovations that cover both nongrowth and social equity should be stressed and headlined. Personal communications should be used, along with audiovisual and printed materials.

2. The federal government should help take some of the risk out of strong local nongrowth-social equity advocacy by attaching a mandated social equity-nongrowth assessment in all of its relevant local grant and loan programs. The main purpose of such a requirement would be to help legitimize the effort in more local communities for those officials and professionals who are interested in coming out in the open. The Housing and Community Development Act would be a good place to start in this regard, because it combines grants through which a community could manage growth and increase social equity.

3. State governments should adopt the new Model Land Development Code prepared by the American Law Institute (ALI) as new state enabling legislation for zoning, subdivision, and other land-use powers. The ALI code endorses the idea of giving more local powers to communities that have more developed and sophisticated plans.

4. States should avoid overriding local development control powers unless it can be clearly shown that the community in question has done absolutely nothing substantial in terms of social equity, especially for its own residents. States should also develop clear and open policies and priorities in close coordination with local communities before moving ahead on any overriding strategy.

5. States should analyze and revise their fiscal and taxing legislation covering local communities to enable these communities to engage in more experiments and more unique approaches to the problems of growth and social inequity.

The emphasis on the local focus raises a question with regard to inequities among various communities. Some communities, such as central cities, have a higher percentage of poor people and less in the way of fiscal resources. Others, such as some suburbs, have a lower percentage of poor people and more fiscal resources relative to their problems. Some areas have more natural resources than other areas. Obviously, some concepts of social equity would not be met by an enhancement or continuation of such patterns,

although it also seems likely that complete interjurisdictional equity
will never be achieved, either naturally or through federal action.
The following recommendations attempt to deal with this problem:

1. Local nongrowth communities should give first priority in
their social equity efforts to their own residents who are less well
off. (This recommendation does not mean that local nongrowth communities must become islands, but it does emphasize that redistribution efforts should first be directed toward those closest to home.)

2. A local community should make specific assessments of
some negative social equity impacts that might result in some wider
region as a result of its nongrowth policies and take some appropriate
positive actions. This response is most necessary where the nongrowth community gains substantial benefits in terms of jobs, parks,
cultural events, and so forth from its neighbors.

Local communities should not be expected to solve or import
all the problems of their region. Nongrowth calls for limits and control. A community should be a responsible neighbor and not continually borrow benefits of size or resources from other communities
without giving anything in return.

The concept of limits on one community's regional social equity
activity has been acknowledged by several leading housing and equal
rights attorneys, including Herbert Franklin of the Potomac Institute.
In a recent book, Franklin noted that many newer outlying areas fear
that if they loosen restrictive zoning policies, they will be inundated
with an unending stream of dense public housing projects, similar to
those they have seen in central cities. After rightly denying that such
would often be the case, he then notes that some of the fair share
housing plans that have been developed "would enable a locality to
absorb a quantity of such [low- and moderate-income] housing in
accordance with a regional allocation plan with the assurance that
some limit on the total will be defined, at least for the planning
period."[3]

Since only a few regional housing allocation plans exist, a concerned nongrowth community should act on its own, when necessary,
to conscientiously determine what its fair share of low- and moderate-
income housing might be, and then stick to that as a maximum.

Communities Should Stress Direct Economic Measures in Their Nongrowth and Social Equity Strategies, Using Their Land-Use and Other Local Powers as Tools

To effectively control growth, and to do it in a socially responsible manner, communities will have to get much more involved in

their local economy. (See Chapters 4 and 5.) Land-use controls over
new housing have been emphasized in the nongrowth movement to
date, but used in isolation from economic policies and strategies,
they often crumble under the pressures of rapid economic growth,
major new industries, and accelerated in-migration.

Nongrowth critics and advocates alike have not adequately considered the individual's total economic well-being, that is, his or her
total income. The movement of hard dollars from one set of hands to
another is a much more effective redistribution strategy than, for
example, the lowering of land-use and environmental standards to
provide slightly cheaper housing. This is where the local economy
comes in.

Precise economic strategies will vary according to the type
and location of the nongrowth community. If a community faces a
substantial amount of private employment growth or turnover, it
could emphasize a policy of slower population growth, especially
from in-migrants, but with continued economic growth. A key to this
strategy would be to hire and train the resident unemployed, rather
than in-migrants.

Local communities can influence and control elements of their
local economy with regard to a number of social equity items (with
potential firms) if they have firm control over the use of industrial
and commercial land. But many other local powers can be used to
shape a responsive local economy. Community utility and transportation policies can be highly important. Local manpower and general
educational efforts can develop a strong resident labor force. A local
public industrial land-banking effort and a local economic development
authority with seed money for the right kinds of industries can also
be helpful.

The following recommendations are designed to help communities gain more control over their local economies in a socially
responsible manner:

1. Local governments should emphasize contracts and purchases
with local firms and suppliers, especially those that offer, or agree
to offer, substantial employment opportunities to the local poor and
minority groups or those that are owned by people in these groups.

2. Local funds should be invested in banks that show consistent
and significant attention to loans and other financial needs in minority
and poor neighborhoods.*

---

*The private economy is the place to start in real nongrowth-
social equity efforts, but as this recommendation shows, the public
economy can interact with the private. A city can also take the

3. Social equity should be increased for the resident poor by
providing more and better public services, including services that
previously were available only in the private market. Local capital
improvement programs and all local physical and social services
should emphasize poorer neighborhoods.* (Such improved, or new,
services could include day-care centers, and meeting places and
special services for the local elderly and handicapped. Residential
bedroom communities could also agree to supply land or other free
services to residential developers who agree to supply lower-income
housing for those in need.)

Key Principle for Local Nongrowth-Social Equity
Efforts Should Be Diversity

The diversity principle is based on the ecological principle
that diverse, pluralistic systems seem to work better in nature. If
every community is the same, then they might all be wiped out by
the same disease or problem, such as inflation, city employee
strikes, or an energy crisis.

Not all nongrowth communities may opt for massive integration
with steady numbers of poor or different ethnic groups moving in.
Some might prefer direct economic transfer payments to poorer
neighboring communities. Nongrowth communities could band
together and contribute to a fund for some kind of revitalization
effort in a neighboring central city. Formal efforts, such as regional
sharing of tax assessments from new development, could also be
established. This has already taken place in the Minneapolis-St. Paul
region.[4] Obviously, if a community does absolutely nothing in terms
of social equity, it cannot hide behind the principle of diversity, and
its nongrowth efforts will probably be subject to legal and political
checks. But communities should have wide latitude and room for
innovation.

---

initiative and put its own fiscal resources to work for social equity.
This would seem to be especially necessary in communities that
are primarily residential and have little private employment—
although most communities have shopping centers or areas that can
be influenced.

*This recommendation applies to the public economy of a non-
growth community.

Local Nongrowth Advocates Should Take Initiative
in Developing Appropriate Social Equity Responses
and in Forging Alliances with Social Equity Advocates

Nongrowth is the newer of the two movements, and its advocates
should take the initiative on social equity, rather than waiting for
approaches or advance pledges of support from equity advocates.
Nongrowth advocates should attend meetings and join organizations
working for social equity. They should provide financial assistance
and volunteer labor for social equity efforts and organizations but,
at the same time, make it clear that they have goals in the area of
nongrowth. Communications and more contact will help a lot, but
unilateral financial donations and concrete contributions to social
equity efforts will be even more helpful to ultimate alliances.

The payoff for nongrowth advocates, at first, may be minimal,
but in the longer run, some actual alliances may start to appear, at
least on specific issues at specific points in time. In addition,
through continuing exposure to the social equity effort, nongrowth
advocates may learn more about their own movement and work
internally to adjust or to change the parts of their nongrowth strategy
that do not seem in harmony with some concept of social equity.

One additional way for local nongrowth advocates to show
initiative and sincerity would be to initiate strategies to reduce their
consumption of energy and materials. It is not encouraging to see
two cars and a camper in every garage in a nongrowth community.
Nongrowth that freezes high and wasteful consumption in place is
bound to be looked upon with suspicion and mistrust. Adjustments in
high consumption patterns might also free more resources for
redistribution to the poor.

NOTES

1. Ed McCahill, "In Mount Laurel, Issues Are Not Black and
White," Planning 41, no. 4 (May 1975): 12-13.
2. Association of Bay Area Governments, "Regional Housing
Plan" (working draft) (San Francisco: ABAG, 1974), pp. 19-21.
3. Herbert M. Franklin, David Falk, and Arthur J. Levin,
In-Zoning: A Guide for Policy-Makers on Inclusionary Land Use
Programs (Washington, D.C.: The Potomac Institute, 1974), p. 77.
4. For a description of the Minnesota program, see Mary
Brooks, Minnesota's Fiscal Disparities Bill, Planning Advisory
Service Memo no. M-9 (Chicago: American Society of Planning
Officials, February 1972).

4

NONGROWTH AND
THE LOCAL ECONOMY

The economics of local nongrowth is tied up in the single idea
that it is a good thing for local communities to control their own
economy. The workings of the local economy are simply too important to all people in the community to be left to chance. And when
speaking of the local economy, both the public and the private
sectors—government, as well as local commercial and industrial
enterprise—are included. But throughout, the emphasis is on the
importance of the private sector.

There are three main reasons why local communities should
exercise control over the local economy. First, workable nongrowth
requires this control, since without it, there would be no restraints
on the principal cause of local growth—the local economy. Second,
controls over the local economy can diminish economic pressure,
which is the cause of inequities in both housing and employment.
Third, controls over the local economy can produce solid economic
gains for the average local citizen.

These three concepts are new to most planners and local
officials. Traditionally, the local economy has been the exclusive
province of such groups as local bankers, the real estate industry,
the local chamber of commerce, and, perhaps, a visiting economist.
For most local governments, the local economy was something to be
left alone. Since local attitudes are still dominated by laissez-faire,
it is important to discuss these three concepts in some detail.

SAY HELLO TO THE LOCAL GROWTH MACHINE

The most serious, enduring, and accurate criticism of local
nongrowth plans is that they are based on economic ignorance.

Failure to recognize simple, basic economic facts leads to strategies that do not affect the local economy, especially the private economy. Not surprisingly, the National Association of Home Builders noted this fundamental weakness:

> The problem is, you can't stop suburban growth with land use policy. The limits on local growth don't have the effect of stopping growth. . . . Communities cannot stop the process of growth by using land use policy because: (1) the economic engine that generates growth is probably still running full blast; (2) the population that brought the sewers to full capacity is still coming because the economic engine is generating more jobs and people are having children.[1]

In the nongrowth setting, land-use controls skirt the central economic issue and, in so doing, fail to confront the single most important cause of growth, the local economy.

It was no accident that nongrowth-planning strategies brought this failure to light. In the past, when the dominant local objective was growth for an increase in tax base, there simply was no impetus, no good reason, to influence the local character of growth. Most planning agencies were principally concerned with beautifying or mitigating some of the more obvious conflicts between land uses. Decade after decade, planners insisted on developing controls over everything but the local economic structure and processes and then began to wonder if the controls really made that much difference. After all, Houston without zoning was not appreciably different from cities with a 50-year history of zoning.[2]

As communities began to question growth and then to consider ways of controlling it, the weak character of the controls over the basic economic structure of the community became more apparent. Suddenly, people such as planner-economist Philip Hammer discovered that

> if we had effective planning, it would be substantially dominated by economics. This is not to say that the only ends of planning would be economic ends; on the contrary, economics would dominate the means, not the ends. Unfortunately, our planning has not been very effective planning, and this is one of the great problems that face us at the local level.[3]

This sentiment was echoed by Wilbur Thompson, the distinguished urban economist: "I am still inclined to the view that the economic base of the urban area is generally the best point at which to manage growth."[4]

While the role of the local economic structure began to receive some attention, planners continued to rely upon standard land-use controls. The land-use controls, themselves, remained directed toward minor features of the local economy, although better packaged and more focused on the principal nongrowth target—the new housing market. As noted in a recent report on urban growth-management systems, the housing market is controlled through time-tested devices: "Perhaps the key conclusion in this examination is that few of the tools being used are new. What is new is the way they have been linked and integrated into management systems."[5] Thus, most of the local managed-growth strategies rely upon new packaging of old devices, combining such time-tested powers as zoning, subdivision regulations, taxation, and capital budgets. The object of their attention is the local housing market, specifically the new housing market.

The new housing market is the most obvious manifestion of growth in population. Without the new housing, conventional planning wisdom has it, there would not be new people. Population growth would be controlled. When this reasoning is coupled with the traditional mix of planner's controls, it is understandable that the force of the nongrowth movement is on the new housing market. The tools are perfectly tailored toward this small segment of the local economy. Whether in Petaluma, Ramapo, or Boca Raton, it is the new housing market that is the object of the growth control attention. And, as far as these new strategies go, they seem to be working.[6] The local housing market is tightly controlled: fewer new units are being built, and population growth is being curtailed. So far so good.

But the real problem arises when the effectively restricted new housing market is thrown up against a freewheeling, continually developing local economy. Since the new housing market or new construction in general makes up roughly 6 percent to 12 percent of the local economy, it leaves the remaining 88 percent to 94 percent unaffected.[7] While the lid on the new housing market is clamped down, nothing is done for the remaining segments of the local economy, such as manufacturing and services. However, since the local engine of growth is fueled by growth in employment, and particularly by employment in manufacturing and services, the nongrowth dilemma is made apparent. Nongrowth strategies aimed at the local housing market are a necessary but not sufficient condition to effectively control growth. To be effective, the housing strategies must be combined with controls over the local economy.

Sweetwater County, Wyoming, provides a particularly clear case of what happens when a restrictive growth policy for new housing is coupled with a rapidly expanding local economy.[8] But to understand

what happened to Sweetwater County, it is first necessary to see
where they were in 1970, the year that the transition began—a transition which would take the county from its dominant rural setting into
a highly urbanized one in the short space of four years.

Sweetwater County is located in the resource-rich southwestern
corner of Wyoming. For many years, its economy was based on
three industries: railroad, coal mining, and trona (a soda ash used
in the manufacture of glass). However, during the 1950s, the railroad
and coal-mining industries declined, while trona mining grew steadily.
By 1970, trona mining was the lead sector for employment, and
Sweetwater County had achieved the easy economic balance that comes
from years of slow transition. Housing was adequate, taxes were
stable, and services were available. It was a good rural life for the
18,000 residents of Sweetwater County, most of whom lived in its
two main cities of Rock Springs and Green River.

But in 1970, decisions were being made, decisions made far
from Sweetwater County—decisions that would change forever the
nature of that rural place. The most important one was the decision
to build the Jim Bridger Power Plant, a $400-million project, which
combined steam-electric power generating plants and coal mining,
sponsored by Pacific Power and Light and Idaho Power Company. At
the same time, the trona industry, itself, was expanding. Taken
together, the trona, power, and coal development placed enormous
growth pressure on the local economy, changing its rate of growth,
size, and composition. In three short years, total employment had
doubled—from 7,230 in 1970 to 15,225 in 1974. Population followed
suit, jumping from 18,000 in 1970 to 36,000 in 1974. Anyone who
had left the county in 1970 and returned in 1974 would have had
trouble recognizing the place.

While the local economy was exploding, major landowners in
Sweetwater County were pursuing some policies of their own. As it
turned out, there existed a de facto controlled-growth policy on new
residential development. Over one-half of the available land around
Rock Springs and Green River was government owned, and the
government was not selling. A good part of the remainder was owned
by Upland industries, and they were not selling either. The major
landowners were keeping the largest, most significant chunks of
developable land off the market. Thus, new residential development
was choked off at the beginning. But the de facto controlled-growth
policy was also supported by other conditions. Labor costs were
extremely high and were getting higher every day. Good labor, in
fact, was becoming difficult to find or hold, since the new energy
development was paying good wages, and new jobs were opening up
all the time. Further, the county suffered from lack of sewage
treatment. It all added up to a very restrictive policy on new

residential development. The policy was not the result of local
government action or inaction but of local market forces operating
quite freely. The local economy of Sweetwater County was allowed
to go its own way, at its own rate, and in its own time—with little
new housing. And the result was not pleasant.

There are now approximately 5,000 mobile homes in Sweetwater
County. Most are yet to be serviced by basic public facilities, such
as sewage treatment. The cost of new housing that is being built far
exceeds the income of the average worker. It is difficult to imagine
traffic congestion in Wyoming, much less problems with air and
water pollution, but it is happening there. The schools are over-
crowded, crime is increasing, and health care is scarce. Productivity
on the job is abysmal—firms cannot keep workers, and absenteeism
is high. There is general dissatisfaction with life in Sweetwater
County on the part of newcomers and old-time residents alike. And
all of this is happening in a relatively isolated, unknown part of what
most people think is a decidedly rural and peaceful place. And until
the local economy is in control, conditions in Sweetwater County will
not improve.

To a greater or lesser extent, the dilemma of the county is
repeated in nongrowth communities across the country. At one end
of the nongrowth continuum are the bedroom communities, with hardly
any local economy to speak of—where most of the residents work and
shop in other communities. In the bedroom communities, the pressure
and potential of the local economy is obviously not that great. But
this is hardly a permanent condition. For example, in the mid 1950s,
Orange County, California, was not much more than a bedroom for
people who worked and shopped in Los Angeles. But by 1975, Orange
County had developed a powerful economic base composed of well
over 700,000 workers, with a total county population of 1.5 million.[9]
The lesson of Orange County, or hundreds of other ex-bedroom communities, should not be lost on those communities that do not now
have a strong or growing local economy. For most of them, it is
only a matter of time.

At the opposite end of the economic spectrum are those communities, like Sweetwater County, which might be called self-contained
economic units. The people who live there, work there; and the people
who work there, live there. In this case, the local economy is capable
of supporting the entire local population. The local economy is the
all-important source of future growth. The community will grow,
decline, or stay about the same, depending upon the growth, decline,
or stability of its economic base. Effective nongrowth begins here.
It is the local economy that causes employment, which brings in-
migration, and which causes more employment and more migration.

It is a cyclical process, economically determined and economically tempered. Pollution, congestion, poor public services, overcrowding, high taxes, and all the other manifestions of supergrowth can be traced to the local economy. There is no getting around it: if communities want to control growth, they must begin to control the local economy.

ADDING EQUITY TO THE LOCAL ECONOMY

The second reason why it is important to control the local economy is that the local economy can increase or decrease social equity. This point has failed to reach the attention of most planners, economists, and sociologists. As seen in Chapter 2, many are quick to criticize land-use controls with respect to their supposed exclusionary basis. While some serious weaknesses in these assumptions were pointed out, there is also the point that it is not land-use controls at all which provide the inequities. It is the pressure generated from the local economy.

Most critics look at the housing market for evidence of the cost effects of land-use controls. If the price of housing is getting outrageous, then something is seriously wrong with the controls and all the policies behind them. But what is often the case is that the local economy is the source of cost pressure on the housing market. New employment opportunities lead to new employees, families of employees, further opportunities for employment, and so on. The new people also enter the housing market. And if there are not enough units available, the price goes up. But the reason the price goes up is the economic expansion. Take away part of the expansion and the price pressure disappears. Thus, the local economy can maintain a more equitable housing market than is currently supposed. Land-use controls are, at best, of secondary importance, except in the most exclusionary context. Most often, it is the local economy that is the driving force behind these highly inequitable results. Evidence of this is found in communities that have experienced severe rates of economic expansion. In these communities—for example Orange County, Santa Barbara, and Boulder—the demand for housing simply outdistances the available supply. Many of the equity problems currently blamed on land-use controls are really not problems of the controls. The problems can be traced back to the local economy, which runs blindly on its way, leaving serious inequities in its wake. Putting equity in land-use controls really means putting controls on the local economy.

More important than the housing question, however, is the effect of the local economy on the character and distribution of employment. Who gets the jobs? What jobs are they? What is the impact of local economic growth on the citizens of the community? And in particular, what does growth mean for the people at the low end of the economic spectrum? This is the truly important equity question.

Poor people are poor because they do not have enough money. Some do not have the money because they cannot work, because they physically cannot work. More are poor because they can work but are not working. The local economy can be turned to the aid of these people. And it is the type of aid that produces lasting gains, which puts money, status, and stability into poor peoples' hands. This is the potential of the local economy, which, for the most part, is yet to be tapped. Local manpower programs try to train workers or give subsidies to industry to do so. These programs rely upon the good will of employers and strategies of program bureaucrats, who often act as if economic growth were not part of the problem or solution. Indeed, they are still at the point of trying to discover if economic growth, local economic growth, can possibly be bad for those who can but do not work. And the answer is yes.

One of the little-researched aspects of local growth is the competition for employment that accompanies it. For example, a new factory or an expanding old one suddenly has 1,000 new jobs opening up. But the availability of the jobs brings in-migrants to the local community in search of new jobs. If the newcomers are better trained, educated, or connected than existing residents, chances are that the in-migrants will get the jobs. And the current resident will be left out. The same holds true when the nature of the local economy changes. For example, Los Angeles County was once a sizable agricultural area. But with the new development, the character of the economy changed. The agricultural base disappeared. And with it went the workers, some skilled and some unskilled. It is not unreasonable to expect that few of these workers would find opportunities for continuing employment in Los Angeles County. The same problem presented itself in Greenville, South Carolina.[10] There, the existing textile industry was threatened by a new tire industry, which had a wage rate much higher than the textile industry. Because the tire industry paid better, there was the possibility that the textile industry would be driven out—textiles simply could not compete in the local labor market. But what of the textile industry workers without the skills to transfer to the tire factory? These people would be the least likely to transfer to the new industries and the least able to move to gain new employment. Thus, the new tire factory could result in increased wages for some, but at a very high cost—unemployment for workers driven from the textile industry.

As the local economy develops, it brings with it new in-migrants. These new people are in competition with the old, not only for the new jobs but for all available work. As is often the case, the new migrants are better educated, trained, and experienced than local workers. When this occurs, the equity problems develop. The problems begin with jobs and then spread throughout virtually every aspect of community life. Employment means dollars. And dollars mean purchasing power over scarce community resources, like housing, education, parks, and transportation. If employment losses are suffered by current residents in favor of new growth, then the equity imbalance occurs.

If the local economy can work against local residents, and it can, then it could also be turned to their benefit. Norton Long wrote that

> a full employment program that makes the fullest and
> best use of the metropolitan area's population, particu-
> larly its youth, makes as much sense as the land-use
> planning that is most commonly cited as a major appro-
> priate objective for metropolitan planning. In fact, man-
> power planning is a necessary condition for the intelligent
> formulation of other plans.[11]

To make the plans work, the local economy must be brought under control. This will be discussed in the following chapter. But the important thing to understand is that the local economy can be used to increase social equity in the most lasting and beneficial way. The economy can be used to provide jobs, income, or training for those who need it most.

MAKING THE LOCAL ECONOMY PROFIT LOCAL RESIDENTS

One of the most difficult hurdles faced by local decision makers is the widely held assumption that rapid economic growth automatically produces solid economic gains for the local populace. Economic growth at the local level is the answer to any economic problem. If per capita income is down, then economic growth will push it up. If unemployment is up, then economic growth will push it down. If the income distribution is top-heavy, then new growth will level it out. But is this really the case? To find out, it might be worthwhile to review the economic performance of some of the fastest-growing areas in the nation. If the assumption is correct, then the fast-growing areas should be solving their economic problems.

In a recent report conducted for the city of Santa Barbara, the authors looked at average unemployment rates first for 25 of the fastest-growing Standard Metropolitan Statistical Areas (SMSAs) for the period 1950-60 and then for the 25 SMSAs with the fastest growth for the period 1960-70. The authors "found that the rates of unemployment in the fastest growing U.S. Standard Metropolitan Statistical Areas (SMSA's) are not different from the aggregate national SMSA unemployment rate. . . . In both cases, half of the fastest growing areas had unemployment rates above the national figure for all urban areas."[12] Thus, the evidence indicates that fast growth bears little correlation to low rates of unemployment.

In another study (for Colorado Springs, Colorado), the SMSAs with the largest population growth during the period 1960-70 were again looked at. This study examined the relationship between these SMSAs and their gains in average per capita income. The report concluded that "in a general way, those SMSA's which experienced the largest population growth during the decade of the 1960's also showed the smallest gain in average per capita income, whereas, those which had the smallest growth showed the highest gain."[13] Here, again, is another very surprising conclusion, and it raises some serious doubts about the assumption that growth will increase average per capita income.

A study conducted by the planning department in Tucson looked at increases in median family income for 14 of the fastest-growing SMSAs in the country during the period 1959-69. It was found that the average rate of income growth for these fast-growing communities was close to the national rate of increase for the period. The study concluded that "it should be obvious that high population growth of and by itself does not seem to guarantee high income growth."[14]

Another important aspect of the "economic growth is good for you" question is the relative one. How do fast-growing communities stand up against other communities across the country that are not having such great rates of economic and demographic expansion? Does rapid economic development improve the relative status of fast-growing communities? The April 1975 issue of Survey of Current Business provides some answers.[15] The article ranked the nation's SMSAs according to their relative status of total per capita personal income for the period 1959-73. By taking the same list of 25 of the fastest-growing SMSAs that had been used in the Santa Barbara study and seeing how they measured up with all other SMSAs, some surprising results were noted. In 15 of the 25 SMSAs, the fast-growing communities had lost ground relative to slow-growing

SMSAs in the nation. Well over one-half of the fast-growing communities had taken a beating in their relative per capita position.

The Anaheim-Santa Ana-Garden Grove area of southern
California had gone from number 1 in total per capita personal
income in 1959 to number 31 in 1973. Also in southern California,
the Oxnard-Ventura area had dropped from number 15 in 1959 to
number 147 in 1973. Nashua, New Hampshire, slipped from the
69th position in 1959 to 105 in 1973. While the supergrowth areas
were gaining people and jobs faster than all other areas in the
nation, many of the supergrowth areas were finding themselves
slipping farther and farther behind. These data show the hazards of
equating economic growth with good economic results. The relationship just does not prove out.

The same assumptions have been applied to the question of
local economic diversity. Growth is somehow equated with diversity
of economic base, which, in turn, is related to increased stability.
Therefore, a growing local economy is equal to a more stable local
economy. But the results of the Santa Barbara study also cast some
serious doubt on this assumption. Presumably, a fast-growing
economy should be getting more diverse and, therefore, more stable.
But the rates of unemployment in these fast-growing areas indicate
otherwise. Recent figures from these SMSAs show rates of unemployment considerably above the national average of 8.4 percent.[16] In
San Diego, California, for example, the rate of unemployment in
October 1975 was 10.5 percent. In Phoenix, Arizona, another growth
winner of the 1960s, the unemployment rate was over 11 percent. In
Miami, late figures show a rate of 11.7 percent. As with rates of
unemployment and average per capita income, there is no consistent
relationship between growth and stability.

There are a number of good reasons why rapid economic growth
is not so good for the local economy as is often imagined. One of the
principal reasons is net in-migration to an area. Consider rates of
unemployment. If a new factory opens in an area and creates 1,000
new jobs, unemployment will only be reduced if the jobs are made
available to current residents who are unemployed. If the factory
merely draws workers from outside of the area, there will be no
effect on unemployment. Thus, an important key to reducing the
rate of unemployment in an area is to get the jobs to the people in
the area who are unemployed. The mere presence of another new
factory, office complex, or research and development firm does not
provide any guarantees. Indeed, quite the reverse may be true. This
could happen if the new source of employment attracted too many
new in-migrants into the area for the number of jobs available. In
this instance, the effect would be a worsening of that condition.

The same can be said for increases or decreases in per capita income.

> Imagine a city with a population of 100,000, a labor force of 50,000, an average income per employee of $6,000 per year, and consequently per capita income of $3,000 per year. Assume that a large new plant employing 1,000 workers and paying an average of $5,000 per employee locates in the city. Let 100 of those new jobs be filled by local workers who upgrade themselves from jobs that had previous average earnings of $4,500 per year, and assume that those very low-wage jobs are lost. Let another 100 jobs be filled by previously unemployed workers and the remainder (800) by new migrants to the city. If those migrants bring families of the same average size as those of previous residents of the city, the situation after the new firm locates will give the city 1,600 new residents, a net increase of $4,550,000 in payrolls ($5,000 x 1,000 - $4,500 x 100), and a resulting per capita income of $2,990 per year.[17]

Now, even if the firm were to offer considerably higher wages than prevailing rates, the effect could be the same. This would happen if a larger number of in-migrants were attracted to the community such that the larger economic pie would be shared by more people— each one getting a smaller piece than before.

Chambers of commerce, utility companies and other development proponents are fond of pointing out that new economic growth increases local stability by diversifying the economic base. But it does not work that way. The really important thing is that diversification and, hence, economic stability have little to do with how fast or how large the local economy grows. Diversification has to do with the business cycle of the existing local industries and how these match up with the business cycles of new local industries. Some industries, like food, are seasonal. Others, such as automobiles, respond dramatically to national recessions. Each major group of industries has its own characteristic business cycles. And within the major group of industries, each subgroup has its own, and so forth. To further complicate things, the degree of stability also changes at the local level, such that a local firm may be running at full capacity while similar firms in other cities are bordering on bankruptcy. Communities can become more stable in a number of ways: by actually getting rid of industries, by getting rid of some industries and substituting others, or by selective pursuit of

industries. There is simply no justification in pursuing new economic growth in the belief that whatever comes will make the community more diverse and more stable. Such policies could easily
lead to the opposite results.

All of these criticisms can be reduced to a single point. There
is no reason to believe that economic growth at the local level will
lead to increases in economic welfare for all citizens of the community. Whether or not economic growth is good for a community
depends upon the specific economic and demographic characteristics
of that place. Each community has developed from a unique set of
conditions, conditions not likely to be duplicated elsewhere. Consequently, economic growth will only prove beneficial to the community
residents if the growth corresponds to precise community needs—
if the development serves the people of the community. Michael
Conroy, in his excellent book The Challenge of Urban Economic
Development, makes this point over and over.

> Neither employment growth nor growth in local produc-
> tion nor, much less, population growth will lead to the
> development of the urban economy unless their nature,
> composition, and relative rates of growth correspond to
> the conditions suggested. . . . Naive "boosterism" that
> proclaims that "more" means "better" in the urban
> economy may be justified because more may mean better
> for some . . . but growth that is indiscriminately encour-
> aged may bring no benefits in terms of higher average
> income while it contributes to the reduction in the quality
> of urban life.[18]

All of this points to some good economic reasons for controlling
the local economy. It has been seen, for example, that increased per
capita income depends upon rates of in-migration, as well as on the
wage rates paid by new firms or expanding old ones. Obviously, if
the objective of local public policy is to increase per capita income
then something should be done about in-migration or average wage
levels of new industries or both. The same holds true for attacking
problems of local unemployment. To do so requires some economic
expansion (or policies of forced outmigration), joined with restrictions on in-migration. It might also suggest some fairly specific
manpower programs, not the usual kind, where job training may or
may not result in a job, but job training resulting in real, guaranteed
employment at the end. Communities could easily set up programs
tied to new development, where permission to develop would hinge
on a close working arrangement with manpower-training programs.

Increasingly, local economic stability is another matter of local concern. Local government action can be taken to increase stability,
but this action requires some careful thinking and selective acquisition programs. Good local public choice can result in some highly
positive economic gains for local residents. But the ability to make
this kind of choice requires some control over the local economy to
ensure that the local economy performs for the benefit of local citizens.

WINNERS AND LOSERS

In light of some of the benefits of economic nongrowth, one
could ask why local governments have not latched on to them before.
While a few local governments have, the majority have not. There
are two main reasons. The first has to do with the growth winners,
the people who benefit most from growth. The second is that local
communities believe they simply do not have the power or knowledge
to do anything, even if they wanted to.

The winners in the local growth setting are easy to identify.
Just see who lines up on both sides of the issue. Basically, the growth
winners are the local monopolists, the people who exercise exclusive
control over a unique local resource. Newspapers are a good example.
The editor of a San Jose, California, newspaper responded to criticism
from environmentalists about the destruction of the famous San Jose
orchards by saying, "Trees don't read newspapers."[19] Newspapers
are big growth winners because circulation goes up with each new
member of the community. And along with circulation come the new
businesses, which means increased advertising space, increased
revenues, more influence, and so on. As David Rasmussen notes:

> On account of the substantial barriers to entering the news-
> paper industry, the new population growth will not encourage
> the formation of another newspaper in the area. With little
> change in costs, the revenue from both sales and advertising
> will increase. Thus, in the case of the local newspaper
> and other businesses that are relatively insulated from
> competition, profits are likely to rise as a consequence
> of population growth.[20]

To the same list of monopolists should be added all large property owners. This is another group that obviously stands to gain from
increased population growth. Every additional in-migrant increases

the demand for the property owner's land, placing the owner in a better position by increasing the value of the property. And, of course, there is the enduring alliance between large property owners and the local banking, real estate, and insurance institutions. Add to this the developers and, to a lesser extent, construction unions, and you have the traditional local power bloc that has dominated local decisions for so long. It is no surprise, then, that local decisions have fostered increased growth, since the decision makers have been so strongly tied to the economics of increased population growth. It was the exceptional planning commission or city council that was not controlled by bankers, developers, insurance men, real estate agents, or lawyers representing all the above.[21] As Conroy has noted, "One is led inexorably to the conclusion that whatever planning of the rate and composition of growth which is undertaken takes place in the board rooms of the banks, developers, and industries which directly induce or produce growth."[22] Thus, in moving to a nongrowth strategy, this group will form the bulk of the opposition, since these people have the most to lose by nongrowth and the most to gain by unfettered growth.

However, this list of winners is hardly complete, for along with the development industry, one must consider a less visible but equally important group of people who are dependent on supergrowth for more and bigger success. Consider, for example, the local city manager. The salary of a city manager often reflects the size of the population and the size of the local bureaucracy.[23] Even a cursory look at salaries in relation to population tells the story. For city managers and other bureaucrats who hold supervisory positions, a bigger city means more money, power, and authority, as well as people to boss. This includes people like the school superintendent, the hospital administrators, the fire chief, the planning director, the director of local water and sewer operations, and a host of other bureaucrats. Salary and population serviced are strongly related. Consequently, it is often the bureaucracy itself that has an interest in growth. And this is particularly true for those holding non-duplicatable positions.[24] The average fireman has no interest in more growth since the city will always hire more firemen. This is also true for teachers, planners, sanitation workers, and other low-level replaceable bureaucrats. The benefits of growth have the distinct tendency to cluster toward the upper end of the income scale—where the managers are.

Now, consider some other local monopoly functions. Local utilities of all types are solidly behind more population growth. The electrical company sees more people in terms of a growing demand for services, a greater power load, and higher electric bills. The same holds true for water and sewer utilities. And what about local television stations? These institutions also benefit from additional growth, so it is not surprising to see where they line up. Radio stations are another population growth winner, since their advertising depends on the number of listeners, which, in turn, depends on population growth.

When looking at the list of winners, it is obvious that it is a powerful coalition. The development industry, coupled with the bureaucracy, coupled with the powerful segments of the media, makes for a sizable, influential progrowth force. This group is likely to be the main source of opposition to any nongrowth plans, since their economic well-being hangs upon future population growth. And they are not particularly interested in quality of the growth—just that it occurs on a regular basis.

Then, there are the growth losers. The big losers are those who are in competition with the incoming population. In terms of local industry, for example, this often means the entire central business district, which is likely to lose out to national conglomerates that are attracted to explosive new markets. Any of the local retail firms whose products are easily imitated are likely to be injured by increased population growth—the hamburger stand that finds a new McDonalds right down the street; the hardware store that finds itself in competition with Angels or Ace; the drugstore that sees the arrival of Walgreens, Safeway, or Thrifty; the Mom and Pop grocery store confronted with the giants, A & P, National, or Safeway. Population growth leads to more and more national firms, which, in turn, places extreme pressure on home-growth retail and industrial developments.

But the biggest losers of all are likely to be people living in the community, who find themselves in competition for jobs, income, education, housing, and health care with the new in-migrants. All too often, the new in-migrants are younger, better trained, better educated, wealthier, healthier, and more employable than existing residents. Old people are particularly hard hit. One thing that growth is sure to bring is a higher cost of living through such things as an increase in property taxes. Fixed incomes and reduced mobility combine to make the effects of growth particularly burdensome for the senior population.

Then, consider what happens when rapid urban development comes to any local community whose dominant economic base is agriculture. Urban development and agricultural production are not compatible. Development leads to the demise of the farm. Yet, the people on the farm have a limited set of skills. These people do not fit well into a local employment picture whose jobs are increasingly

located in nonagricultural pursuits. There are many other examples.
The textile industry was driven out of New England (and into the
South) by virtue of a changing economic base. The result for New
England is a string of depressed mill towns, with high unemployment
and few immediate prospects for recovery. Thus, new development
can change huge segments of the local economic base, which means,
in practice, that many people will be thrown out of work. The people
are big growth losers.

WINNER OR LOSER? THE CASE OF CONSTRUCTION WORKERS

One of the most volatile issues in the growth-nongrowth contro-
versy is the status of construction workers. Many people, especially
developers and union chiefs, assume that the lines are clearly drawn,
that growth is good for construction and nongrowth is not. But there
are a number of impressive reasons why nongrowth could help them.
The first and most obvious point is that nongrowth does not
mean that all new construction stops. Houses will continue to be
built, roads paved, hospitals erected, schools put up, and so forth.
Nongrowth simply means that local communities should take a hard
look at new development to discover for themselves which development
works for the community and which does not. This could hardly be
interpreted as a call for the cessation of all growth. Indeed, a review
of some of the local nongrowth studies shows that communities are
prepared to accept and plan for new development. In Orange County,
California, the recommended population would increase by over 1
million people by the year 2000.[25] Between 1975 and 1990, Davis,
California, will add 20,000 to its current population.[26] And the
Petaluma, California, system would allow more new people per year
than had been coming into the city previous to the plan.[27] Thus, for
construction workers, the conclusion should be obvious. There will
be work available.
When the population growth estimates are translated into new
housing units, there are some comforting findings for the construction workers. In Orange County, for example, the population growth
would indicate that approximately 330,000 new units will be required
by the year 2000. Davis, California, will require some 7,000 new
units before the year 1990. These figures point up an extremely
interesting point. And that is that most nongrowth plans represent
an attempt to level off growth rather than to stop it altogether or to
reverse it overnight. This means that employment in the construction industry—specifically, in new housing construction—will not

suffer. Workers who are now working will have sufficient work available for the foreseeable future. There are large differences between the words "growth," "stability," and "decline." Nongrowth will push the construction industry in a local community toward stability rather than toward continued growth. But all this means is that the number of working carpenters, plumbers, roofers, and electricians will remain the same.

There is another important point that bears heavily upon the quantity and quality of work that will be available for construction workers. Buildings get old. Houses begin to fall apart. Office buildings show the strains of age. Old courthouses become firetraps. This means that the nature of construction work changes over time, along with the quality of the buildings. As buildings get old, they must be renovated or replaced. Suburban areas, generally speaking, have yet to face the problem of getting old. Nongrowth communities will get old, too. And as they do, new opportunities open up for the construction industry. Remember the example of the number of new units that would be required in the nongrowth plans? To this should be added the number of units that will be renovated or replaced. And if one assumes that buildings have an average life of 50 years, a full 2 percent of the total existing housing stock will have to be replaced each year. In Orange County that would add another 10,000 units per year to the approximate 12,000 new units per year that are being planned for. Together, they add up to almost 33 percent more per annum than the Orange County average for the last ten years.[28] Clearly, there will be no shortage of work.

The controlling influence of requirements for new housing and other new uses, plus the growing effect of renovation and renewal, adds up to a sizable amount of construction work. Studies done in Orange County, Santa Barbara, Marin County, California, and Tucson, Arizona, all show that employment in construction will either increase or remain the same under the recommended nongrowth plan.[29]

There is, however, one very tiny segment of the construction industry that would be hurt by nongrowth policies. These are the union chiefs, the leaders of construction unions, who have seen their membership continue to expand. Like the newspaper editors, city manager, large property owners, bankers, the union chiefs have a strong interest in continued union growth. As with the others, the interest is also anchored in more power, status, and money. Since it is likely that nongrowth will induce some stability in union membership or at least level off the growth, the strategies are certain to run against the interest of the union leaders.

While nongrowth will not harm construction workers, it just might do them some good. One of the major problems with the

industry is that it is one of the most recession-prone in the country.
Almost everything affects construction. Interest rates go up, and new
construction slowly diminishes. If the weather gets bad, the workers
go home. Costs of land, taxes, building materials, labor, and financing
all combine to make this an extremely insecure field of work. The
average worker has little confidence in anything except the current
job, and often little confidence in that. And adding to all this insecurity
is a particularly knotty problem for local construction firms. They
don't know what anyone else is doing.

Here is a typical local construction scene. Ten firms decide
independently to build 10 new housing units each for a total of 100
units. Their market research, such as it is, has shown that the community will need at least 50 and maybe 70 new units. All proceed to
break ground and erect the units. Come opening day, there are 100
new units available. Unfortunately, only 50 or 70 buyers are interested.
Someone is stuck with 50 or 30 vacant, unsold, and expensive units.
Next year, just after everyone takes a beating, each decides independently to build only 1 new unit. On opening day, 70 buyers show
up and trample each other for the 50 units available. This is a very
common condition of local construction industries. The industry
runs from overbuilding to shortages and back again. One year, there
might be more than enough new units, and by the next year, they would
have all disappeared. Thus, the industry in a local area runs from
recession, to boom, to recession. It is all a big game of chance.

One of the real economic strengths of nongrowth strategies is
that they can take some of the chance out of the industry. Nongrowth
strategies can do so by means of new housing allotments for any one
period. This strategy, as is now the case in Petaluma and Davis,
California, calls for the construction of a certain amount of new
housing units for a particular time period. By providing the industry
with some solid figures on the number of new units that can be built
in any one period, they introduce an element of certainty which was
not there before. The industry now knows exactly how many units
will be built and can then match this figure against their buyer estimates. They will then be in a much better position to know whether
or not their development will be successful before they commit all
their resources. Thus, nongrowth strategies may help solve one of
the most difficult problems the industry faces.

For the average construction worker, nongrowth could provide some highly useful results. In taking out some of the wild
fluctuations of the industry, the strategies might provide more
stability than construction workers have seen in some time. Since
this is one of the major problems faced by construction workers,
and one that has defied corrective measures, any improvement would

be a great improvement. When stability is coupled with a continuing supply of jobs, it is apparent that the construction worker has nothing to lose and quite a bit to gain.

THE TECHNICAL BIND

The second major reason why local governments have not been overly anxious to control their local economy is that the experts tell them that it either should not, or could not, be done. On the "should not" side, the experts point out that nongrowth makes the central cities worse off than they are at present. On the "could not" side, the experts argue that communities simply do not have the power to control their local economy, much less the proper experience or talent.

The great central city ripoff argument goes something like this. Scheming suburbs want to keep people out, especially central city people. To do this, they adopt nongrowth strategies. And in doing so, the central city people are locked out of the suburbs and locked into the central city. "A suburb may be able to keep population or industry out," states William Alonso, "but it can do so only by directing it to other suburbs or by keeping it cooped up in the central city."[30] Because of this, all of the central city problems will increase—the pressure in the pressure cooker will continue to rise. Thus, nongrowth is just another twisted version of "I'm all right Jack," or "I just got aboard, so let's pull up the gangplank." Alonso writes:

> Local policies for zero population growth ultimately run
> into the problem that ours is a highly interconnected
> society and economy. No state or city is an island, entire
> unto itself. Local policies may try to limit population by
> passing restrictive zoning, limiting housing permits, and
> the like. This is the I'm-all-right-Jack-and-bar-the-
> door version, much favored by suburbs, which forces out
> the young and is regressive.[31]

So, based on its (moral) bad taste no one should do it.

At the public relations level, the central city ripoff argument has its merits. But a closer examination would reveal some strange assumptions, little evidence, and bad thinking. First, the whole concept of nongrowth is tied to the idea that each community should determine for itself what it wants to do and where it wants to go—

central cities included. The last thing one would expect is that all
communities would choose to do the same thing. It is extremely
unlikely that an entire set of communities would band together to
effect any kind of unified policy, much less a unified nongrowth
policy. In the Tucson area, for example, the city is pursuing a nongrowth policy, but Pima County seems to want little to do with it.
Petaluma may choose to let in 200 new units per year, while its
sister cities might allow 500. Thus, the premise for the argument
that all suburbs band together to exclude everyone else is on shaky
grounds.

Second, nongrowth strategies are not the exclusive province of
suburban jurisdictions. Tucson is hardly a suburb. Neither is
Toronto. And Los Angeles is not one either, although it, too, is considering nongrowth. As will be seen in the next chapter, some states
have adopted the basic concept. Consequently, the assumption that nongrowth is first, last, and always a suburban plot does not hold up.

Third, economists looking into the effects of nongrowth suburbs
on the central city theorize that they will be positive. One paper, for
example, pointed out that a ring of nongrowth suburbs may lead to
the point where "fewer households [will] choose the suburbs and the
central city . . . should remain a more heterogeneous, viable
entity."[32] Nongrowth would help the central city by stemming the
flight of its most valued resources—the people. This would be no
small contribution toward keeping the central city a worthwhile place
to live. While it's important that the central city keep its people, it
is also important that they keep their jobs. The fiscal zoning approach
favored by some nongrowth communities could result in "the central
city [retaining] more firms . . . suburban large-lot zoning may also
'bottle up' a profitable industrial tax base and many nonpoor families
in the central city."[33] Clearly, if the central cities were able to
hang on to more of their people and more of their employers, they
would be in a considerably stronger position. Another economist
pointed out that the nongrowth strategies in the suburbs could result
in resource transfers back to the central city.[34] When nongrowth
communities make potential industrial employers pay a high price
for moving in, the employers are encouraged to go elsewhere in
search of lower prices. An obvious choice is the central city, particularly if many of the suburban areas adopt similar policies toward
industry. In this case, the suburbs would lose the tax advantages, as
well as employment advantages, to the central city. In this way,
resources would be transferred from the suburbs to the central city.
This is a policy long favored by big-city mayors and liberal politicians
of all types, as well as by many academics. Make the suburbs pay is
what it amounts to, and nongrowth may do exactly that.

The fourth point in the ripoff argument is that nongrowth could lead to a more stable national economy, a condition that would benefit the entire country. This would require controls over the local economy that are not, as yet, in place. But the main idea, developed by Conroy in his book Regional Economic Growth, is that if local communities were able to make their own local economies less recession-prone, the national economy would follow suit.[35] In Conroy's words:

> With the industrial portfolio approach, it is possible to
> see how a city might be more diversified than the nation,
> how the reduction of instability . . . would not necessarily
> mean competition for the few stable industries, and how,
> in fact, careful diversification programs nationwide could
> tend to reduce national fluctuations.[36]

These counterarguments point out a few of the weaknesses of the ripoff argument. But they go further. They provide a glimpse into some of the positive reasons why local communities should adopt nongrowth. If nongrowth is good for communities, if nongrowth is good for central cities, if nongrowth could strengthen the national economy, then who, aside from usual growth winners, is the loser?

The second technical argument strikes directly at the thesis of this chapter—that communities should, and can, control their local economy. The core of the argument is that even if local communities wanted to control their local economy, they cannot, since they do not have the economic power to do so. The critics generally pick up on Alonso's previous point about communities being very small cogs in a very large, complex, interdependent economic system. Witness, for example, the statement of Conroy:

> The position of every urban economy within the national
> economy and the intricate relationship that its economic
> structure has to the economic structure of other urban
> places in its region both suggest that the amount of lever-
> age that residents in any single city have over their own
> economic structure is severely limited.[37]

Because the odds are stacked so heavily at the national level, there is hardly any point for local communities to do much of anything.

This type of thinking is much in favor with consultants, as well as with nearly every one of the growth winners. It attempts to force communities into a passive economic stance, where, because of the decisive influence of the national economy, they must simply and meekly accept whatever comes their way. It is the doctrine of

predestination, dressed in growth winner's clothes. "We have come,"
writes Norton Long, "largely to regard our cities and their citizens
as powerless. This acceptance of the powerlessness of cities and
individuals accounts, to a considerable extent, for the uncritical
assumption that socioeconomic structure is not susceptible of meaningful alteration."[38] This argument fosters the subtle destructive
logic that if cities have no real economic power, then they have no
real responsibility. And if there is no local responsibility, then
there are no local problems—only local symptoms of national problems. Air pollution in Los Angeles, traffic congestion in Denver,
unemployment in San Jose, and underemployment in Tucson are all
national problems. Someone else, not the local community, is responsible. And the someone is the federal government, big enough and
rich enough to do almost anything. Thus, the burden of any kind of
social, environmental, or economic performance is lifted from the
puny shoulders of local government.

The no-power argument is often backed up by the professional
bias of urban economists. To begin with, urban economics itself was
not considered a serious subdiscipline of economics until the early
1960s. And even then, economists considered it with some disdain:

> Local government positions are regarded as of relatively
> low prestige and interest among economists, compared to
> academic, national government, and business jobs. . . .
> Hence, the best economists have usually avoided local
> government jobs. Moreover, those [economists] in it
> [local government] are forced to grapple with what many
> economists consider "grubby, everyday problems,"
> rather than "global issues" that pure academicians can
> pursue with mathematical fantasies.[39]

But more serious than professional snobbery was the fact that the
tools of urban economic analysis, the evaluative methods and techniques, were themselves geared in a national direction. This includes
input-output models, simulation methods, as well as basic-nonbasic
analysis, and the foreign trade multiplier models. The common
assumption with all of these fundamental urban economic tools is
that local economic growth, its size, rate, distribution, and composition are all determined by outside forces—from what was going on
at the national level. The clear implication from the tools themselves is that local governments cannot really do much, since the
local economy is so much the creature of national economic determi-
nants. As James Heilbrun, an economist himself, notes, "This way
of looking at the local economy inevitably focuses attention on

matters over which local authorities have no control . . . while distracting attention from the very thing they can influence—the nature and attractiveness of the local economic environment."[40]

The professional bias of economists and the analytic bias of urban economists have resulted in a strange (and to communities a harmful) outcome. On the one hand, the economics profession pushes promising students away from urban economics and into the more highly regarded, tenured roles as watchdogs of the international, national, or private business economy. And the urban economists themselves help the process along by continuing to work with and on the analytic devices supporting the proposition that whatever happens to a local economy is the product of the national one. Finally, urban economists contend that the subject, urban economics, is so complex and demanding that it should be left to the experts who understand it. It all adds up to continued support of the no-power argument. Any way one looks at it, cities just do not have the power. Long captures this idea and its implications:

> The cities' leaders and the cities' inhabitants have been taught to believe that the unwalled cities of the nation-state no longer possess significant power over their economic fate. At most they are local housekeeping agencies who must beg handouts from superior governments when their revenues fall short and pinch. They are regarded and regard themselves as without significant power to favorably alter their economic fate by efforts of their own.[41]

For nongrowth strategies, this is, perhaps, the most important question. Do cities have the power to really do anything? Can they really control population and economic growth? Can they make growth of population and the economy work for the local residents?

A good place to begin is with a brief analysis of the much-used case of foreign countries. Alonso is fond of this one:

> It might be easier to limit growth than to promote it, but this is not the case according to a rich experience of national policies in Europe and the socialist countries. Moscow, Paris, London, and Warsaw are among the centers where vigorous policies have been followed to contain and even reverse growth. The means at hand have often appeared foolproof, including not only the tax incentives and disincentives, subsidies, land use regulations, and other devices familiar in American experience, but also direct command over the location of jobs and people

through state control over many enterprises, location
and expansion permits for industry, residence permits,
and job and housing assignments for people. Even
so, these centers have continued to grow, although
perhaps less than without these measures. These
powerful tools have failed in the face of more powerful
social and economic currents.[42]

Alonso stayed home, but not James Sundquist. Sundquist spent
a year of study in Europe looking at how the programs were working
and found that

as for the total effect, it seems clear that the European
governments have interfered successfully with the normal
working of the economy—jobs have been moved from con-
gested areas to decongested areas, particularly new jobs.
Migration has been slowed and population stabilized in
areas of out-migration. The proudest boasts in these
countries now are that, probably for the first time in
modern history, there is a net migration from the London
region, from the Paris region, and from the provinces of
North Holland and South Holland. In the case of the Stock-
holm region, there was not only a net out-migration in
1972 but an absolute decline in population.[43]

Yet, the "Moscow tried and it does not work" criticism persists in
high academic places. But the academics are wrong.

Local government has two main types of power that, if exercised, translate into raw economic power. The first is fiscal, that
is, the power to spend and the power to tax. In 1972, the gross
national product (GNP) was $1.150 trillion. Local government, in
that same period, had revenues of $113.162 billion.[44] That is over
9 percent of total GNP and over one-half of the total federal revenue
for the same period, which is a lot of money and even more economic
power. These revenues are used for employment, capital outlays,
subsidies, and other expenses. Local government is a major economic
actor whose economic power has continued to grow.

But more important than the hard dollars are local police
powers. This is what really sets local government apart from state
and federal governments, as well as the private sector. Local governments control the power of location. It is a monopoly power vested
in local government, which gives them, with few exceptions, virtually
absolute authority over the use of land in the community. The local
community literally grants permission or withholds it from anyone

seeking to change the use of land. Local government controls the
nature, characteristics, timing, and location of all new development.
From the factory to the houses to the used car lots, everyone must
get permission from the local government. By carrying out its plans
and regulations, the local government sets the basic urban form,
including its economic and social characteristics. Police power makes
the community a monopoly, the only one of its kind. And like all
monopolies, local government can, if it so chooses, exercise these
monopoly powers for the benefit of its residents. It can require
specific types of performance from all new development, performance
that might lead to less pollution, more low-income housing, more
open space, or, for that matter, to a stronger and more stable and
equitable local economy.

In recent years, the power of local communities has been
strengthened by both the courts and the federal government. The
courts, in the case of Petaluma, Ramapo, and Belle Terre, have
expanded what constitutes local health, safety, and welfare.[45] In so
doing, they provided additional legal leverage for the plans and regulations of local government. Local governments can expand the range
of local objectives that they can attempt to achieve through their
police power. And the federal government has acted similarly. New
federal laws, such as the Water Pollution Control Amendments of
1972, increase the power and responsibility of local governments for
the protection of local environments. New revenue-sharing programs
can be used for a variety of purposes. The number of strings attached
to the federal dollar is at least leveling off, if not decreasing. Finally,
the states have moved to increase this power. Ten states have passed
what amounts to comprehensive land-use legislation, which does two
things.[46] First, it increases the state power over land use where the
local governments refuse to act. Second, and more important, it
increases the local power and responsibility of local government to
act to achieve a range of positive local objectives, like a quality
environment, a good economic base, solid land-use planning, and
reasonable social programs.

Local governments have the kind of raw, simple economic and
legal power that can get things done. With the power comes responsibility, responsibility to achieve locally determined objectives. Far
from advocating a do-nothing approach, it argues strongly for local
intervention in local problems. As one economist noted:

> If planning has any meaning at all, it is to be found in the
> inadequacies of a totally unrelated system. The extent
> to which the planner can intrude upon the workings of the
> marketplace depends upon many things, including the

condition of the law, the social philosophy of the times, and the state of his own art. But intrude he must.[47]

We have a long history of local government that has shown, until recently, a unique ability to say yes—yes to every new development proposal, regardless of its consequences for local citizens, who sometimes paid dearly. Local governments are just now beginning to acquaint themselves with the word "no" in the case of those developments that do nothing for the citizens. Mistakes will be made, but as Long wrote:

> Many governments might prefer to make these decisions consciously. And this is the best of reasons for having a government to make decisions consciously—so that hopefully one can at least learn and in the process improve one's practice. The task of government is to take one out of the state of nature and change the intended play of forces into an ordered set of intended and corrigible outcomes.[48]

This is what the economics of local nongrowth is all about. The next chapter suggests what communities can do to achieve it.

NOTES

1. National Association of Homebuilders, "Land Use Policy Must Consider Need for Development," Local Government Affairs 6, no. 1 (1975): 3.

2. See Bernard H. Siegan, Land Use Without Zoning (Lexington, Mass.: D.C. Heath and Company, 1972), pp. 23-76.

3. Philip Hammer, "Economics in the Planning Process," Institute on Zoning and Planning (Dallas, Texas: Southwestern Legal Foundation, 1968), p. 71.

4. Wilbur Thompson, "Planning as Urban Growth Management: Still More Questions Than Answers," American Institute of Planners Newsletter 9, no. 12 (December 1974): 10.

5. Michael E. Gleeson et al., Urban Growth Management Systems: An Evaluation of Policy Related Research, Planning Advisory Service Report nos. 309, 310 (Chicago: American Society of Planning Officials, 1975), p. 4.

6. Manuel S. Emanuel, "Ramapo's Managed Growth Program," Planners Notebook 4, no. 5 (October 1974): 7, 8.

7. Michael E. Conroy, The Challenge of Urban Economic Development (Lexington, Mass.: D. C. Heath and Company, 1975), p. 36.

8. See John S. Gilmore and Mary K. Duff, The Sweetwater County Boom: A Challenge to Growth Management (Denver, Colo.: University of Denver Research Institute, 1974), app. A.

9. Research Department, Security Pacific Bank, Monthly Summary of Business Conditions 54, no. 8 (August 1975): 6.

10. See Bert A. Winterbottom, "A Growth Management Strategy for Greenville County, South Carolina" (Paper delivered at the 57th Annual Conference of American Institute of Planners, Denver, Colo., 1974), p. 4.

11. Norton E. Long, The Unwalled City: Reconstituting the Urban Community (New York: Basic Books, 1972), pp. 103-04.

12. Richard P. Appelbaum et al. (Santa Barbara Planning Task Force), Santa Barbara: The Impacts of Growth, vol. 1 (Santa Barbara, Calif.: City of Santa Barbara, 1974), pp. 6.12, 6.14.

13. Richard C. Bradley, The Costs of Urban Growth: Observations and Judgements (Colorado Springs, Colo.: Pikes Peak Area Council of Governments, 1973), p. 11.

14. Tucson, Arizona, Planning Department, The Comprehensive Plan (Tucson: City of Tucson Planning Department, 1975), economy section, pp. 16-17.

15. Regional Economic Measurement Division, "County and Metropolitan Personal Income," Survey of Current Business 52 (April 1975), p. 33.

16. "A Look at Business Across the Country," U.S. News and World Report 79, no. 16 (October 20, 1975): 71, 73.

17. See Conroy, op. cit., p. 54.

18. Ibid., p. 63.

19. Stanford Environmental Law Society, San Jose: Sprawling City—A Study of the Causes and Effects of Urban Sprawl in San Jose, California (Stanford, Calif.: Stanford Law School, 1971), p. 17.

20. David W. Rasmussen, Urban Economics (New York: Harper and Row, 1973), p. 166.

21. Marion Clawson, Suburban Land Conversion in The United States: An Economic and Governmental Process (Baltimore, Md.: The Johns Hopkins Press, 1971), chap. 12, pp. 106, 253.

22. Michael E. Conroy, The Challenge of Urban Economic Development: An Evaluation of Policy Related Research on Alternative Goals for the Economic Structure of Cities (Austin: Center for Economic Development, University of Texas, 1974), p. 11.

23. Research and Development Center, The Municipal Yearbook 1973 (Washington, D.C.: International City Management Association, 1973), pp. 134-53.

24. See Rasmussen, op. cit., p. 166.

25. Orange County, California, Planning Department, People, Policy & Growth: A New Direction? (Santa Ana, Calif.: Orange County Planning Department, 1973), p. 31.

26. Davis, California, Community Development Department, General Plan (Davis, Calif.: City of Davis Planning Department, 1975), p. 10.

27. See Gleeson et al., op. cit., pp. 18, 19.

28. Orange County, California, Planning Department, Orange County Progress Report (Santa Ana, Calif.: Orange County Planning Department, June 1972), p. 88.

29. See the following reports: Orange County, California, Planning Department, People, Policy & Growth: A New Direction?, op. cit., p. 49; Tucson, Arizona, Planning Department, op. cit., pp. 62-66; Baxter, McDonald & Smart, Inc., Economic Impact of the Marin Countywide Plan, Technical Report (San Francisco: Baxter, McDonald & Smart, 1974), p. 47; and Santa Barbara Planning Task Force, op. cit., p. 6.20.

30. William Alonso, "Urban Zero Population Growth," Daedalus 102, no. 4 (Fall 1973), p. 196.

31. Ibid., p. 204.

32. Michelle J. White, "Fiscal Zoning in Fragmented Metropolitan Areas," Fiscal Zoning and Land Use Controls, ed. Edwin S. Mills and Wallace E. Oates (Lexington, Mass.: Lexington Books, 1975), p. 99.

33. Ibid, p. 99.

34. See Niles M. Hansen, The Basic Economics of Metropolitan Growth and Development Goals: An Evaluation of Policy Related Research (Austin: Center for Economic Development, University of Texas, July 1974), p. 178.

35. See Michael E. Conroy, Regional Economic Growth: Diversification and Control (New York: Praeger, 1975), p. 112.

36. Michael E. Conroy, The Challenge of Urban Economic Development (Lexington, Mass.: D.C. Heath and Company, 1975), p. 75.

37. Ibid., p. 37.

38. Norton E. Long, "Have Cities a Future?," Texas Town and City 61 (April 1974), p. 11.

39. Anthony Downs, "How Cities Could Use Economists: Why They Don't; What to Do About It," Public Management 53 (June 1971), p. 11.

40. James Heilbrun, Urban Economics and Public Policy (New York: St. Martins Press, 1974), p. 168.

41. Long, The Unwalled City: Reconstituting the Urban Community, op. cit., p. x.

42. See Alonso, op. cit., pp. 195, 196.

43. James L. Sundquist, "Europe Stops the Urban Swarm," The Brookings Bulletin 12, no. 1 (Winter 1975): 9.

44. U.S. Department of Commerce, Bureau of the Census, Statistical Abstract of the United States: 1974, 95th ed. (Washington, D.C.: Government Printing Office, 1974), p. 248.

45. See Construction Industry Association of Sonoma County v. City of Petaluma, 375 F. Supp. 574 (N.D. Cal. 1974), rev'd, no. 74-2100 (9 Cir., decided August 13, 1975), 522 F. 2d 897; Golden v. Planning Board of Town of Ramapo, 30 N.Y. 2d 359, 285 N.E. 2d 291 (1972), app. dis., 409 U.S. 1003; Village of Belle Terre v. Boraas, 416 U.S. 1 (1974).

46. William J. Toner et al., Information/Data Handling Requirements for Selected State Resource Management Programs (Washington, D.C.: U.S. Department of Interior, forthcoming).

47. Leslie E. Carbert, "The Economist as Planner or Visions of a Dismal Science," State Planning Issues, ed. H. Milton Patton and Merlin M. Hackbart (Lexington, Ky.: Council of State Governments, Secretariat, 1975), p. 18.

48. Long, "Have Cities A Future?," op. cit., p. 12.

5

WORKABLE NONGROWTH: GETTING THE LOCAL ECONOMY IN CONTROL

This chapter is about the ways that local communities can control their local economy. It may come as a surprise, but local communities can control their economies by using the powers they now possess. There is no need for new institutions, legislation, or massive injections of bureaucrats. On the contrary, it is merely a matter of using the current assortment of powers that every community has.

As seen in the previous chapter, there are three main reasons for controlling the local economy: (a) effective nongrowth requires control over the local economy; (b) controlling the local economy can increase social equity by transferring income, jobs, or other resources to local people who need them; and (c) controlling the local economy can result in solid economic gains for local citizens, a more stable local economy, higher incomes, and the like. Recent statements and actions of public officials around the country show that these ideas are beginning to take hold. Elected officials are beginning to discover and exercise the power that they really have.

Witness, as an early example, the statement of Tom McCall, who as governor of Oregon said:

> Now we Oregonians are at the point where we can look
> at some tremendously good firms and maybe we can let
> a limited number into the state. . . . We are in a position
> to pick. We can go down to Los Angeles and say, "If
> you want to become a member of our club we'd like to
> have you, but we don't like rattle and bang and smoke and
> dirt." . . . That's our whole philosophy, instead of
> panting madly.[1]

Unlike many governors, McCall had the good economic sense to
realize that Oregon was holding some very important, powerful
cards. By virtue of its natural resources and excellent national
image, Oregon was an attractive state for many firms looking for
new locations. And McCall was going to use this advantage to make
sure that the new firms would serve the people of Oregon in an
environmentally and socially sound fashion. If firms wanted to build
new plants in Oregon, they would have to pay the environmental price.

Taking the position of Governor McCall one step further was
the state of Hawaii. In Hawaii, the state with the strongest land-use
control powers in the nation, the elected officials decided to embark
on a new program of selective economic growth.[2] In practice, this
meant that the state would use its fiscal and police power to direct
new economic growth away from the heavily developed island of Oahu
and toward some of their less-developed islands, which together
comprise the state. Moreover, the officials decided to slow the
growth of their most explosive industry, tourism, and try to strengthen
other economic sectors, like agriculture. According to Shelly Mark,
former Planning and Economic Development director, "With slower
growth the state can maintain a relatively healthy economy . . . and
a possible reduction in vulnerability to severe state recessions."[3]

The new position now being taken by Hawaii illustrates a key
point. Hawaii's economy is tied to tourism. And the reason that
tourism is so important a part of their economy is because the state,
and Oahu in particular, are extremely beautiful places. But by over-
promoting and overdeveloping the tourist industry on Oahu, the state
runs a sizable economic risk. The risk is that the tourist industry
itself will literally destroy its reason for being—the natural beauty
of the island state. Recent visitors to Oahu can testify to the high
environmental price being paid. In Honolulu, hotels and motels jam
the once open beaches and the island cities' air is polluted. Water
pollution has destroyed exquisite aquatic areas, and tourist generated
growth chews up agriculture and open space. So by tempering the
development of the tourist industry in Oahu in favor of other sectors like agriculture, the state is really strengthening both the
tourist and agricultural industries. The policy of selective economic
growth makes good economic sense.

Contrast what Hawaii is doing for its tourist industry with what
Anaheim, California, has done to its tourist industry. As the home
of the original Disneyland, Anaheim had a national tourist attraction.
People liked Disneyland, wanted to go there, and were willing to pay
for it. But along with the people came the explosive growth of the
tourist industry. By now, the tourist industry has literally swamped
its foremost attraction—Disneyland. Disneyland can hardly be seen,

much less enjoyed, because of the huge expanse of hotels, motels, signs, fast food centers, bars, gimmick shops, and convention facilities. Instead of protecting Disneyland, the city's most important economic resource, Anaheim let just about everything happen. And it did. Hawaii, in contrast, had the foresight to know why its tourist industry was successful and has taken steps to keep it that way. It really is not difficult to see that Hawaii will do this by controlling the very thing that Anaheim did not—the local economy.

In Atlanta, Georgia, Mayor Maynard Jackson, Jr., took some direct economic action.[4] Jackson is using the city's spending power to ensure that its underemployed black population gets part of the local economic pie. Mayor Jackson knew two things. First, he knew that blacks in Atlanta, as in most other places, were not getting and holding their share of good jobs. Second, Jackson knew that each year the city spent millions to build buildings, highways, and other public facilities. So what he did was to require that any business winning a city contract share 15 to 25 percent of the jobs with the city's blacks. Thus, if you win a city contract in Atlanta, you must show solid social performance, performance that means jobs to underemployed or unemployed blacks.

The interesting aspect of Mayor Jackson's program is that it was quickly developed in response to an obvious problem. There was no need for extensive research, long lead times, huge bureaucratic staffs, or even federal dollars. Yet, there is no mistaking its direction or outcome. More blacks will be getting good jobs. Firms receiving city contracts will suddenly discover ways of hiring and training blacks that they couldn't seem to find under other, more voluntary programs. By using raw economic power of the kind that every city has, Atlanta will achieve two objectives. It will get the work done, and it will employ more blacks. There is no reason that the same kind of program could not be used to employ more Mexican-Americans in Los Angeles, Puerto Ricans in New York, or poor whites in Appalachia. It is all a matter of exercising the controls that communities do have over the local economy.

But Oregon and Hawaii are very attractive states, and Atlanta is an attractive city. They all have a lot going for them by virtue of their location, image, and natural resources. They are nice places to live and have no shortage of people willing to move there. It is easy to see how Oregon, Hawaii, and Atlanta could control their local economy, since it is a clear case of having many economic actors vying for their approval. So, it is instructive to look at a few other communities that are in a very different position. The first is Cleveland, Ohio, and the second is Franklin County, Florida.

Cleveland is one of those old eastern metropolitan centers that, like Detroit, has seen better days. It is one of the places to be from rather than to go to. As with most of the eastern central cities, Cleveland is in deep economic and social trouble. In the official bureaucratic tongue, "disinvestment" has set in. People and jobs are leaving Cleveland faster than they can be replaced, and the city contains every type of economic and social malfunction.

Yet, in Cleveland, the city's planners have adopted a "strange" attitude toward new economic growth.[5] Like Hawaii, Oregon, and Atlanta, the planners take the attitude that economic growth is only good if it helps the people who need it most. They have one basic guideline that is used to evaluate new development, and that is, What will the development do for the people of Cleveland and, in particular, what will it do for the people who need help most?

This question provides a whole new way of looking at new development. For example, in a recent case, the Cleveland planners evaluated a $350-million scheme for a downtown office-commercial complex. The city was to subsidize this development to the tune of $10-15 million. By evaluating the development on the basis of what it would do for or against the people of Cleveland, the planning staff found that

> the proposal offered no guarantee of additional property
> or income tax revenues. Nor was there a firm commit-
> ment of jobs for the unemployed. In fact, detailed analysis
> of the market for office space in downtown Cleveland and
> the probable impact of Ohio's new property tax abatement
> legislation suggests that the project might result in a net
> tax loss to the City.[6]

The planners went on to recommend against the proposal, since the proposed development offered so little in the way of jobs or tax revenues to the city. In taking the position that the local economy should work for the city, the planners came to this conclusion, a conclusion wholly in line with getting the local economy in control. But it hardly corresponds to conventional planning or economic wisdom.

Lying about a thousand miles to the south is a very poor and very rural place called Franklin County.[7] Franklin County, Florida, sits in the panhandle on the Gulf Coast, about 80 miles from Talla-hassee, Florida's capital. In Franklin County, the economy rests on the fortune of a single industry, the oyster industry. For over 100 years, the people of Franklin County have earned their living by harvesting and selling the oysters that grow along a long, thin barrier island called St. George. St. George is part of Franklin County and lies about two miles off the county's coast.

The oyster industry does not pay very good wages. If a person earns $5,000 a year, he is rich by Franklin County standards. Oysters can only be harvested nine or ten months of the year, and even then, no one really knows how good the harvest will be or what price the oysters will fetch. Because of its economy, Franklin County exhibits most of the problems that plague rural areas across the nation—high unemployment, poor health care, substandard housing, low income, and out-migration of the young. What Franklin County really needs is more economic development. And most people would think that a new proposal to build a $100-million commercial and residential development would be just the thing. But it did not turn out that way.

The problem was that the new development was going in on St. George Island, a very short distance from where the oysters grow. Oysters are funny creatures. They just cannot tolerate any kind of ecological interference, like water pollution. The Franklin County commissioners, mostly oystermen themselves, knew this. They knew that if the development went in as proposed, it would eventually destroy the oysters, through water pollution. For the people of Franklin County, this would have been disastrous. They had one set of skills. They knew how to find and harvest oysters. It is not the kind of skill that makes it easy to get up and move and do the same thing in other towns. Indeed, save for Franklin County, development had all but wiped out the oyster industry throughout Florida.

Yet, the development was extremely attractive from an economic point of view. It would provide construction jobs and following that, a whole set of retail and service jobs. The new jobs might even stem the out-migration of Franklin County's young. So the commissioners tried to make the development ecologically failsafe. For example, they wanted the development to have tertiary sewage treatment so there would be no contamination danger to the oysters. They also demanded controls over the use of pesticides on the island, required building setbacks to keep the development off the beach, and made certain that all drainage occurred away from the precious oysters. In short, the commissioners decided that the development could go in, but if it did, it would have to be compatible with the environment, just like the oysters. Unfortunately, the developers found the commissioners' conditions too restrictive. Being far more interested in profit margins than oysters, the developers pulled out.

The action of the Franklin County commissioners was economically and environmentally sound. They knew that the people depended upon the oyster industry. If the oysters did not survive, the people would be out of work. The development, as attractive as it was to this poor place, put the oysters in jeopardy. So, when the commissioners looked at the proposal in terms of what it would do

for the people of Franklin County, their choice was clear. The
development would go in only if it would not harm the oysters. Had
the commissioners allowed the development without the safeguards,
it is probable that they would have destroyed their main economic
strength.

The experiences of these local communities and states suggests
that much is at stake when spending public money or when evaluating
large new developments. Often, the decision means the difference
between prosperity and depression, between stable employment and
increased instability, between increases and decreases in family
income, between economic gains for those who need them most and
economic setbacks for the same group, and between a healthy public
treasury and one approaching bankruptcy. The actions of these communities point out two main features of local control over the local
economy. First, communities can control their economy through
their annual expenditures, that is, fiscal power, the simplest and most
direct application of economic power. Second, communities can control their local economy through their police power, zoning, subdivision regulations, and the like, which give them near-absolute
authority over the location of major new developments. Taken
together, the union of fiscal and police power is a formidable one.

ECONOMIC GUIDELINES FOR LOCAL NONGROWTH

What sets places like Hawaii, Atlanta, Cleveland, and Franklin
County, Florida, apart from most others is that they have developed
a unique perspective on new growth—a nongrowth perspective. Local
decisions reflect a different way of thinking about themselves and
about new growth. These communities and states see themselves as
having something worthwhile of their own, something worth preserving
or something worth serving. And they see new growth in this way—
that if new growth is to occur, it will preserve or serve what the
citizens want or it will not be encouraged. In most cases, the communities have yet to write that thinking down. But if they would, they
would find many of their basic attitudes reflected in the following set
of guidelines. The guidelines are not iron rules, but they do set a
direction, a way of thinking about what the community has to offer
and a way of thinking about what new growth should offer the community.

Growth Is Not Important—People Are

Until recently, most local economic goals were miniature versions of national ones. The dominant national goal, "GNP Pollyanna," was that increases in gross national product (GNP) meant increases in the economic welfare of people. Conversely, if GNP slipped off, the people's welfare suffered. At the local level, GNP Pollyanna translated into economic goals that had, at their core, simple quantitative increases in such things as jobs, incomes, or goods and services. Local economic goals were being achieved if employment was expanding, if total income went up, and if more goods and services were being produced.

However, there is no automatic association between quantitative economic gains and qualitative advances in the welfare of people. More is not better, it is simply more. As seen in the previous chapter, many of the areas with the greatest quantitative increase in people, jobs, and total income experienced no increase in net economic welfare. Indeed, in nearly one-half the cases, per capita income fell, the areas lost ground compared with other slower-growing areas, and unemployment stayed about the same. In short, quantitative increases had little to do with the real economic welfare of most citizens.

There is only one way to make sense out of local quantitative economic goals. And that is to add people to them—local people. The first responsibility of each community is to its own citizens, not those of the region or the nation but its own citizens. Thus, increases in employment are only meaningful for specific local population groups, particularly the unemployed. The simple addition of more jobs will often fail to decrease rates and levels of unemployment unless the jobs are taken by local citizens who are currently unemployed. When more jobs simply mean more in-migration, not much is accomplished for the local citizen who has no job. The same point holds for all economic goals. This means that local economic goals should be tailored to local people, to specific segments of the local populace.

One of the major points being made by planners in Cleveland, Mayor Jackson in Atlanta, and the commissioners of Franklin County, Florida, is that the local people, the citizens of the community, are the most important element. And if economic growth is to mean anything at all, it should help local people by increasing their job opportunities, by increasing their average income, by working for them instead of against them. The economic goals of these governments are people-oriented. That is really the only kind worth having.

The Local Economy Is Unique

It is difficult to get this concept across to most planners and public officials. Planners and public officials do not see their local economy as being particularly unique. Indeed, they believe themselves to be just like everyone else, all striving after the same economic objectives, all competing for the same types of development. Nevertheless, every local economy is unique.

First, the people comprising the labor force in each community make that labor force different from all other community labor forces in the country. Differences in age, sex, education, training, race, skills, health, and a host of other characteristics make any single labor force different from all others. In any community, the types, amounts, and character of the goods and services produced will be different from those produced elsewhere. This is due to the many kinds of firms and different types of markets that these firms serve. Third, the natural resources of any community are different from others. One community may house large gravel or coal deposits, while another may have highly productive agricultural soild. One community may have relatively pristine air and water quality, while another might have good supplies of timber or sunshine. Fourth, and most obvious, each community has a distinct location, a location different from that of all other communities.

All of these factors join together to make each local economy a distinctly unique product. There is no other just like it. Some may be similar, but there is no duplication. Every local economy is the product of a very special set of forces, forces growing out of a community history that continue to operate in changing the economic character of every community. Amongst these forces are its economic, natural, regional, labor technological, and government history, plus a whole set of events that defy rational explanation. Taken together, they make a unique product—a local economy different from all other local economies.

There are several lessons from all of this. One of the major ones is covered in the next section ("Think and Act as a Monopolist Would"). But another lesson is that it does not make good economic sense for any community to try to pattern itself after any other or to try to compete with all others. As Michael Conroy points out: "The past, present, and expected future development of each city is likely to be more closely related to the individual locational history and present characteristics than to any common pattern of development among cities of comparable size or economic structure."[8] This means, for example, that it is not sound practice for a community to use others of similar population size as a basis for comparison or, worse, as a basis for designing their own economic strategy. And yet, one of the most common sights in economic planning is the wholesale copying of economic strategies from city A to city B. Everyone, for example, seems to want research and development industries, especially nonpolluting ones. What someone once spotted as a good idea for Boston (because of its collection of high-powered universities) is suddenly the rage all over the country. But the fact is that Boston, New York, and the San Francisco Bay area will continue to dominate research and development industries and everything in between will not. Thus, what needs to be done is for each community to look at itself closely to determine just what its potential is. And communities will discover that, indeed, they are unique.

Another reason why uniqueness is important is that it does wonders for the local self-image. It is really strange that most communities do consider themselves special in every way except economically. In southern California, for example, where the word "suburb" achieved a whole new meaning, each one considers itself distinct. Garden Grove and Anaheim grew up about the same time, have shared many of the same community experiences, and are side by side. Yet people in Anaheim find vastly superior reasons for living there, as opposed to Garden Grove, and people in Garden Grove have discovered that they, too, have their own identity. But oddly enough, when it comes to the local economy, they just cannot find any difference worth exploiting. As far as local officials are concerned, they are in competition. Thus, the concept that each economy is unique liberates communities, since it takes them out of the competitive mold—the image that one city is just like another and all are chasing the same resources. Because each community has a unique local economy, it need not concern itself with what all other communities are doing but, rather, with a relatively specific economic future. The simple fact is that each local community is a specific economic entity. Each one has its separate and distinct potential, a potential as distinct and separate as the local economy itself.

One way to appreciate this concept is to look at the way that major corporations go about selecting a new site for a major new plant.[9] Usually, the search process occurs in a four-step process. First, the firm does a national search to decide on a region, a multistate area of the country that meets basic corporate needs—needs such as proximity to market, to resource supply, or to availability of transportation. Second, the firm looks within the multistate region to pick out a particular state or region within a state.

Once again, the firm picks the state or region on the basis of its particular needs. Third, the firm looks at a subregion to determine which one looks best—what land is available, which utilities are in, closeness to freeways, and so forth. Once a particular site is spotted, the firm is ready to talk to the community in which it is located. By this time, the firm has looked at the potential of many communities. Since they are interested in particular characteristics, they are able to narrow the field down, usually to a few sites arranged in priority. Thus, the firm has examined the local economy to see if the local economy matches up to the firm's needs.

Now, this is a vastly different outcome from that which would occur if local communities were really in competition. For example, if all communities were really competitive, the firm would just see which community of all communities would give them the best deal. But firms cannot do this since they need particular things—a special labor force, a unique natural resource, special transportation needs, and so forth. The firm needs a particular location in a particular place. The more specific and narrow the needs of the corporation, the more specific and narrow the type of local economy that can support it. Thus, a unique local economy points the way for a change in local thinking. Each community has something special to offer. Because of this, each is in a position to make some demands on new development that it could not otherwise make.

There remains, of course, the fact that some communities are more attractive to developers than others. There is a range—some communities are extremely attractive to a whole host of new firms and others attractive to a very few. But this does not change the basic idea. All communities can use their unique economic setting to make the local economy work for the local citizen.

Think and Act as a Monopolist Would

A city, virtually any city, has enormous economic power. The power, as seen exercised in places like Atlanta and Cleveland, breaks down into police power and fiscal power. Both can be exercised over new development or, even, expanding old development to ensure that it performs for the benefit of the community. In doing this, the city is acting very much like a monopolist—exacting a higher price from new development than a community could get if operating under competitive conditions.

To understand why cities can act like monopolists, it is necessary to understand just what a monopolist is and then to compare that to the power which cities have. Economists define pure monopoly "to mean the case of a single seller, enjoying absence of competition of any kind, with complete control over the supply of the product, including control over entry into the industry."[10] There are two sides to monopoly, a monopolist (a single seller) and a monopsonist (a single buyer). The word "pure" is used to show that this is an extreme case, too extreme to be found in practice and the very opposite from pure competition, where there are a host of buyers and sellers.

In the case of a city, there is only one seller and one buyer. No one but the city itself can give permission (can sell) the product called "location," which the city may or may not make available to new development. The same is true from the monopsony side—there is only one buyer of products for the city. If a firm wants to sell goods, like schools, highways, or hospitals, the firm must go to one place, city hall. The fact that each city is unique, that its special resources and character cannot be duplicated elsewhere, also means that it is pretty much without competition from other cities. There is really only one Boulder, Colorado; one Savannah, Georgia; one Tucson, Arizona; one Kitsap County, Washington. The final part of monopoly is that the monopolist must have complete control over the supply of the product, including control over entry into the industry. Obviously, each city controls its land use, and there is no danger that some disgruntled developer could set up a whole new land-use authority to replace the one that exists. The only recourse for the developer is to change the decision or to change the people who made the decision.

When all these factors are put together, it can be seen that cities look very much like monopolists. A city is the single seller of location, through its land-use controls, and the single buyer, through its fiscal power. It presents a sharp contrast with the usual self-image of cities, especially in economic affairs, where they see themselves in hopeless competition with everyone else.

Some critics have charged that cities cannot really act like monopolists, since if they do, they will lose all new development to other cities. But the argument misses a major point, which is that cities have something to offer, something special, which just cannot be duplicated elsewhere. The most obvious thing, of course, is a specific site, since there are no others exactly like it. But there are a host of other reasons: the quality of its labor force, its educational institutions, an airport, its water supply, or any number of others. It is this combination of things, this resource package, which the community really has to offer. And developers know it. So the idea is for communities to use the resources they have to ensure that the major new development works for its citizens.

There is no doubt that some communities are more attractive
to developers than others. But they all have something. For most
cities, this means that some firms will be very interested in locating
there, others will only be mildly interested, and others would prefer
someplace else. Thus, each city has some bargaining power, monopoly
power, with the firms who really want to locate there. These firms
will be willing to make concessions to have the special location that
they need.

There are many examples. In Chicago, for example, one of the
high-growth areas is near O'Hare International Airport. The cities
close to the airport are powerful by virtue of their location, a location that separates them from all other communities in the Chicago
area. Firms that need airport access need these communities. Thus,
these cities are in an extremely powerful position. They have something that no one else has—a location close to an airport—and they can
use this to make new developments perform in any way they choose.
If developers want the airport, then they have to go to these cities.
At the other end of the spectrum are places like the southside of
Chicago. It is not really close to the airport. Not too many developers
are interested in the southside. So to get them interested, a subsidy
of some sort is in order. But the subsidy, like the location close to
the airport, can be used for the same monopolistic purpose. The
subsidy can be used to make development perform for the citizens.
Here's a working example.

Boston, as with many eastern cities, had been losing its manufacturing industries to the suburbs and replacing them with service
industries. However, the trouble was that the service industries
were employing mostly suburbanites, leaving many of the city's
residents unemployed. So the city set up the Boston Economic Development and Industrial Corporation, empowered it to establish small
neighborhood industrial parks in the city, and gave it $7 million worth
of bonding.[11] The development corporation has since been using this
money to set up small, light industrial parks in various city neighborhoods. Having accomplished this, the development corporation
required that prospective industries give preferential hiring treatment to neighborhood people who were unemployed. Thus, the Boston
development corporation first offered the industries a light subsidy
by preparing the neighborhood parks for industrial occupancy. But
then they acted like monopolists when they required new industry
coming into the park to hire locally. Had Boston considered itself in
deadly competition with surrounding suburbs, it obviously could not
have afforded to make this type of demand. But with the subsidy and
its control over location, it was able to make demands, exacting a
price of jobs for the city's residents.

On the monopsony side, where there is the single buyer, the
case of Atlanta has already been cited, where Mayor Jackson required
that city contracts be shared with a certain percentage of minority
workers. Clearly, the city is using its unique economic power for
the benefit of its citizenry. Had Jackson visualized Atlanta as just
another buyer in the marketplace, the results would have been much
different.

A monopolist is used to getting high prices for the products
sold and low costs for the products purchased. The objective of
getting cities to think like monopolists is to take them out of the
competitive mold, a mold that makes them the victim of national
economic trends and prevents them from using the real power that
they have. In thinking and acting like a monopolist, a city can control the local economy and make it work for local citizens.

Getting Yourself Together Again

One of the real impediments to getting the local economy in
control is that so many groups are involved. Worse, they are often
working at cross purposes. Inevitably, most of the groups consider
themselves to be the lead economic development agency. Everyone
is in charge.

In Tucson, for example, the city and Pima County have created
a development authority that is supposed to broaden and stabilize
Tucson's economic base. But while the development authority is
going about broadening and diversifying Tucson's economic base,
the local Chamber of Commerce is doing it too, or so they say. And
while not fighting between themselves, two local groups are working
in manpower planning. One is a Model Cities creature and the other
is the bureaucratic offspring of the U.S. Department of Labor. While
they do their manpower work, they rarely talk with the development
authority or the Chamber of Commerce. But that might be good,
since the city's Planning Department now has some economic capability (of course, local banks and industrial and commercial developers
do, too). Then there is a local community college training people for
all types of jobs; they, too, seem unaware of what others are doing.

Tucson is not one isolated example. The U.S. departments of
labor and commerce have set up local programs all across the
country. Most communities have chambers of commerce, and
hundreds more have set up economic planning and development
groups. Community colleges provide job training, utility companies
have development programs, and so do banks. When you put it all

together at the local level, there are often as many as eight separate economic planning and development organizations. That means there are roughly seven too many chiefs.

With all these chiefs, odd things begin to happen. The manpower programs somehow divine the answers to manpower problems, train people for jobs they hope will exist, and set up whole new programs for an ever-expanding operation. The local chamber of commerce, of course, has its own ideas of what the community needs and proceeds to do such things as placing advertising in the back of travel magazines that tout the economic highlights of the city. Banks and utilities go about trying to drum up whatever business suits them, while the city's development agency has discovered the grand economic design and proceeds to carry that out. In the meantime, the local economic planner working in the planning department has come up with ideas of her own and incorporates those into the community general plan. The result is a series of half-baked, half-workable schemes, some mutually supportive and others at opposite poles. It is a waste of money—all of it.

The thing to do is for the local general government to take charge. In order to get the attention and, perhaps, grudging cooperation of utilities, banks, and the chamber of commerce, the local government will have to set itself up as the real chief. Initially, this will mean that the local government will have to step on toes, perhaps by cutting off promotional funds to the chamber of commerce, just to show it means business. And within the general government itself, it is necessary to put someone in charge, so that the manpower and development agencies and economic planners know what the others are doing. In order to get the attention of these small but powerful bureaucracies, it will be necessary to cut a budget or two and to place budget review authority in the hands of a single person. This means that there would not be a series of single departments but, rather, that the three groups would be placed in a single department, or at least under one unified authority.

Only by creating some order in economic planning and development will the community really be able to make the local economy work for its citizens. You cannot, for example, expect manpower programs to really work when they have no idea of the future jobs that will be available; they could do a lot better if they were directly tied into the land-use control process. Why not give manpower programs direct access to new firms? Why not put manpower goals directly into the decision-making process over new commercial and industrial developments? And what about the now separate development authorities? Many of their programs now run contrary to manpower goals; some might be supportive, but who knows? And what about the relation of the manpower development agency to the basic

community plan? Does anyone really know whether the two are supportive or whether the community plan stresses one action while
the development agency does the exact opposite? In order to have
the local economy work for citizens, local governments will have to
get rid of some economic planning, especially by private groups, and
put the rest together under one authority—the local general government. Otherwise, it will not work.

Add the Word "No" to the Local Vocabulary

Many planners and elected officials make the incorrect assumption that virtually any proposal for economic development must be
good economically and that, somehow, even if it is not, its failure
could not possibly harm local citizens. Thus, they are free to say
yes to a wide variety of economic development proposals. Yet, many
new developments do little for the local citizens, and may actually
harm them. In Boston, for example, the development rush to service-
oriented industries in high-rise structures hurt the prospect for
the city's industrial growth. Yet, industrial growth would have provided the types of jobs, those requiring low and intermediate skills,
that were needed by many of Boston's citizens. Because the land
was going for high-rise development, such as banks and insurance
companies, it was becoming difficult to package land for new industries. As a consequence, "Surveys showed that two thirds of the
jobs in high-rise office buildings go to suburbanites, whereas industry probably would employ more Boston residents."[12] This city's
decision to support high-rise, service-oriented industries has had
two bad consequences. First, it has added to the employment problems of many Bostonians, and second, it has increased the prospect
that Boston will follow the path of other dying central cities. It is
simple: if people cannot find work, they will leave. Clearly, here is
a case where new development hurt all residents of the city and
placed particular burden on the city's unemployed.
　　Many new economic developments, regardless of their individual success or failure, can be harmful to the local citizen.
Because of this, it is important to understand that there are at least
three outcomes to every local economic decision: yes, a conditional
approval, and no. Local communities have the power to say no,
finally and completely, without any backsliding or reservation. That
such a choice would lead to some positive economic results is a
real surprise to local communities. But it can.

Do Not Worry About Small Entrepreneurs;
Save Yourself for the Big Ones

All local communities have less time, money, staff, and other resources than they would like. Because resources are short, it is important to focus on those economic decisions that are really important. Thus, only a few types of industrial, commercial, and residential development warrant serious public attention. There is neither need for, nor justification of, a detailed examination of each new development proposal. The principal focus should rest on those key decisions with the potential for changing the economic nature of the local place. These major economic events are also likely to change other fundamental qualities of the local community, such as its social structure, tax structure, political makeup, service costs, and environmental setting.

On the other side, there is very little to be gained, and a lot to be lost, in subjecting every small property owner, retail merchant, or small manufacturer to the kind of rigorous examination that should be reserved for the truly large development proposals. Aside from the infringements on personal liberties, the proponents of small economic proposals can often offer or succeed in developing the unique economic qualities of a local community.

For example, with three employees, the Shelter Institute, in Bath, Maine, capitalized on Maine's special character as a haven for many people who want to get to the country, live simply, and enjoy Maine's natural resources.[13] The institute specializes in showing people how to build low-cost, environmentally sensitive housing, and the people build the housing by themselves. The Shelter Institute conducts classes, publishes manuals, and has itself built some housing. Clearly, here is a small organization that knew the special needs of Maine's citizens and worked to satisfy them. The interest in the housing products of this institute suggests that it will continue to grow and that its products will begin to take hold in other states. But it began with an idea, a few people, and a very special, small, identifiable market. It is not the kind of thing that even enters the thinking of large housing corporations. Jane Jacobs makes the case for small entrepreneurs: "It is not the success of large economic organizations that makes possible vigorous adding of new work to older work. Rather, when this process operates vigorously, it depends upon large numbers and great diversity of economic organizations, some of which, of course, grow large in their heydays."[14]

The history of cities in economic trouble is replete with examples of those relying too heavily on large economic enterprises

to the exclusion of the small. The current predicament of cities like
Detroit, with its automobiles, or Seattle with Boeing, or Gary,
Indiana, with steel, is sufficient to show the hazards of too much
reliance on size and a single industry. Jacobs compares the experience of two English cities: Birmingham and Manchester. Manchester,
in the mid-1800s, was dominated by immensely efficient and profitable
textile mills. Birmingham, in contrast, "had a few relatively large
industries, although nothing remotely approaching the scale of
Manchester's, and even these accounted for only a small part of
Birmingham's total output of work and total employment. Most of
Birmingham's manufacturing was carried out in small organizations
employing no more than a dozen workmen."[15] By the 1960s,
Manchester had become a depressed and stagnant place. Birmingham,
on the other hand, prospered, since "its fragmented and inefficient
little industries kept adding new work, and splitting off new organizations, some of which have become very large but are still outweighed
in total employment and production by the many small ones."[16]
Smallness breeds diversity and long-term economic health. Cities
should encourage it.

There is, however, substantial justification for a rigorous
examination of those industrial, commercial, and residential applicants with the potential for changing some fundamental community
characteristics. This includes not only individual applicants but also
key decisions on major economic directions of the community. For
example, in the case of Boston, the city at some point decided to
support high-rise, service-oriented industries. Clearly, this was a
major decision that should have been subject to more extensive
examination. The main objective of such an examination should be
to evaluate the proposal in terms of the basic community goals, that
is, to establish whether community change is worth the specific
economic, social, or environmental by-products of the new development.

The Toughest Question To Be Asked

The single most important economic question to be answered
by large-scale economic development is simply, Who wins, who
loses, for how long, and by how much? The answer to this question
enables the local community to make some economic sense out of
the proposal, yet this tough question is almost never asked, and
when it is, rarely answered.

Chambers of commerce, industrial brokers, and developers'
spokesmen have come up with a standard litany as an answer to

almost any economic question. They will point out, for example, that
the development is certain to add to property tax revenues and will,
of course, pay for itself. The more industrial the development, the
more it will pay. Yet, even with this widely held assumption, some
studies have shown industrial development to be a net tax loser.[17]
If the tax angle comes under fire, the spokesman will highlight the
addition to the community's income in the way of employee wages.
But it was seen earlier how questionable this income assumption is.
While the development may add to total income, it might decrease
median family income. Beyond the income and tax benefits, the
spokesmen then go to discuss the development's positive influence
on the local economic structure. Usually they point to the "diversifying" effect of their proposal on the local economy. But most local
communities, much less developers, have no idea of what "diversification" really means, and one of the things it does not mean is that
whatever is new adds to diversification. Inevitably, the last line of
defense is that the proposal will add jobs to the community and that
these jobs will, in turn, create others. The net effect, one expects,
is a greatly reduced level and rate of unemployment. But it has been
seen that new development may actually increase the number of unemployed and rate of unemployment if it attracts more in-migrants than
the number of jobs it creates.

    All of these criticisms of the usual justification for major new
development bring us back to the beginning. Just who is going to
benefit by it, who is going to suffer from it, for how long, and by how
much? It is not so much a question of what the development will do
for the community at large (or the region) but, rather, what it will
do for very specific identifiable groups of local citizens. What, for
example, will be the hiring practices? Where will the jobs be advertised? Who will get the job preference? Will any special consideration be given to local citizens? What are the job skills required, and
how will these match up to those of the existing population? What
about income? What kinds of jobs will be available for the local
citizen, how many, and what will they pay? Will the development
really serve the locally unemployed or merely serve to attract more
migrants? If local citizens take low-level jobs, are there avenues
for advancement or opportunities to gain a special skill?

    Communities should not assume that a new development, by
virtue of its existence, will do much of anything for the local population. In order to find out what it means, questions will have to be
asked. Vague public relations promises of "reducing unemployment"
or "increasing tax base" should not be substituted for the hard,
essential question of who wins, who loses, for how long, and by how
much.

Land Gives and Development Takes Away

Land is the basic capital of any community. It is the single
limited, exhaustible resource that the community really controls.
By using combinations of police power and fiscal power, the community determines the use of land. But once the land is put to urban
uses—uses that cover it with all manner of commercial, residential,
and industrial enterprises—the community's control disappears. The
future of the community is then in the hands of whoever is using the
land.

The land that is open and not developed or land which is available for development is really the working capital of the community.
It is the flexible community resource that can be directed at any
number of community objectives. This land is money in the community bank. It is the reserve account that can be brought to bear on
any problem that the community might want to solve. The developable
land is what gives a community choice, the opportunity to choose.

However, once this land is given over to urban development, it
is no longer the flexible instrument of community control. It can no
longer serve the range of public purposes that it could before it was
committed. And as the supply of developable land disappears, the
community will find that it has less and less control over its character (both current and future). The power shifts to the users of the
land. This is the reason that planners like those in Cleveland spend
less and less time with land-use regulations. Suddenly, there just
are not any new uses to regulate. They are all old. Thus, development can be seen as a resource-intensive process that diminishes
the future choices which the community can make. The community
loses control over its future.

Compare, for example, a city like Chicago with a city like
Boulder, Colorado. Chicago, for the most part, has spent its basic
land capital. Its urban form has been set and will not change for a
long time. The number of choices open to Chicago are considerably
less than those available to Boulder, since Boulder has retained
more of its land resource. The problems of a big city like Chicago
are more difficult to solve, since the number of things possible for
Chicago depend, to some extent, on the amount of developable land
available. If, for example, Chicago decided to decentralize its
industrial development into various city neighborhoods, they would
be faced with enormous costs of gathering and clearing sufficient
land to make it a worthwhile proposition. However, had the city
retained more of its basic land resource, the problem would be
considerably less severe. Once the land is spent, the community

forecloses on future choice. The advantage in holding off, in waiting
for the right type of development, is that the number of alternatives
increases.

Too many public officials believe that land not put to use and
sold for something is wasted land. If it is not covered with buildings
and asphalt, it is a drain on community resources, a drag on economic development. But the truth is exactly the opposite. The land
available for development is the most important community resource,
since this is the major resource that the community controls. It is
also the resource that gives the community its special, unique urban
character, which makes each community different from all others.
The land is its distinctive feature. Keeping flexible suggests a go-
slow approach rather than speeding to any and all development
proposals.

Consider the case of the Northern Cheyenne. This Indian
nation, some years ago, leased its mineral rights to several coal
companies. Not too long thereafter, the energy crisis flared up, and,
suddenly, everyone needed more coal. The value of coal deposits
exploded, and the Northern Cheyenne were left holding the bag. They
are now trying to break the leases. But the point is that holding off
on the leases would not have hurt them. Hindsight is wonderful, but
economic history indicates that virtually all resources, and especially
land, increase in value over time. There is little danger that holding
off means losing out. Rushing to development is like spending all
resources immediately to get a new car, house, trash compacter, or
snowmobile. When the hard times come, there is nothing left. It is
a powerful reason to go slow.

BEGINNING POINTS IN LOCAL CONTROL

Workable nongrowth, as seen, requires a close working relationship between controls on the local economy, on the one hand,
and controls on new residential development, on the other. To date,
most nongrowth communities have placed almost exclusive emphasis
on the residential side, which is the most obvious manifestation of
new growth but not the most important factor to control. Even here,
we are beginning to see some hopeful, important changes on the part
of local communities.

In the 1960s, San Jose, California, had the dubious distinction
of being compared to Los Angeles. A local newspaper publisher
declared: "They say San Jose is going to become another Los
Angeles. Believe me, I'm going to do everything in my power to

make that come true."[18] San Jose's citizens were less enthusiastic.
By electing local officials on growth control platforms, the citizens
were able to bring San Jose up considerably short of Los Angeles.
Amongst the people they elected was Norman Mineta, who, until
recently, was the mayor.

Mineta understood that if growth control were to work, it
would have to work through the local economy. The local economy,
in Mineta's view, was too important to be left alone: "Communities
must strengthen their capacity to influence their economic base.
Traditional industrial and commercial promotion is no longer adequate. Current program activity must be solidly based on the community's perception of 'what the community is, where it is and where
it wants to go.' "[19] San Jose wants to go to controlled growth, a
balanced controlled growth that would keep the industrial, commercial, and residential sectors in steady equilibrium. The City Council
recently considered such a growth policy, one that would "restrict
excessive residential growth in order to achieve an economic balance
between industrial, commercial and residential development."[20]
The growth policy goes on to explain that

> while encouraging industrial growth, the City should limit
> the number of acres zoned for new residential development
> to a number sufficient to accommodate the households
> attracted to San Jose by the new industrial and supporting
> jobs generated in San Jose. Before zoning is approved for
> residential development, it must be determined that suffi-
> cient jobs have been generated in San Jose to justify further
> residential development.[21]

If San Jose adopts this policy, the city would be basing its
strategy on the workings of the local economy, which makes good
sense. First, San Jose would have much more control over growth,
since its strategy would be anchored in the local economy. Second,
the city would be better able to keep a balance between the residential, commercial, and industrial sectors, since residential
development would be tied to new job formation. Third, the strategy
would strengthen the local economy, since new housing construction
would be related to new job formation. The strategy promotes new
housing construction when the demand is there to support it. This
is in contrast to the usual situation, where new housing construction
falls into a regular pattern of overbuilding, followed by underbuilding,
and so forth. Thus, the San Jose approach strengthens local control
over growth and promotes a more stable local economy by using the
local economy as the key to its development strategy.

Four hundred miles to the south is the city of Santa Barbara.
In 1974, the City Council asked a group of citizens, the Santa Barbara
Planning Task Force, to help the council determine an optimum population for the city. The citizen Task Force responded with the most
impressive local nongrowth study that the present authors have seen.[22]
The study highlights the role of the local economy, noting that the
local economy was the prime growth mover and that the growth which
Santa Barbara had experienced was the product of the local economy.
To control growth, it followed that the place to begin was with the
local economy. "By controlling the job-producing capacity of the
local economy," the report stated, "one controls much of the potential for population growth. As we have reiterated a number of times
thoughout this document, the population of an urban area increases
primarily in response to growth of its basic economic base."[23]

The Planning Commission was convinced. Following the citizen
report, the commission adopted a resolution that should help bring
the local economy into a central role in the city's growth control
policies. The resolution read, "In order to bring the demand for
housing into balance with the supply, it is necessary to evaluate and
adjust the various factors which make up the demand. The primary
factor affecting housing demand is employment."[24] With that, the
commission went on to state that "to limit growth, it is necessary
to examine the present commercially and industrially zoned land, to
determine the amount of each needed, and to adjust each, where
appropriate, so that the housing demand allowed complements the
reduced housing supply."[25] The commission has since revamped
the city's zoning policies in order to get the commercial, industrial,
and residential sectors into better balance and better control. As
with San Jose, the city of Santa Barbara has put its finger on the
most important, yet most often overlooked, growth-control factor—
the local economy.

Boulder, Colorado, was one of the first cities in the nation to
actively pursue nongrowth strategies. It was also one of the first
to recognize the importance of controlling the local economy to
achieve nongrowth goals. In some ways, Boulder's economy is
easier to control than places like San Jose. This is because it is a
relatively free-standing city, with large segments of its employment
in professional occupations—professors, lawyers, doctors, consultants, and so forth. Because of this, there is not too much growth
pressure from internal expansion; the doctor's office is unlikely to
turn into a hospital, individual consultants will not turn into mega-
corporations, and so on. But Boulder was still attractive to many
commercial and industrial operators. It is a nice place to live, and
the labor force is highly skilled. In order to control this outside

pressure, Boulder took an active role in controlling new commercial
and industrial development. Many were discouraged from locating
in Boulder, because as Bill Lamont, the ex-planning director, stated:
"Boulder believes that part of its control policy is regulating employment opportunity. This cautious attitude towards receiving new industry has become necessary to prevent new multiplier effects which
employers exert upon metropolitan and regional economies."[26]
    Back in California, a consulting firm suggested a novel growth-
control approach for Marin County, a highly urbanized county in the
San Francisco area. The consultant was reviewing the county's controlled growth plan and made two important points. First, the consultant agreed that the county needed a growth-control procedure in
order to make the plan work but "it [the plan] need not emphasize
the number of residential units that can be permitted in any year.
An alternative growth-control procedure that calls for balanced
achievement of all Countywide Plan goals, and for greater dependence
on the private market, should be evaluated and adopted."[27] Obviously,
the consultant was aware how a one-sided residential approach to
growth control could easily get out of hand, since it left the economic
side untouched. But more important was the fact that the economic
side, the local economy, could be used to attain a number of local
objectives. So, the consultant recommended

> a policy of balanced achievement where the goals of the
> Countywide Plan officially receive equal standing and
> the growth control mechanism be applied only at times
> when growth in the county was not maintained in balance.
> . . . The control would be that the housing and employ-
> ment targets must, within reasonable limits, remain
> in-balance.[28]

This would mean, for example, that if Marin County were
meeting its goals for new housing but not those for new employment,
then the new housing market would be curtailed through normal
police powers, like zoning. According to the consultant, "only
projects that help to re-establish balance in employment would be
approved until balance was re-achieved . . . projects that did not
contribute employment would not be approved."[29] The interesting
thing about this approach is that it gives the private market maximum freedom. And it gives the private market leeway so long as
it continues to meet the Marin County goals. But once things begin
to get out of hand, the county police power is applied to bring employment and new housing back into balance.
    Prince George's County, Maryland, was in a situation similar
to that of Marin County. Being in close commuting distance to

Washington, D.C., Prince George's County found itself to be the
home of thousands of new Washington bureaucrats each year. In
the 1960s, the county almost doubled its population, going from
350,000 to 660,000 people. But the trouble was that the only thing
that Prince George's County was getting was new, expensive housing.
And along with the flood of house-hunting bureaucrats came sharp
increases in the cost of housing and, also, in the tax rate. The industrial and commercial sectors were lagging much too far behind to
achieve any kind of economic balance. So the county developed a
growth-control system that, in effect, limited the construction of
new, expensive housing. But at the same time, it encouraged the
construction of low-income housing, as well as new commercial and
industrial development. This strategy will lead to a much better
balanced county, socially and economically. But more important
than this is that Prince George's is using the local economy to get
the kind of development that it needs and wants.[30]

The common feature shared by all of these local nongrowth
approaches is that they are placing more importance on the role of
the local economy. The growth machine is fueled by the local economy, and if a community wants to keep things in control, this is the
place to begin. Unless the community is 100 percent bedroom and
fully developed, new housing development must be joined by controls over the local economy. There are, as will be pointed out, a
number of methods to do that, but first, it is important to review
the one thing that communities must do in order to have any effective
control whatsoever. And that has to do with the basic zoning.

One of the least discussed, yet most common and important,
planning problems is overzoning—the tendency for communities to
zone for more commercial and industrial land than they could con-
ceivably need. And on the other side is the result—not enough land
zoned for other uses, like agriculture. Consider, for example, the
city of Aurora, Colorado. In this city of 107,000, there will shortly
be enough "existing industrially zoned land coupled with pending
annexations [to] place Aurora second only to Denver in the region
as to the amount of total land zoned for industry."[31] And this is so
in spite of the fact that only 10 percent of this land is currently
being used for industrial purposes. Such local policies, a very
common event, make bad economic and growth-control sense.

The economic side is simple to explain. Each community has
only so much land available for all types of uses. If the community
zones too much land for one use, such as industry, there will not be
enough available for other uses, such as agriculture. In dollar terms,
it means that industrial land will be considerably cheaper than other
types. Overzoning creates a monopoly of one type of land and a

great oversupply of another type. It will make some people very rich and keep others not so rich.

There is also a property tax side. Property tax is based on two things, the market value of the land (or some percentage thereof) and the improvements to the land, such as buildings. If the city has a great oversupply of industrial land, it means that the per capita property tax for industrial land will be low, since the supply will far outrun the market demand. But consider the owners of other types of land. If the market is tight for residential or agricultural land, the taxes on this property will be considerably higher. And the reason that this happens is that the city has been zoned for far too much industrial land. Thus, overzoning creates inequities in the property tax structure, inequities which usually mean that owners of industrial and commercial land pay relatively lower property taxes than homeowners or farmers.

Overzoning of industrial and commercial property is also a key problem with growth control. Blanket industrial or commercial zoning leaves the community wide open to a whole range of possible uses, uses that may effectively destroy any attempt at growth control or that could damage the local economy. Once the zoning is given, especially if a large number of uses are allowed in the zone by right, the community really forfeits the most important control that it has over the local economy. In most cases, the community is left with only one approach and no real power, that is, "jawboning" with new developers, literally asking the developer to do something that he is not legally required to do. Moral suasion is simply not effective in controlling new development.

A study that was done of the zoning in ten major West Coast cities shows just how disastrous overzoning can be.[32] The study did three things: first, it looked at the amount of land zoned for industry in each city; then, it estimated, on the basis of past performance, the amount of land that would be developed each year; and finally, it estimated the population that would accompany the industrial land if it were developed. In Orange County, California, it was found that the industrially zoned land, if developed, would mean a population of 6.5 million versus the current population of 1.6 million. Moreover, to use up the land currently zoned for industry would take 51 years. And the results get worse as one goes up the coast. In Portland, Oregon, the development of the industrial zoned land would mean a population of 5.1 million versus the existing population of 1 million, with 152 years to deplete the supply of industrial land. Worse yet was Seattle, Washington. In this city, the development of the industrially zoned land would generate a population of 1 million compared with the current 500,000, and the industrially zoned land would not be exhausted until well into the twenty-second century.

Clearly such policies are so much nonsense. They leave the cities wide open for virtually any type of development, and they place large tax burdens on other property tax payers. Not only is this true, but they also increase the cost of other types of property. For example, in cities like Portland and Seattle, someone is paying the price. Some property owner is literally subsidizing the industrial land tax burden and, in the process, is charging higher prices to the public. If there is a shortage of agricultural land, since so much land is zoned for industry, then prices for agricultural land are higher than they would otherwise be. If there is a shortage of residentially zoned land due to too much commercial or industrial land, then homeowners and homebuyers are paying higher taxes and higher prices for housing than they would otherwise. Overzoning means that someone is getting ripped off, and typically that someone is the local homeowner.

Overzoning is a common problem. And it has only one solution—to change the zoning. In practice, it means changing industrially zoned land and the commercially zoned land to "residential" or "agricultural." The property owners usually scream about having to pay industrial and commercial taxes for all those years, as well as suffering a loss in value to the property. But the real losers are the people who have been subsidizing the tax loads for the holders of industrial and commercial excess land. The real losers are the people who have had to pay higher prices for housing or for food than they would have if so much land had not been zoned for industry or commerce.

By changing the zoning, and, thus, by ridding the community of the vast excess of commercially and industrially zoned land, the community accomplishes three things: (a) it allows the community to get the local economy in control; (b) it lets the private market work to smooth out artificially high prices for residential and agricultural land and artificially low prices for industrial and commercial land; and (c) it makes the property tax far more equitable by putting the burden where it belongs—reducing, in most cases, taxes on homeowners and farmers and increasing it on commercial and industrial property owners who still have the land zoned for that purpose.

There is no getting around it. If a community wants to control growth and wants to foster equitable prices and equitable taxes, then it will have to change the zoning to reduce the ever-present, common overzoning of industrial and commercial land. And by doing this, the community will be in a position to apply land-use controls, which really work to control growth and to make the local economy work for local citizens.

BITING THE BULLET: POLICE AND FISCAL POWER
IN THE LOCAL ECONOMY

Police power and fiscal power have been around for a long time. Local officials know, and are comfortable with, zoning, subdivision regulations, and planned unit development ordinances, as well as annual budgets and capital expenditures. Simply put, these fiscal and police powers are the most attractive, effective, efficient, and politically acceptable control devices that local governments have.

But with the surge of growth control, there has been a change—not a change in the basic features of the controls but a change in the way that the controls are being combined. The control devices are being used as packages, as combinations of controls, to achieve specific objectives, like growth control. Zoning and subdivision regulations are being joined with the fiscal power of the capital expenditures to implement growth-control plans. What is being created is a new organization of some old workable tools to achieve some new ends.[33]

The same type of controls can be used by the local economy. Doing so requires no new state enabling legislation, nor does it require extensive local economic expertise. It does require a change in local thinking, a change that puts the local economy to work for the citizens.

One of the first things that the community has to do is to develop some economic common sense. Economists would have people believe that urban economics is a subject fraught with serious technical pitfalls, where the smallest incursion into the local economy often leads to disastrous results. In the view of most professional economists, it takes years of study to master exotic analytic techniques, not to mention the convoluted body of theory. But the awful truth is that sophisticated urban economic analysis is about as sophisticated as housing analysis or environmental analysis—which means that it is not that sophisticated.

In contrast to all other planning subjects, economic data are both good and plentiful and are available from a host of private and public organizations. On the private side, one of the best sources is the local utility, especially the electric and gas utilities. These companies have special research divisions whose job it is to analyze the detailed economic characteristics of communities and to tell the utility what kind of power load to expect. Thus, their land-use and economic data are quite detailed. Real estate brokers, especially those specializing in industrial and commercial properties, are another good source. They often conduct detailed analyses of selected sites or of whole industries in the area. The government has even more data. First, there is the huge amount of data collected and published by the Bureau of the Census. Then, there is the special census, as well as the specialized data collected by other federal departments and agencies, such as the departments of Labor, Commerce, and Treasury. State employment offices collect and publish data on employment that shows numbers employed by industry over considerable periods of time. Then there are the local agencies, planning departments, the assessor's office, administrative offices, economic development agencies, as well as other local line departments. Data simply are not a problem. The information exists for the types of problems that are important.

By using available data, the community can begin to know itself in economic terms. The city would want to know, for example, who is employed and who is not and about the skills and education levels of both. What about income? How stable is the local economy—does it go into an economic coma with each national recession? Do particular sectors, like construction, experience wild fluctuations regularly? How is income distributed? How is income distributed relative to other areas? What sectors of the economy have been growing rapidly? Which ones have not? What is the outlook for the local economy? What do the business people think of the future? The answers to these basic questions are sometimes found in books and reports but are also found in the offices, streets, and factories of the area. It is not really difficult to get them, and once they are acquired it is not difficult to proceed.

The reason it is not difficult to proceed is that the local economic objectives have to be modest. There is no attempt here at fundamental alteration of the economic structure and processes of the local economy. What is wanted is control of the aggregate rate of development and the way that certain segments of the local economy work for citizens. Here is an example.

Cities like Petaluma, California, and Novato, California, have already adopted a growth-control plan which limits the total number of houses that will be built in any one period.[34] As explained earlier, this approach increases the stability of the highly volatile construction industry. The control procedure makes the construction industry more stable by increasing the knowledge about the housing market. The industry knows how many units will be built, and each company can plan its program around that knowledge. Thus, by virtue of the growth-control program, the cities have increased the economic stability of the construction industry and, consequently, of the entire local economic base. It did not take a lot of analysis to figure this out, nor did it take great tons of data. The process was simple, direct, efficient, and effective.

Now consider the application of fiscal power instead of police power. In a hypothetical example it is postulated that Petaluma and Novato have discovered that the Mexican-Americans of their city want to get into construction and have the basic skills or capability to do it. These cities could easily do what Mayor Jackson of Atlanta already did. By executive order, the City Council could require that all jobs coming from city construction contracts be shared with some percentage of the cities' Mexican-Americans, or low-income population, or any other group that needs a chance. Once again, almost any manpower agency, poverty agency, employment agency, or community leader would be able to identify who needs work and to make a reasonable judgment about the kind of work they could do. It is a short step from there to a working program put into effect through executive order. There would not be any fundamental restructuring of the local economy, and there would be a working program for a specific group of people who need it. No monstrous bureaucratic machine would be required, and the local economy would be used to help the local citizens.

What about when a major new industrial developer comes to town, and the developer needs a change in zoning, a city subsidy, or perhaps a special permit to get into business? Would it be possible for the city to make economic performance part of the deal? One condition of the special permit might be one of the following: (a) jobs would have to be advertised locally—before being advertised on a national or regional basis, (b) the developer would hire and train so many of the community's unemployed, or (c) the developer would provide some hard cash for manpower development, facilities, or land. The point is this: making the local economy work for local people is not a difficult, time-consuming, or resource-intensive proposition. What is mostly required is a change in thinking, a change to thinking about what the local economy can do for the local citizens.

It is easier for the community to put its fiscal powers to use serving the community than it is to use police power. This is so because the community has exclusive control over its fiscal resources—the city council passes the yearly budget, as well as the capital budget. The main actors in the process are the bureaucracy and the elected decision makers. The size of the expenditures is tempered by the revenues produced. The budget is drawn and passed. So, injecting economic performance into the budget, the operating budget, and the capital expenditure budget is a comparatively simple process, namely, identifying what people need help and putting the budgets to the task by simple executive order. But the application of police power to economic matters is slightly more involved. When applying land-use controls to the local economy, there are two parties involved—the private sector and the public sector.

The private sector can be divided into two broad categories: large developments and everything else. The reason for this seemingly arbitrary division is that large developments are the ones that offer the greatest economic, environmental, and political threats. Small developments do not. Indeed, it is the small developments that bring a host of worthwhile characteristics to the local community. They are, for example, locally owned and operated. This means that the owners are in direct and daily contact with the community. They know the community needs or at least are more aware of them than an absentee stockholder. Small developments also hire locally. They also keep the community free from the kind of economic dependency that comes with major economic developments. Taken together, small developments exhibit the kind of economic health and vitality that makes the difference between one-horse economic cities, like Detroit, and a diverse, stable local economy, like that of Cedar Rapids, Iowa, with its avionics, gas-heating, road equipment, food-processing, and agricultural industries.

Large developments, on the other hand, have the opposite features. Absentee ownership makes for a less responsive industry. Could anyone seriously suggest, for example, that the International Telephone and Telegraph Corporation (IT&T) would change its corporate policies when they conflicted with local needs? Indeed, could anyone even get to the president of IT&T to tell him that the problem even existed? And what of political pressures that big firms generate? Often, major industries dominate the local decision-making process, especially when it's a one-industry town. Is Henry Ford II, for example, or Leonard Woodcock, president of the United Auto Workers, more important in Detroit? And then consider the economic dependency that large developments often generate. One-horse economic cities depend on the fortunes of that industry. And once that industry begins to fall off, so, too, the whole economic structure of the city—just ask people in Seattle or Detroit.

There are even more problems. Large industries consume enormous amounts of resources—all types of resources. And in the process of consumption, they often destroy other sectors of the local economy that previously have depended on those resources. In parts of Wyoming and Montana, for example, ranchers and farmers are falling victim to the water demands of the newly emerged energy industry. There simply is not enough water to go around. Large developments also have a way of putting people out of work by destroying historically important natural resources. In Maine, for example, it is altogether probable that if the state's coastline is used for refineries and superports, the fishing industry will be seriously harmed. Refineries and superports pollute the water, and water pollution kills fish, which puts the fishermen out of business. In addition to the pressure placed on natural resources, large developments also strain economic ones. In Greenville, South Carolina, the local economy is heavily dependent on the textile industry, a low-skill, low-wage, labor-intensive industry. Recently the Michelin Tire Company took an interest in Greenville and considered opening a plant.[35] But the differences in skill and wage levels between the tire and textile industries would have created serious economic trouble for Greenville's textiles. The textile industry simply could not compete, since Michelin would draw all the skilled labor with its higher wages, leaving it with even fewer skilled workers. Further, wages in the textile industry would have to go up, or it would be driven out. But in its wake would be the people with too few skills for other employment. Thus, major new developments also strain local economic resources and, in the process, often destroy important sectors of the local economy.

Finally, it is the large development that sets the growth machine in motion, often overnight.[36] A good example of this is the pipeline development in Alaska and the coal developments in places like Rock Springs, Wyoming, and Colstrip, Montana. Large corporations are quite capable of moving thousands of employees on short notice to any number of locations. Once the movement begins, secondary supportive developments follow—everything from housing to small retail operations. Thus, for every one employee of the large development, there might be two or three others in supportive roles. In addition, large developments often begin a process called "agglomeration," where a series of associated industries follow the major industry. For example, a tire manufacturer might be followed by someone making tire chains, or an aerospace manufacturer might be followed by an industry that makes special electronic parts for aircraft. It adds up, often to a scale that makes the initial development small by comparison.

"Large," of course, is a relative term. Each community must apply its own definition, based on its special economic characteristics. A community hooked to aerospace, for example, would want to give new aerospace developments special attention. Likewise, any development that would add more than 1,000 jobs to the community should be reviewed. In smaller communities, this figure might be reduced to 500 or 200. The major point is that each community should tailor its definition of "large" to its special needs. With this definition, the community is prepared to review these extremely important developments. And land-use controls are perfectly suited to do that.

The economic impact statement is a good place for communities to begin. Recently, a group of citizens in the Reno, Nevada, area were

asked by their elected officials to study their local economy and its
relation to growth. The citizens found that

> economic growth and population growth are closely related.
> Growth in the area's "basic" industries creates jobs and
> increases revenues accruing to the area from other re-
> gions. New jobs attract population in-migration, which,
> in turn, creates jobs in construction, retailing, and the
> public sector to meet the needs of the new in-migrants.
> Thus, there is a multiplying effect at work.[37]

From this, the citizens went on to recommend a way of controlling
the new growth or, at least, a way of discovering what the new growth
really meant—the economic impact statement.

> One way to manage local population growth would be to
> require that any proposed new commercial or industrial
> project which would directly employ more than 25 em-
> ployees should produce an impact statement. This state-
> ment would describe the likely population as well as
> economic, social and ecological effects of the project.
> Approval or disapproval would be based on compatibility
> with long-term growth objectives.[38]

The economic impact statement is an excellent educational
device and is easily adapted to other land-use controls. The purpose
of the statement is to get the hard economic facts about the project,
facts that relate the project to the needs of the community. Like the
environmental impact statement, the economic one should show three
things: (a) the existing condition of the economy, (b) the condition of
the local economy after the development has gone in, and (c) the relationship of the economy's postdevelopment condition to local community goals.

The impact statement should be required before the issuance of
any building permit. All small developments would be exempt, and
all large or questionable projects would have to prepare them. The
community should make the developer pay for the cost of the statement but should not let the developer prepare it (or even pay directly
the person who prepares it). The developer should give the money
to the local agency and let the agency decide whether to do it itself
or hire it out.

The main thing that communities should do is to decide on the
questions and economic objectives that are important. Two publications would help the representatives of the communities ask the right

kind of questions. The first, Measuring the Impacts of Land Development, by Thomas Muller and Philip Schaenman, suggests measures for evaluating impacts on the local economy, as well as on housing, social conditions, public services, and the natural environment.[39] This is a good introduction to the subject and should be used with others, like Conroy's The Challenge of Urban Economic Development, in order to get a better idea of the type of information that is important.[40] The second, Local Impact and Requirements of Manufacturing Industries, published by the Delaware State Planning Office, summarizes the economic, environmental, and energy characteristics of 414 four-digit standard industrial classification (SIC) industries.[41] This report is useful, since it paints a quick picture of the average firm within the 414 types of industries. The study suggests some of the kinds of things that communities can expect from various types of industries and, by doing that, provides an independent perspective on the likely performance of the firm. For example, it tells what percentage of the industries' employees are female and, also, covers average worker wage rates. Thus, if the community wants to increase labor force participation of women or to achieve some increase in average worker wage, this study will tell them about the average firm's performance in that industry. This allows the community to isolate major concerns in advance—to get them on the table—while the firm is going through the permit process.

One step up the land-use control ladder from the impact statement is the major development control ordinance. The basic idea with this ordinance is that it is designed to control all large developments, commercial and industrial, above some minimum size. Smaller developments would continue to be controlled through the normal zoning process, but at this larger scale, the applicants would be subject to more intensive evaluation and standards before the permit would be issued. The difference between the impact statement and the major development control ordinance is that, in the case of the latter, the evaluation would be the major criterion for decision making. The decision about the large development would be made on the basis of the evaluation.

In metropolitan Dade County, Florida—that is, the Miami area—the Board of County Commissioners recently passed an ordinance establishing a Development Impact Committee. This committee reviews and makes recommendations to local government on large-development applications.[42] "Large," in this case, is judged by the size in acres of the development or by the off-street parking generated by the development. Commercial developments larger than 20 acres or having more than 1,000 off-street parking spaces are included, as are industrial developments of more than 50 acres or 500 off-street parking spaces. The review committee looks at the development to see if it conforms to the comprehensive plan and then makes recommendations on the environmental, economic, fiscal, and public service impact of the development. The local government must, in turn, consider the recommendations when making its final decision.

This system could easily be used to build some positive incentives, economic as well as environmental, into the review process. For example, if the ordinance language were changed to include specific local objectives, developers would have a much better idea of what the community really wants and what the community would accept. This would influence the developers to pay attention to the particular types of development that would meet community needs. For example, if the ordinance stated that the community had specific economic needs, such as more jobs for the female population, or better-paying jobs for low-income population, or more stable industries, or more industries in the central city, developers would have the incentive to meet those needs in order to get approval. If the development industry knew that the community will look favorably on developments that do things for the community, the development industry would have the incentive to produce that type of development.

An example of developers responding to particular community needs identified in the land-use controls is found in the small community of Columbia County, Wisconsin.[43] Here, the people were trying to preserve their agricultural base and prevent leapfrog development. To do this, they developed a system that had, at its core, a short series of standards for new development. Each development application was evaluated in terms of the following: Is the new development on prime agricultural land? Is the new development adjacent to existing water and sewer lines? Is the new development next to already developed areas?, and so forth. The community found that, in the beginning, most developers acted as they always did—bringing in virtually any type of application, even if it did not meet the local standards. But after being turned down for bad proposals, proposals that did not meet the standards, the developers saw the light. Since those early days, the applications have been geared to the criteria. Now applications come in with developments that meet the community needs, that is, they preserve agriculture and promote compact development. Thus, as more exact standards and guidelines are developed for evaluation, developers will become more aware of what is worthwhile and what is not. Such an event would lead to better, more community-oriented developments, for Dade County, Florida, and other communities anxious for results.

The point system is another candidate for strong local police power over the local economy. The concept behind this system is

that applications for new development are evaluated according to a
set of criteria established by the local community. The criteria that
are used can extend over a large range. In Ramapo, New York, it is
mainly tied to the capital improvement plan.[44] In Davis, California,
it is mainly tied to a residential needs analysis and then to a housing
development priority program. The purpose of the program "is to
establish a formal review and approval process for housing applications."[45] The applications are evaluated periodically and weighed
against a set of specific housing goals for that period. Applications
responding best to the local goals receive highest priority. The
Petaluma, California, point system is similar.[46]

It does not take too much imagination to turn this system to the
local economy. For example, if the city of San Diego, California,
wanted to control its economy, it could first evaluate it, identifying
important strengths and weaknesses—particularly weaknesses. It
could then use these problem areas as the basis for its point system.
If the problem were low per capita income or persistent unemployment in the teen-age black population, then these important community
needs could form that year's main criteria for evaluating new industrial or commercial development. If the city were to decide that it
needed a certain number of jobs, then new developments could be
judged, one against the other, in terms of their contribution to San
Diego and its economic problems. Those developments that did something about the problems would be approved, while those which did
nothing or made the problems worse would be disapproved.

Smaller communities might consider the use of a special permit
system for the larger developments. The community might zone
itself as residential and set aside a special permit process for industrial and commercial developments. These types of development
would be required to obtain a special permit. To get the special
permit, the development would be evaluated against a set of local
economic needs.

As should be evident, the community has sufficient police power
to regulate the local economy. All that is required is that the communities develop some economic common sense, so that they really
get to know themselves in an economic sense. Beyond that, it is a
simple matter of going to traditional local powers, powers easily
adapted to control the local economy.

CONCLUSION

By using the power that every community possesses, three
things can be accomplished. First, communities can achieve effective

nongrowth, since the prime growth mover, the local economy, is in control. Second, communities can increase social equity by controlling the local economy, using the local economy to transfer jobs, dollars, training, or other resources to the people who need them. Third, communities can produce solid economic gains for their citizens through controlling the local economy.

All of this, however, is a new idea. Most communities simply have not worked that way. But if the local nongrowth movement shows anything, it is that communities are willing to try. To control the local economy, communities do not need any new legislation, vast bureaucratic resources, or long lead times. The powers that communities now have, their fiscal and police powers, are wholly sufficient to the task. It is merely a matter of directing these controls to a new end. Clearly, there is a lot to be gained in the process.

NOTES

1. Tom McCall, quoted in Charles E. Little, The New Oregon Trail (Washington, D.C.: Conservation Foundation, 1974), p. 35.

2. State Department of Planning and Economic Development, State of Hawaii Growth Policies Plan: 1974-84 (Honolulu: Department of Planning and Economic Development, 1974), pp. 53-84.

3. Shelly Mark, quoted in George Chaplin, "Hawaii Weighs the Future," Cry California 9, no. 3 (Summer 1974): 7.

4. "White Business Balks at Sharing the Work," Business Week, November 17, 1975, p. 47.

5. Norman Krumholz et al., "The Cleveland Policy Planning Report," Journal of the American Institute of Planners 41, no. 5 (September 1975): 298-304.

6. Ibid., p. 302.

7. William J. Toner, "Oysters and the Good Old Boys," Planning 41, no. 7 (August 1975): 10-15.

8. Michael E. Conroy, The Challenge of Urban Economic Development (Lexington, Mass.: D.C. Heath and Company, 1975), p. 89.

9. Henry L. Hunker, Industial Development (Lexington, Mass.: Lexington Books, 1974), p. 80.

10. H.H. Leibhafsky, The Nature of Price Theory (Homewood, Ill.: The Dorsey Press, 1963), p. 247.

11. Anthony J. Yudis, "BEDIC—Getting Jobs to Neighborhoods," Boston Sunday Globe, August 12, 1973, pp. 61, 62.

12. Anthony J. Yudis, "City Work Park Plan the Next Trend in Development," Boston Sunday Globe, July 21, 1974, pp. 65, 68.

13. Jack Aley, "The Shelter Institute's Instant Success," Maine Times, December 5, 1975, pp. 20-21.

14. Jane Jacobs, The Economy of Cities (New York: Vintage Books, 1969), p. 79.

15. Ibid., p. 87.

16. Ibid., p. 89.

17. Charles E. Garrison, "New Industry in Small Towns: The Impact on Local Government," National Tax Journal 24 (December 1971): 493-500.

18. Stanford Environmental Law Society, San Jose: Sprawling City—A Study of the Causes and Effects of Urban Sprawl in San Jose, California (Stanford, Calif.: Stanford Law School, 1972), p. 17.

19. Norman Mineta, "Organizing for Economic Development," New Directions in Local Economic Policy . . . a Report on a CUED Seminar, San Francisco, Calif., Sept. 1974 (Washington, D.C.: National Council for Urban Economic Development, 1974), p. 18.

20. San Jose, California Planning Department, Urban Growth and Development Policies, Final Draft (San Jose, Calif.: February 1974), p. 32.

21. Ibid., p. 32.

22. Richard P. Appelbaum et al. (Santa Barbara Planning Task Force), Santa Barbara: The Impacts of Growth 1974, vols. 1, 2, 3 (Santa Barbara, Calif.: City of Santa Barbara, 1974).

23. Ibid., p. 10.4.

24. Jeanne Graffy (Chairperson, City Planning Commission), Recommendations for General Plan and Zoning Ordinance Amendments, based on the comprehensive population impact study and on public discussions (land-use zones analysis) (Santa Barbara, Calif.: City of Santa Barbara Planning Commission, 1975), attachment D, p. 10.

25. Ibid.

26. "Report on Boulder, Colorado Workshop" (Summary Workshop Report delivered at National Conference on Managed Growth, Chicago, September 16-18, 1973), p. 27.

27. Baxter, McDonald & Smart, Inc., Economic Impact of the Marin Countywide Plan, Summary Report (San Rafael, Calif.: Baxter, McDonald & Smart, Inc., 1974), p. 6.

28. Ibid., pp. 42-43.

29. Ibid., p. 43.

30. Michael E. Gleeson et al., Urban Growth Management Systems: An Evaluation of Policy-Related Research, Planning Advisory Service Report nos. 309, 310 (Chicago: American Society of Planning Officials, 1975), pp. 21-22.

31. Aurora, Colorado, Department of Planning and Community Development, An Economic Analysis of the City of Aurora (Aurora, Colo.: Aurora Planning Dept., 1973), p. 20.

32. Alfred J. Gobar and Christine Coman, "One Aspect of Neo Mercantilism at the Regional Level" (Paper delivered at the 46th Annual Conference of the Western Economics Association, Simon Fraser University, British Columbia, Canada, August 1971).

33. See Gleeson et al., op. cit., p. v.

34. See Appelbaum et al., op. cit., vol. 3, Technical Appendices, pp. 152-53.

35. Bert A. Winterbottom, "A Growth Management Strategy for Greenville County, South Carolina" (Paper delivered at the 57th Annual Conference of the American Institute of Planners, Denver, Colorado, October 1974), p. 4.

36. John S. Gilmore and Mary K. Duff, The Process for Policy and Objectives for Growth Management in Sweetwater County, Wyoming (Denver, Colo.: University of Denver Research Institute, 1974), pp. 3-21.

37. Blue Ribbon Task Force, Growth and Development in Reno, Sparks and Washoe County, Nevada (Reno, Nev.: The Regional Planning Commission of Reno, Sparks, and Washoe County, 1973), p. 38.

38. Ibid., p. 39.

39. Philip S. Schaenman and Thomas Muller, Measuring the Impacts of Land Development: An Initial Approach (Washington, D.C.: The Urban Institute, 1974), pp. 45-55.

40. Conroy, op. cit., p. 8.

41. Bruce L. Hudson, Local Impact and Requirements of Manufacturing Industries (Dover, Del.: Delaware State Planning Office, December 1974), pp. 1-34.

42. Board of County Commissioners of Dade County, Florida, Ordinance No. 75-47 (Dade County, Fla.: June 18, 1975).

43. Charles Deknatel and Susan Harris, Zoning to Preserve Agriculture: Columbia County (Madison, Wis.: State Planning Office, Bureau of Planning and Budget, Department of Administration, December 1974).

44. See Gleeson et al., op. cit., pp. 22-23.

45. Davis, California, Community Development Department, General Plan—City of Davis 1974-1990 (Davis, Calif.: 1974), p. 56.

46. See Gleeson et al., op. cit., pp. 18-19.

Typically, the people who influence decisions about the
future of cities have acted on the simple-minded axiom:
the bigger the better. This is most notably true here in
America where the rational prospect of great gain
encourages an almost pathological obsession with the
virtues of sheer bigness, as if the very bigness of the
city, the height of its buildings, and the crowds on its
streets must somehow outweigh all squalor and ugliness.
There seems to be a fear, too, that the moment we stop
growing we start to die, a half truth that overlooks the
fact that in nature the mouse and the sparrow have out-
lasted the brontosaurus and the sabre-toothed tiger.
There are, I suspect, all sorts of devices we could use
to control the growth of a city when it reaches the
optimal range. These need to be explored, but they will
be of little use until we decide that this is what we really
want to do.[1]

Both as a state of mind and as a program of action, nongrowth
has applications beyond concerns of land use, social equity, and economic development. Nongrowth has important organizational and
administrative implications for the local bureaucracies—primarily
municipalities but, also, counties and a variety of other jurisdictions
below the state level—that are the prime means our society uses to
deal with the problems of its cities. Just as many of our cities have
grown in an uncontrolled way, so many of our local government
bureaucracies have grown—in size, in numbers, and in costs—to the
point where it is no longer clear that the public has any actual control over them. Just as the growth of our cities has frequently made

the lives of many of their residents less pleasant, so the growth of local bureaucracies has hardly improved the quality of the services they give citizens or, even, of the working life they offer their employees, who are, of course, increasing in number. The problem of bureaucratic growth is an essential part of the problem of urban growth.

Dealing with the problem of bureaucratic growth ought to be a key concern of the nongrowth movement, but thus far, it has not been given high priority. Nongrowth advocates have been preoccupied with the issues discussed previously in this book. And local political and administrative leaders, caught up in day-to-day operations and inevitably concerned with defending and enlarging their powers, have shown no great interest in fighting the evils of bureaucratic growth. Indeed, many local leaders—for example, bureaucrats in supervisory positions and businessmen whose livelihood depends on city contracts—have welcomed and profited from the bureaucratic growth that population and geographic growth usually necessitate.[2]

It is surprising, however, that many of the most prominent students of organizational and administrative behavior have generally neglected the problems that bureaucratic growth brings. In their studies of both public and private institutions, they appear to assume that all organizations are good, that big organizations are better and more efficient than small ones, and that all organizations should, therefore, grow as much as they can.[3] They unthinkingly identify sound management and effective leadership with organizational growth. The possibility that organizational nongrowth might, in some situations, be a preferable approach—that some organizations may sensibly decide not to grow, that others ought to be kept from growing—apparently does not seriously occur to them.

This widespread inattention to issues of organizational nongrowth is unfortunate. Citizens, officials, and academics should all be thinking in terms of organizational nongrowth, but none of them are. This blindness is especially regrettable since economic difficulties, energy shortages, and environmental constraints are likely to bring on a state of organizational nongrowth at the local level, regardless of whether our cities are ready for it.

This forced state of nongrowth, crudely imposed by outside pressures, need not necessarily lead to disaster. But it would be far more desirable if citizens and local government officials were to come to appreciate the advantages and opportunities that a planned, deliberate policy of organizational nongrowth can offer, and to prepare to capitalize on them. Nongrowth perspectives represent a highly useful approach for understanding and improving the operations of urban bureaucracies (and of other bureaucracies, as well). This chapter outlines the emergence of the large urban bureaucracy, shows the external and internal effects of these bureaucracies, and suggests what nongrowth advocates can do about the more baleful of these effects.

THE RISE OF THE LARGE URBAN BUREAUCRACY

The twentieth century, it is often said, is the age of the large organization. The organizations cited as examples are usually private corporations and federal agencies. But in fact, as Werner Hirsch writes, "The largest and fastest-growing industry in the United States today is government employment, especially at the local and state levels."[4] He points out that by mid-1970, the total number of employees on government payrolls had reached 12.6 million, or about 15 percent of the total labor force—up from a 1940 figure of 3.5 million, which represented 6.5 percent of the labor force. Four-fifths of the 1970 government employees worked for state and local governments.[5] In 1945, the total payrolls of the federal government and of state and local governments were both about $6 billion a year. By 1975, the federal government's annual payroll had risen to about $35 billion, while that of state and local governments had risen to about $110 billion.

A brief look at some of the results of the 1972 Census of Governments confirms this growth. In 1971/72, state and local governments had total revenues of $804.59 for each member of the population—up from $87.39 in 1946 and $12.46 in 1902. In 1971/72, local governments had total revenues of $105.2 billion—up from $9.6 billion in 1946 and $.9 billion in 1902. They spent, for example, $5.4 billion on hospitals in 1971/72, compared with $.3 billion in 1946 and only $22 million in 1902. Massachusetts's local governments had 242 employees per 10,000 population in 1953; by 1972, this figure had risen to 332. And this kind of increase was paralleled in less urban states: in Kansas, for instance, the same figure went from 212 to 337 in the same period.[6]

Another, less statistical way to appreciate the growth of local bureaucracies is to look up a city government in the telephone book. In a city of any size, there are long listings and sublistings for agencies whose very functions few big city governments—or any other governments—were performing even 25 years ago. In the 1974 Chicago telephone book, for example, one finds the Citizens' Complaint Registrar, the Consumer Sales Department, the Economic and Cultural Development Board, the Environmental Control Department, the Human Relations Commission, the Human Resources Department,

the Manpower Department, the Model Cities Committee, the Senior
Citizens' Office, and the Urban Renewal Department.

The growth and increased cost of local government are caused
by more than the accretion of new functions, however. Historically
rising incomes have produced larger tax revenues; this has allowed
local government to expand, to spend more, and to try to do more
than was possible a quarter of a century ago. Inflation, urbanization,
increased public expectations, higher levels of technology, and the
increased need for highly trained professional and administrative
personnel are other obvious factors adding to this bureaucratic and
financial growth.

In addition, city employees are increasingly forming unions,
whose activities naturally—and for the most part, constructively—
tend to increase wages and decrease working hours (thus, making it
necessary to hire new employees at the higher wages). By 1970, the
number of organized municipal employees exceeded 2 million, and
they had become a serious political force. In cities whose population
was over 10,000, three out of five city workers belonged to unions.
The biggest union, the American Federation of State, County, and
Municipal Employees, had nearly half a million members. In less
than a decade, it had moved from being the 19th to the 7th largest
affiliate of the American Federation of Labor-Congress of Industrial
Organizations.[7]

For most of late 1975, until New York State and the federal
government assumed a good part of its financial affairs, New York
City was on the brink of bankruptcy. Much of the blame for the city's
plight was due to former Mayor John Lindsay, whose strong profile
on talk shows concealed a glass jaw in bargaining with employee
unions. The city was obligated to pay more than $1 billion a year—
approximately 10 percent of its budget—into employee pension funds.
Its 34,000 policemen were receiving salaries and fringe benefits that
averaged $24,000 a year, and its firemen and sanitation workers were
not far behind.[8] Many of its other employees were receiving wages
considerably in excess of what they could have obtained for the same
work in the private sector. Retirement benefits were often excessive.
Between civil service and welfare costs, one New Yorker in three
was being supported by the taxes of the other two.

No other major city—with the possible exception of Detroit,
where unemployment was nearing 25 percent—was in as bad a financial situation as New York. But so many large cities were paying so
many employees such high wages or were otherwise overcommitted
that it seemed likely, as of late 1975, that some of them would
eventually suffer New York's difficulties. In addition to Detroit,
possible candidates were Newark, Cleveland, Buffalo, Hartford,
Philadelphia, and Oakland. And a large number of other cities were

considering or undertaking cutbacks—such as closings of facilities, reductions in pay or pay increases, and even outright dismissals— intended to prevent them from undergoing New York's trials.

Civil service unions aside, the federal grant system, whose effects on local government will be examined in greater detail in the next chapter, has contributed substantially to the growth of urban bureaucracies. Federal aid as a percentage of total local and state government expenditures had risen from about 2 percent in 1930 to about 22 percent of vastly larger expenditures in 1974.[9] Federal aid to New York City, which had been $56 million in 1952/53, had risen to over $2 billion in 1973/74. It had been under 4 percent of the city's budget in 1952/53, but it was nearly 20 percent of a much larger budget in 1973/74.[10] The city's government had surpassed the state governments of California and New York to become the nation's second-largest government.

The impact of federal aid on the growth of local bureaucracies is even more dramatic if one focuses on specific urban activities the federal government has wished to encourage. In the early 1950s, there were fewer than 250 active city planners in the entire country, many of them in the private sector or academic life.[11] But since then, federal legislation, beginning with the Housing Act of 1954, which created the 701 program that provides money for local planning efforts, and continuing through more contemporary housing, welfare, public works, transportation, and environmental legislation, has utterly transformed the field of city planning. All this legislation requires that localities prepare plans in order to qualify for federal grants. By 1964, every city with a population of over 100,000 had a planning agency. Some 92 percent of the cities with a population of over 10,000—that is, 1,261 cities—had a planning agency, a figure that had tripled since 1957.

By mid-1972, more than 200 metropolitan regional planning agencies had been established, and more than 4,000 development plans had been prepared. By mid-1975, the total number of active American city planners was, to estimate from the membership figures of the American Society of Planning Officials and the American Institute of Planners, approximately 20,000—a figure that indicated an annual increase in the number of planners in excess of 20 percent every year since 1954. Naturally, most of these planners worked for local agencies.

Similarly, striking growth at the local level as a result of federal grants could be demonstrated for other fields and activities. Public health specialists, doctors practicing community medicine, poverty lawyers, welfare workers, librarians, manpower specialists, schoolteachers and administrators, policemen, and urban researchers

are other examples of workers whose career opportunities have been
greatly enlarged by federal grants, in particular, and the growth of
city government, in general.[12]

EXTERNAL EFFECTS: ADMINISTRATIVE IMMOBILITY
AND THE PROVISION OF SERVICES

In the abstract, there is a great deal to be said in favor of big
urban bureaucracies, as there is in favor of large bureaucracies of
other kinds. They perform a wide variety of useful tasks that might
not otherwise be performed. They offer a means of harnessing
technology—whether scientific, administrative, or financial—for
socially desirable ends. They are full of talented, dedicated people.
They offer their staffs a comforting sense of both usefulness and
belongingness, as well as an anonymity that many people find reassur-
ing. Furthermore, they pay their people regularly and, often, well.
Regardless of their virtues, big city bureaucracies are here to stay.
They are the way we, as a society, have learned to do things we want
to do. In any case, no substitute for them is at hand. It is romantic,
atavistic, and ostrichlike to wish they would go away. They will not.

With all these points conceded, however, it is clear that
describing the good features and the irreplaceability of large urban
bureaucracies is not likely to be an inspiring task. The organizations
themselves are hardly inspiring. They cost too much and deliver too
little. They move too slowly and often in such a way as to prevent
the resolution of the problems they are supposed to deal with; given
enough time and money, they usually become an inherent part of these
problems. They tend to respond only to other large organizational
forces, such as other public agencies and big corporations, and they
lose touch with small, individual influences—for example, neighborhood groups, citizen organizations, small businesses, and otherwise
unaffiliated residents. Their sense of accountability to the public
atrophies. And as a result of frequently rigid civil service rules
that confer easy, early, and unassailable tenure on comparatively
new employees, their political accountability, their responsiveness
to the mayors, other elected officials, and department heads who are
supposed to run them, often dwindles, as well.

They tend to become accountable only to themselves. They consist mainly of red tape, petty rivalries with other agencies, clumsy
coordination, and an excessive dominance of those who administer
over those who do not. The organizations are primarily interested
in defending their past actions, however harmful or ineffective, and

carrying them on indefinitely. They are much less interested in performing their assigned functions or taking on new ones as they become necessary. The organizations have a life of their own. And since they are public organizations, they are deprived of whatever invigoration competition based on the profit motive can offer.

Like other big organizations, large urban bureaucracies are far better able to deal with the tangible problems of administration, finance, law, and technology than with the more amorphous problems of politics, culture, or society. In any big city, the sewer and highway systems are likely to work well, but not the schools, the welfare department, or the public housing. The planning that occurs is likely to be either the straight-line projection of existing trends into the future or the production of papers no one reads—probably both. Large urban bureaucracies tend to be good at measures of consolidation and codification—which naturally induce further bureaucratic growth. They are poor at measures of innovation—something that, because it may be antagonistic to other large organizations, may well hinder further bureaucratic growth. The great disadvantage of relying on these large organizations is that they are often, in administrative terms, almost immobile. Change and adaptation do not come easily to them. They find it very difficult to respond to outside challenges. Sometimes, they can barely respond to the outside world at all.

These characteristics are, as indicated above, always prevalent to some extent in large organizations.[13] But today's local bureaucracies must face serious new problems, including economic difficulties, energy and environmental constraints, and rising dissatisfaction on the part of the taxpayers and consumers, who ultimately have to pay the bills. These agencies already suffer from substantial restraints—large size, civil service rules, aggressive unions, rigid procedures, and lack of real competition—which may sometimes be praiseworthy but will invariably have the effect of limiting the agencies' freedom of action. The question is whether they will be able to respond constructively to all these frustrations. The agencies have grown rapidly for the last few decades, but now continued bureaucratic growth can no longer be taken for granted, especially since the results it has produced have hardly led to universal satisfaction.

From the point of view of the ordinary citizen, what is at issue is the quality of the services provided by the city. The services that large city bureaucracies deliver are now widely regarded as inadequate. Yet, the only way the bureaucracies can find to improve them is to become bigger and more costly. But larger size and increased cost offer only the most tenuous promise that the services will actually improve, and voters rightly see no reason to believe in it. The

problem seems real and apparently has no solution. Elliott Medrich
writes that consumers of public services

> want "more" for "less." On the other hand they are
> skeptical that service sector agencies really could de-
> liver the kind of "service package" they want, no mat-
> ter how much is spent. But even so, we expect
> improvements in programs despite the fact that we
> seem less willing than ever to pay. . . . The struggle
> is played out in the face of rising costs, marginal im-
> provements in efficiency, and terribly slow response
> to demands for new kinds of programs.[14]

There is no question that the services provided by and through
large city bureaucracies are not what they should be. The persistent
image is that of the four or five underoccupied city workers who
show up to fix a street light or fill a pothole months after the job
first needed to be done.

There is also no question that most of the attempts of the last
ten years or so to alter the way urban services are delivered have
come to very little—other than to increase the size of the bureaucracies delivering them. These points have been documented in field
after field, but with particular attention to education, police work,
housing, and antipoverty activities.[15] The failure in the provision of
services and the proliferation of ineffectual agencies are especially
poignant in the case of the social programs begun by the Johnson
Administration. Allen Pritchard, executive director of the National
League of Cities, writes:

> Before 1960, public policy emphasized the tangible inputs
> to problem-solving—if people lived in deteriorating neigh-
> borhoods, housing projects were constructed; if they were
> victimized, 100 additional police officers were hired; if
> they were sick, a wing or two was added to a hospital.
>
>   By the mid-sixties, we began to understand that
> all this building of things was not an unmixed blessing.
> Neighborhoods and communities were ripped apart by
> urban renewal and highway construction. Children in
> brand new schools were not learning any better. We
> created a surplus of hospital rooms, but health care was
> not improving.
>
>   Policy responses to these understandings were
> vigorous but had a peculiar frantic quality . . . Head
> Start . . . War on Poverty . . . Black Capitalism . . .

> Citizen Participation . . . Manpower Development and
> on and on.
>> More was promised than could be delivered.[16]

But perhaps the dilemma of increasingly unsatisfactory services
provided by increasingly immobile bureaucracies does have a solution. It is entirely possible that the problem is not really a matter of
economic constraints, unrealizable expectations on the part of the
public, the nature of the services the city agencies are trying to deliver, the behavior of the people receiving them, or broad social
conditions the agencies cannot affect. The problem may in large part
simply be that most city agencies—especially, the ones in our largest
cities—have grown so large and are so clogged, so inefficient, and so
immobile that it is no longer realistic to expect them to be responsive
to public or political control. They are inflexible to the point of being
unmanageable.

They have become so weighted down, so insulated by their sheer
size, that they cannot perform their functions to anyone's satisfaction. Often, as when school systems become places to contain rather
than places to educate adolescents, or when planning agencies become
tools of development interests, or when police departments become
massive shakedown operations, they abandon their ostensible functions
and adopt more perverse ones. The solution for the bureaucracy that
has become so large that it can no longer perform socially useful
functions is not to beef it up but to slim it down. The agency that has
grown to the point where it no longer does anything worthwhile or has
become a positive public menace is an obvious target for the application of nongrowth approaches.

What these approaches might be are suggested in the last section of this chapter; for the present, it will be shown how the growth
of a city bureaucracy—particularly its brute size and immobility—
can deform the services it is trying to provide and, sometimes, even
negate these services entirely. There are few studies that directly
compare, for example, the quality of the police or educational services
provided by cities or city bureaucracies of different sizes.[17] But
there is a great deal of evidence that suggests that organizational
growth—as measured by increases in budgets, staff sizes, or the
number of administrative units—only rarely improves city services
and, often, makes them worse.

For example, studies of specific large urban bureaucracies
always seem to uncover an impressive variety of organizational
pathologies that clearly get in the way of the performance of the
ostensible tasks of the bureaucracy. David Rogers's excellent
study of the New York City school system, 110 Livingston Street (the

Brooklyn address of the Board of Education), found that a key cause
of the generally mediocre performance of the schools was the insula-
tion of the bureaucracy administering them. Its officials, he concluded

> have been isolated for decades from the city and from any
> outside review, and now they are under constant attack and
> tend to be inordinately suspicious of any outsiders. The
> system has taken on an almost "paranoid" tone in recent
> years. . . . The system is a "total institution" for its
> officials and they are preoccupied with its internal politics
> and status order. They are at the same time withdrawn
> from and often suspicious of or arrogant toward outsiders.[18]

New York's educational bureaucracy has systematically, and
for the most part successfully, fought decentralization and other
reform efforts. The Board of Education

> has organizational defenses that allow it to function in
> inefficient, unprofessional, undemocratic, and politically
> costly ways without evoking more of a revolution or push
> for radical change than has yet emerged. It has an almost
> unlimited capacity for absorbing protest and externalizing
> the blame, for confusing and dividing the opposition, "seem-
> ing" to appear responsive to legitimate protest by issuing
> sophisticated and progressive policy statements that are
> poorly implemented, if at all, and then pointing to all its
> paper "accomplishments" over the years as evidence of
> good faith and effective performance. . . . The system is
> much like a punching bag. Protest groups can hit it in
> one place, and it simply returns to an old equilibrium.
> Even hitting it in several places has not helped effect
> basic structural change. It has been able to maintain its
> archaic programs, not solely for protectionist motives,
> but by its normal cumbersome workings.[19]

But the undesirable manifestations and outcomes of these
"protectionist motives" and "normal cumbersome workings" ranged
from the trivial to the tragic. The central headquarters of the board
was the only administrative unit that could provide light bulbs, door-
knobs, and erasers. The board's bureaucracy deliberately clogged
the agenda for board meetings with unimportant items that kept the
lay board so busy that it did not have time to set policy, much less
find out what was going on in local schools, districts, or headquarters.

There were numerous cases where teachers with new curricula, which had often already worked elsewhere, were not able to get their material into classrooms or were harassed once they did. Seemingly impartial civil service tests were little more than devices to give preferment to insiders. Many principals, flooded with directives from Livingston Street and angry at the board's ignorance of local conditions, had concluded that headquarters could generally be ignored. There were large numbers of wasteful programs, ones that supplied books to children at a cost of $2 apiece, when the same books could be bought in stores for $.50. Reading test scores were unavailable to parents, even after a superintendent's order that they be made accessible. The scores were often deliberately distorted, sometimes by giving the tests several times and, on occasion, by outright doctoring. Principals consistently mistreated students and parents, sometimes disregarding their constitutional rights. Many schools sabotaged even mild desegregation plans. Potentially innovative programs of all kinds were repeatedly ignored.[20]

Other studies of other large urban bureaucracies have produced similar results. Diana Gordon's study of the New York City Department of Social Services found that the caseloads of the department's 12,000 workers were too heavy to allow even the pretense of personal service to clients. Paperwork requirements for the simplest modification in a client's status were so great that caseworkers either refused help or offered it only grudgingly. Regulations for different levels of payment were often so complex that no one in the department understood them—which led, of course, to both inequitable differences in payments to clients and the use of the regulations by caseworkers for their own personal ends. Field mutinies by caseworkers were common; sometimes, they were tinged with racism. Managing the department was an impossible task. Gordon quoted a former commissioner:

> I will always remember two things that were told to me
> by the staff—"Commissioners come and Commissioners
> go, but we stay on forever." The other thing I heard was,
> "Be sure to be nice to the elevator operator, he may
> become Commissioner some day." I've known staff who
> have laughed when I told them to do something. The atti-
> tude was, why should we listen? He'll be around next
> week, next month, maybe next year, but not longer than
> that![21]

Gordon also examined the New York City Health Department's response to evidence of increasing lead poisoning among slum

children in the city and found a bureaucratic *stasis* comparable to
that of the Social Services Department. When the City Housing
Authority asked the Health Department for an opinion on some
applications from families who maintained that the risks of lead
poisoning in their apartments justified giving them priority for
placement in public housing, it took the Health Department over a
year to reply. The department's commissioner took nine months to
approve a warning poster. Fifteen months were needed to get approval
of simple notices that were to be sent in envelopes containing welfare
checks.

A pamphlet on the dangers of lead poisoning took another 15
months to get written; and when it was, it turned out to be full of
complicated technical language suitable for a physician rather than a
welfare mother. An official sent community newspapers a draft editorial about lead poisoning, but failed to follow up on it, so it got no
play. The department accepted an untainted gift of 2,000 valuable
testing kits with only the greatest reluctance, and it seemed unwilling
to distribute them. Only when a Village Voice journalist began to
publicize the lead-poisoning issue did the department shake off its
lethargy.[22]

All these cases exemplify the mature urban bureaucracy. It is
not just a matter of New York City's bureaucracies, although New
York's seem particularly bad. Most large, stable urban bureaucracies
operate in much the same ossified way. So, at only slightly reduced
ossification, do many stable bureaucracies in smaller localities; it
is not uncommon to find departments of 5 people in small cities that
are about as rigid, as overgrown in relation to their tasks and performance, as departments of 50 people in big cities.

Moreover, many of the same undesirable patterns appear in
local bureaucracies that have not yet reached their mature size,
which are growing rapidly, with no particular limits yet in sight.
The growth problem is not that the bureaucracies have grown to the
point of obesity, but that their rate of growth is cancerous. The problem is not so much that the bureaucracies have grown immobile
(although, often, they have) but that they are growing too swiftly, too
much beyond any real control. The sheer fact of growth becomes a
replacement for any useful public function the growth might serve.
And a variety of unforeseen side effects, most of them negative, begin
to occur.

This pointless kind of bureaucratic growth is surprisingly
common. As mentioned earlier in this chapter, city governments
have expanded rapidly in recent decades, but can anyone seriously
maintain that the public is happier with their services, or that the
services have improved in any substantial respect (as opposed to

technical or cosmetic ones)? There are many more city planners than there used to be, but it is hard to find any evidence that cities are better planned, or even that the increase in the number of planners has made the slightest difference in the substance of how cities are planned or grow.

For example, Ralph Nader's study group report on land use in California, Politics of Land, undertook a detailed examination of Santa Clara County, which contains the extremely fast-growing city of San Jose, and found that the county has one of the nation's finest planning staffs and one of its worst patterns of urban development.[23] William Wheaton, dean of the University of California at Berkeley's planning school, makes the point, "One could compare Houston, which has had no planning, with any of a score of cities of comparable size and recency of development, which have had the most advanced planning, and find no discernible important differences."[24] And the same might be said of the performance of other kinds of urban professions and professionals whose numbers have exploded in recent years.

There are other examples. In the mid-1960s, the heyday of programs like the War on Poverty and Model Cities, local bureaucracies carrying out the programs sprang from nonexistence to considerable size, often within a few months; in the case of the War on Poverty, the new bureaucracies were specifically intended to counter the inaction of existing local agencies. But the rapid bureaucratic expansion merely created more frenetic versions of the same old social welfare agencies, with some new and more hectic vices. It produced highly imaginative forms of corruption, vicious and often racist varieties of radicalism, meaningless charadelike citizen participation activities, a confirmation of existing power structures in low-income areas, much wider career opportunities for middle class professionals, and somewhat widened opportunities for the better-endowed segments and hustler elements among the poor. But it did very little for most of the deprived populations the programs were supposed to help.[25] All these effects of rapid bureaucratic growth, of course, discredited the new programs, while making it difficult to arouse support for better programs to replace them.

In time, the new programs mellowed. The rapid pace of bureaucratic expansion could not be kept up indefinitely. The high-speed ineffectuality of the early days gave way to the more phlegmatic inefficacy of the ordinary urban bureaucracy. When federal funding for the quickly aging programs was largely cut off, the older city agencies easily absorbed many of their more digestible functions. The change was purely one of bureaucratic nomenclature. The spectacularly objectionable results of the high-growth period of the programs made little difference in the long run. They quickly became the less obviously objectionable results of the traditional urban agencies. These agencies just kept on growing, more slowly than the new agencies, but also more inexorably.

Jane Jacobs's 1961 classic, The Death and Life of Great American Cities, suggests another example of how rapid bureaucratic growth can impede and prevent the delivery of the services the bureaucracies are ostensibly providing.[26] The urban renewal attempts of the 1950s, Jacobs argued, were an attempt to undo blight by means of "cataclysmic money." This money quickly produced large local (and federal) housing bureaucracies, as well as precisely the low quality of housing one would expect from such bureaucracies. Socially stable, low-rent, relatively safe neighborhoods built on a livable scale were repeatedly bulldozed to make way for unstable, sterile, higher-rent, unsafe public housing projects built on an inhumane scale. Such projects deteriorated quickly and, sometimes, as in the case of Pruitt-Igoe in St. Louis, had to be torn down. But they continued to be built at a great rate long after their deficiencies were widely recognized by people less perceptive than Jacobs.

Were it not for external events, such as the recent economic downturns and the reluctance of the Nixon and Ford administrations to push the federal government further into the urban housing market, the projects Jacobs found so atrocious would still be springing up today. If the recession lifts or if a Democratic president is elected, they will probably start to spring up again. For the housing bureaucracies, with all their administrators, planners, and architects, have continued to proliferate all the while—not at the halcyon rate of the late 1950s and early 1960s but, nonetheless, at a substantial pace. It did not matter whether these agencies built much housing or not, nor did it matter how bad the housing was or how many poor people it displaced. The bureaucracies just kept on expanding.

INTERNAL EFFECTS: THE QUESTION
OF THE QUALITY OF WORKING LIFE

A burgeoning literature on the quality of American working life strongly suggests that large organizations of any kind are in many ways undesirable, even destructive, places to work. While little of this literature specifically focuses on big city bureaucracies, its applicability to them is clear—and distressing. Their internal effects may well be worse than their external ones.

Work in America, a brilliant, highly publicized, and heavily documented special task force report to then Secretary of Health,

Education and Welfare Elliot Richardson, concluded that

> significant numbers of American workers are dissatis-
> fied with the quality of their working lives. Dull, repeti-
> tive, seemingly meaningless tasks, offering little challenge
> or autonomy, are causing discontent among workers at
> all occupational levels. This is not so much because work
> itself has greatly changed; indeed, one of the main prob-
> lems is that work has not changed fast enough to keep up
> with the rapid and widescale changes in worker attitudes,
> aspirations, and values. A general increase in their edu-
> cational and economic status has placed many American
> workers in a position where having an interesting job is
> now as important as having a job that pays well.[27]

Jobs in large institutions pay well enough, but they rarely seem particularly interesting, much less engrossing. Work in America cited a study that asked different workers: "What type of work would you try to get into if you could start all over again?"[28] The persons who would choose again to do the same kind of work they were doing tended to be people who did not work in large institutions. If they did, they worked primarily in small groups within those institutions. Some 91 percent of the mathematicians, 83 percent of the lawyers, and 82 percent of the journalists would choose the same occupation, but only 43 percent of a general cross section of white-collar workers. Among working class occupations, printers tend to work outside big organizations, and 52 percent of them would choose the same work again. But only 24 percent of a cross section of blue-collar workers would do so.[29]

Work in America then reviewed a variety of data on the rise of large organizations of all kinds and on the "diminishing opportunities to be one's own boss." The big organizations

> typically organize work in such a way as to minimize the
> independence of the workers and maximize control and
> predictability for the organization. . . . Yet, the more
> democratic and self-affirmative an individual is, the
> less he will stand for boring, dehumanized, and authori-
> tarian work. Under such conditions, the workers either
> protest or give in, at some cost to their psychological
> well-being. Anger that does not erupt may be frozen
> into schizoid depressed characters who escape into drugs
> and fantasies. More typically, dissatisfying working
> environments result in the condition known as alienation.[30]

In effect, the large organization turns off—repels—some of its potentially most productive workers. They take refuge in psychically destructive forms of dropping out, even if they happen to stay physically in place at their jobs. This is not just a problem for assembly line workers or other blue-collar workers or secretaries or young employees; it hits mature managerial and professional workers, as well. Middle-level managers in big bureaucracies—a large and important group of workers—seem especially susceptible to this discontent. Work in America offers a description of the sources of the discontent that anyone who has ever been in serious contact with a large urban bureaucracy has to recognize:

> Characteristically, middle managers perceive that they
> lack influence on organization decision making, yet they
> must implement company policy—and often without suffi-
> cient authority or resources to effectively carry it out.
> They must then compete to gain the attention of top
> management for support for their particular projects or
> functions. This leads to tension, conflict, and unproduc-
> tive and frustrating in-fighting in that spectrum on the
> organization chart with responsibility for planning,
> integrating, and controlling the entire managerial sys-
> tem. The managers' discontent thus spreads throughout
> the organization. For example, managers without power
> often establish a style that consists of applying inflexible
> rules and procedures—thus, they bureaucratize an insti-
> tution and frustrate change down the line.[31]

The middle managers in a large bureaucracy may not agree with an organization's policy and may have had no role in setting it, but they have to carry it out anyway. They inevitably react to this frustration by making the organization more rigid. And all this stiffening inside a bureaucracy eventually affects the bureaucracy's external work. For example, Work in America cited a 1972 Gallup poll that asked whether respondents believed "they could produce more each day if they tried."[32] Of those questioned, 57 percent thought they could. This striking figure rose to 70 percent for professionals and businessmen—that is, the people most responsible for the functioning of big organizations.[33] The middle and upper levels of these organizations, along with the lower ones, would appear to be rotting with tedium and disaffection, which inexorably translate into immobile organizational performance.

The findings and conclusions of Work in America are totally supported in a work that could hardly be more removed in tone and spirit from a government-supported piece of social science: Studs Terkel's best-selling Working.[34] Terkel's book, which consists of interviews with people in different occupations, shows in the most vivid, intimate, continuing detail that large bureaucracies of any kind are essentially unhealthy places to work. In reading the book, one cannot avoid being repeatedly struck by the fact that the people whose work is most satisfying and sustaining—the people with whom one would most happily trade places—do not work for large organizations. They are fulfilled precisely because they do not do so.

Literally dozens of Terkel's 123 interviews confirm the point. Particularly striking was the quite tangible happiness expressed by Terkel's stonemason, piano tuner, bookbinder, saxophonist, hockey player, carpenter, baby nurse, small-school librarian, community college teacher, pharmacist, community organizer, jockey, tennis player, farmer, alternative school teacher, free-lance press agent, and publisher of a small magazine. All of these people plainly enjoyed their work. All of them obviously felt productive and useful in it. None of them worked in a large bureaucracy.

On the other hand, Terkel interviewed plenty of people who worked in big organizations; these were people with whom one would never want to trade places. Most of them were unfulfilled in their work. If they did enjoy it, it was only in terrifying ways, ones that were often socially objectionable, as well. Especially impressive was the awfulness and unhappiness of the lives of Terkel's auditor in a large accounting firm, copy chief in a big advertising agency, ex-president of a conglomerate, who is now a consultant to top corporate management, stock broker, editor in a big bureaucracy (called "the Institution") that publishes health care literature, and government bureaucrats.

The borderline people Terkel talked to—people who spent part of their lives inside big corporations and part outside—also tended to confirm the comparative joylessness of life inside large bureaucracies. The policeman and fireman Terkel interviewed showed very little interest in the administrative procedures of their organizations, but came alive when talking about occasions when they and a small group of co-workers coaxed a would-be suicide off a bridge or rescued a child from a burning building; these times easily made up for the tedium of the rest of their jobs.[35] The inspiring people who made the most of a second chance in their lives—the advertising copywriter and salesman who became a farmer, the house counsel for a large insurance company who became a storefront lawyer for poor people, the television producer who became a librarian in a small school, the butcher for a big packing company who became a stonecutter—are invariably people who found happiness by leaving large organizations for small ones or for no organization at all.[36]

The government bureaucrats Terkel interviewed had no difficulty conveying the dismaying quality of their working lives. They gave a good sense of the inevitable frustrations of being an employee of a large public institution. In the words of Steve Carmichael, a project coordinator with a Chicago antipoverty program:

When I was with VISTA my greatest frustration was dealing with administrators. I was working in a school and I saw the board of education as a big bureaucracy, which could not move. I was disdainful of bureaucrats in Washington, who set down rules without ever having been to places where those rules take effect. Red tape. I said I could replace a bureaucrat and conduct a program in relationship to people, not figures. I doubt seriously if three years from now I'll be involved in public administration. One reason is each day I find myself more and more like unto the people I wanted to replace.

I'll run into one administrator and try to institute a change and then I'll go to someone else and connive to get the change. Gradually your effectiveness wears down. Pretty soon you no longer identify as the bright guy with the ideas. You become the fly in the ointment. You're criticized by your superiors and your subordinates. Not in a direct manner. Indirectly, by being ignored. They say I'm unrealistic. One of the fellas that works with me said, "It's a dream to believe this program will take sixteen- and seventeen-year-old dropouts and make something of their lives." This may well be true, but if I'm going to believe that I can't believe my job has any worth. . . .

My suggestions go through administrative channels. Ninety percent of it is filtered out by my immediate superior. I have been less than successful in terms of getting things I believe need to be done. It took me six months to convince my boss to make one obvious administrative change. It took her two days to deny that she had ever opposed the change.[37]

Lilith Reynolds, a project coordinator with a regional headquarters of the federal Office of Economic Opportunity, had recently become active in an employee union in a way that had angered the regional director:

When management [in government] wants to get rid of you, they don't fire you. What they do is take your work

away. That's what happened to me. He didn't even tell me
what my new job would be. They sent somebody down to
go through my personnel file. "My God, what can we do
with her?" They had a problem because I'm a high-grade
employee. I'm grade 14. The regional director's a 17.
One of the deputy directors told me, "You're going to be
an economic development specialist." (Laughs.)
I'm very discouraged about my job right now. I
have nothing to do. For the past four or five weeks I
haven't been doing any official work, because they don't
really expect anything. They just want me to be quiet.
What they've said is it's a sixty-day detail. I'm to come
up with some kind of paper on economic development. It
won't be very hard because there's little that can be done.
At the end of sixty days I'll present the paper. But because
of the reorganization that's come up I'll probably never be
asked about the paper.[38]

These are distressing, unsatisfying, eventually deadening lives.
But they are clearly typical of those led by people in the confines of
large bureaucracies. And at least the interviewees still have the
strength to fight the bureaucracies and to care about what the bureaucracies do. Moreover, there is no reason to believe that local government bureaucracies are any better than other kinds; in some ways,
they may actually be worse. The conditions of such lives are, in the
perceptive words of the late social critic Paul Goodman,

exquisitely calculated to increase tension and heighten
anxiety. It is not so much that the pace is fast—often it
consists of waiting around and is slow and boring—but
that it is someone else's pace or schedule. One is continually interrupted. And the tension cannot be normally
discharged by decisive action and doing things one's own
way. There is competitive pressure to act a role, yet
paradoxically one is rarely allowed to do one's best or
use one's best judgement. Proofs of success or failure
are not tangibly given in the task, but always in some
superior's judgement. Spontaneity and instinct are likely
to be gravely penalized, yet one is supposed to be creative
on demand.[39]

All these massive bureaucracies are full of people who are
continually getting in each other's administrative and psychic way,
who are jerking each other's working lives about in the most arbitrary, mutually unsatisfactory fashion. And many of these people

are apparently trapped for life. How can the lives of such people possibly be happy? How can the city bureaucracies that employ these people ever be made to work? The next section offers some answers that the perspectives of organizational nongrowth provide.

PROMOTING NONGROWTH IN CITY BUREAUCRACIES

The beginning of wisdom in dealing with the growth problems of urban bureaucracies, which provide inadequate services and stifle the lives of their employees, is to realize that reform will not occur naturally. It will not arise spontaneously from within the bureaucracies. They are (institutionally) unlikely to view their expansion as a serious social problem; those of their employees who have misgivings about their growth are not usually in a position to do anything about it. Similarly, an abatement of bureaucratic growth will not necessarily come about as an inevitable result of economic constraints, such as inflation or recession. And in the unlikely event that it does, the bureaucratic cutbacks are likely to be so brutal and so arbitrary that continued uncontrolled growth might well be preferable. But what would be more desirable than either of these alternatives would be a carefully planned, deliberately pursued policy of controlled organizational nongrowth.

Since the forces that animate bureaucratic growth and produce its objectionable results are too strong to be spontaneously overcome from within bureaucracies or from the economy at large, they must be thwarted by direct acts of political will. These acts must spring from citizens concerned with growth problems of all kinds and from their elected representatives, who are, after all, charged with the direction of the organizations whose operations have become so objectionable. The execution of these acts of will is, at present, one of the key unaddressed tasks of the nongrowth movement.

To be successful, these acts will have to be suffused with a particular cast of mind. Although, at present, many nongrowth proponents are a bit leery of city agencies, they must learn to become highly distrustful of these bureaucracies, suspicious of even their most normal, innocuous, or well-intentioned acts. As part of this distrust, nongrowth proponents must not allow themselves to be deluded into thinking that problems of bureaucratic growth can be solved by more funding, higher levels of technology, younger or better-educated city employees, or more female or minority employees. Nor should they believe that the introduction of managerial techniques—such as cost-benefit analysis or management by objectives, that are, by now, orthodox in the textbooks of public adminis-

tration—will make any difference. More radical consciousness-
raising techniques, such as encounter groups, will not help, either.
It is the bedrock bureaucratic functioning of the large local public
agency that is at fault. It is the growth and extension of this functioning that must be brought under control.

What, then, should nongrowth proponents be trying to do? How
can they use their perspective to prevent bureaucratic growth and its
undesirable consequences? A good general principle that comes to
mind is the following: oppose any proposal or procedure that has
bureaucratic initials and acronyms all over it. Such schemes almost
invariably turn out to consist of nothing but alphabet soup and compli-
cations. They can usually be considerably simplified; often, they
need not be undertaken at all. Some more specific suggestions, all
of them adaptable to particular local circumstances, are offered
below.

Wariness of Expansions of All Kinds

Enlargements of public functions, whether administrative or
geographic, should be opposed unless they appear absolutely necessary
and completely unavoidable, except at the risk of the most dire consequences. In administrative terms, these strictures apply to new agencies, larger staffs, increased budgets, additional programs, heavier
technology, new constructions, the creation of special districts or
public authorities, and the floating of bonds. None of these administrative expansions should be undertaken simply because expansion
seems natural. There must be a decent possibility of real accomplishment. Each expansion should only be pursued if something truly
terrible—rather than just some bureaucratic befuddlement—will
happen if it is not.

All expansions must be preceded by serious study and justification to make sure that they must be performed by public rather than
private agencies and to be certain that they will do more in the long
run than add costly administrative fat to already immobile local
bureaucracies. The necessity for the new public undertaking should
be totally clear—as it is, in the case of nongrowth efforts for rapidly
growing communities, provided they do not produce growth-control
bureaucracies that are themselves overgrown.[40] In some situations,
a Jeffersonian tenure-of-statutes approach, sharply limiting the life-
span of the proposed administrative creation, may be useful.[41]

In geographic terms, the strictures against expansion apply
for similar reasons to annexations, new developments, and any other
proposals that are likely to contribute to urban sprawl. In the long

run, all are likely to cause more problems and to create more costs
than can be foreseen when they are first proposed. And in the end,
local government will be left holding the administrative and financial
bag. None of these undertakings should be approved unless there is
no alternative.

Improvement of the Quality of Working Life
in Large Local Bureaucracies

Many jobs at all levels of big local public agencies should be
redesigned so as to reinvigorate their occupants and to improve the
performance of the bureaucracies. The private sector, unlike the
public sector, has accumulated a fair amount of experience with job
redesign. Generally speaking, this experience suggests that employees are happiest and most productive when they are working in the
following situations: (a) in small, autonomous groups; (b) in charge of,
and seeing, all aspects of their own output; (c) undertaking challenging
assignments; (d) being rewarded for learning from, and teaching, each
other; (e) being supervised by nonauthoritarian leaders; (f) making
various kinds of management decisions; (g) governing their work-
places themselves; and (h) working in an enjoyable physical setting
that does not emphasize status differences (for example, one without
reserved parking spaces for top staff). In other words, if work is to
be made enjoyable and organizational output improved, workers must
feel that they are participating in a serious way in managerial tasks
and controlling the most important aspects of their working lives.[42]
Because this approach to job redesign tends to eliminate the
more onerous and unproductive features of middle- and upper-
managerial jobs by spreading the objectionable tasks among a large
number of people, it probably will eventually win the support of such
managers. Although initially, it may be attacked by unions as a covert
way of exploiting employees and reducing the work force, progressive
union leaders are likely to accept it, since they are at least as likely
as management to want to humanize work. Local bureaucracies
should attempt to apply all this experience to their own operations.
Another approach to improving working life would be to try to
break the thrall in which large local bureaucracies hold and dispirit
their workers. Among the possibilities here are the following:
(a) four-day weeks and other arrangements for flexible hours;
(b) portable pensions that would allow experienced workers to switch
jobs without losing accumulated benefits; (c) programs for midcareer
change; (d) sabbaticals and other means of getting away from work

for periods long enough to permit self-renewal; (e) changing the organizational mores that make it hard for workers to get new jobs after 40 and which mandate that all workers must retire by a specified age; (f) loosening up rigid civil service systems, which tend to impale people in their jobs and to make paper qualifications and seniority ends in themselves at the expense of performance; and (g) giving some forms of preference to employees who do difficult, dangerous, or specialized work as opposed to general purpose administrative employees (policemen in emergency squads rather than those doing clerical work in station houses).

Decentralization

Nongrowth proponents should support all attempts to decentralize the operations of large local bureaucracies. Such attempts might loosen the administrative structure of big agencies—by, for example, creating little city halls, such as those in Boston and Atlanta. Or it might turn the agencies into federated coalitions or break them up entirely. More radically, such attempts might aim at the creation of neighborhood governments—a whole new level of multipurpose government below the municipal level. Preliminary experiments with such governments in a number of cities of different sizes suggest that they perform reasonably well, are not costly, are capable of a surprising number of functions, stimulate existing city agencies, and foster a previously dormant sense of community.[43] Private or semipublic neighborhood corporations can also be a useful way to decentralize some of the present functions of city agencies. In extreme cases, neighborhood nongrowth proponents may wish to consider carrying decentralization to its logical end point by seceding from the municipality altogether.

Evaluation

A key task of the advocates of organizational nongrowth is to assess the performance of existing local bureaucracies. Such evaluations could come from within the bureaucracies, but they are more likely to come from journalists, citizen associations, or Nader-like public interest research organizations. They might even come from grand juries, as in Orange County, California, where a jury annually conducts an evaluation and issues a report on randomly chosen county agencies. Charles Peters, editor of The Washington Monthly, gives a good sense of the nature of the task:

> Organizations need to be evaluated, not by computers, as Robert McNamara and his disciples tried to do, but by human evaluators, who combine investigative, analytical, and literary skills, so that they can find out what the organization is actually doing, figure out whether it's worth doing or could be done better, and report in a way that can be read and understood. . . .
>
> Organizations need to be evaluated from the inside— by employees whose independence should be guaranteed both by their own talent and by a three- to four-year limit on how long they can work for the organization—and from the outside by newspapers and magazines. Journalism could find a new role in evaluating government agencies.[44]

A good place for evaluation efforts to start is with the most basic question of whether particular functions of local government need be performed at all. Will tourists stop coming if the city does not have a tourism bureau? Does the city need a convention bureau? Is the commerce department doing anything? Is the human relations commission more than just an ornament? Has the manpower department accomplished anything of substance? Do taxicabs need to be licensed? Should the city be in the business of issuing all those licenses and permits? Should the present license and permit procedures be changed? Does each department of local government really need separate public relations, purchasing, or personnel operations? Does the city derive any good from all the plans it produces? None of these functions are likely to have especially strong political constituencies. So if the answer to any of these questions is negative— and in many cases it probably is—then the functions in question can be abolished or cut back and those who perform them transferred to more useful tasks.

Evaluation efforts should look into other questions, too. Which local agencies need more resources? Is each agency pulling its weight? Are its hiring practices nondiscriminatory? Do they benefit local residents or a more national, amorphous pool of potential employees? Do the requirements for obtaining a job actually measure qualities needed for performing the job? Do local agencies pay their employees more than the same people could get for the same work from another employer? Are retirement benefits a bonanza? Or would it be worthwhile to alter such benefits to encourage early retirements? Should particular functions of local government be transferred to other levels of government or the private sector?[45]

A caveat should be inserted at this point. It would be tragic if evaluation projects were used as a cover to dismantle valuable welfare, educational, environmental, or consumer programs simply because such programs, since they are of relatively recent vintage, have not had the time to sink into the bureaucratic structure. Evaluations should not provide employment for reactionaries, racists, or people who know nothing but budget cutting. But there is a need for honest, fair-minded investigation, for citizens and politicians who are willing to visit local agencies and to ask embarrassing questions that may offend powerful constituencies. There is also a need for inspector-generals in each agency and for local equivalents of the federal government's General Accounting Office; both should have evaluative responsibilities beyond purely financial areas. Agencies should hire the sort of short-term evaluators Peters describes. And all agencies should be subject to sweeping evaluations by city or county councils roughly every five years.

Improvement of Individual and Organizational Productivity

Nongrowth advocates should support all attempts to increase the productivity of local bureaucracies. The measures suggested previously to improve the quality of working life in these agencies and to decentralize and evaluate them are among the possibilities here, but there are many others. For example, wage rates could be made incentives to performance in a way that neither demeans employees nor encourages undesirably manipulative adaptations on the part of employers or employees. Such incentive arrangements have been successfully put into effect in the case of police personnel in Orange, California, and sanitation workers in Flint, Michigan; when certain types of crime drop or garbage collection becomes more efficient, wages are increased.[46]

In addition, public agencies should be made to announce their performance goals six months to a year in advance and should be held responsible for any shortfalls from these commitments. Administrative and political leaders should hold frequent public accountability sessions in different areas of their jurisdictions, where citizens can directly question them about their performance in an unstructured, unmanipulated setting. Systematic citizen complaints about bureaucratic performance to the consumer "action lines" maintained by many newspapers, television stations, and radio stations can, on occasion, also be effective.

On the working administrative level, local bureaucrats should be encouraged to acquire a useful humility and perspective, by

frequently visiting or, even better, living for periods in the areas for
which they are responsible. The Board of Education official who has
spent some time in a schoolyard, the planner who has lived in a
housing project, and the police commander who has ridden in an
ordinary squad car or rented a room in the neighborhood he patrols
will all return to their desks with a quickened sense of what they are
trying to do and how they might best do it.

The same principle can also be applied within bureaucracies.
People at the top of local agencies should periodically do the jobs of
those they supervise. Chiefs of fire departments should fight fires.
Office managers should become secretaries. Physicians should work
as orderlies. Budget officers should work in the line agencies whose
finances they rule on. Again, all these experiences will give local
bureaucrats a sense of reality that should improve the performance
of the agencies they administer.

There are other measures that would improve individual or
organizational productivity. Acceptable performance by employees
should be rewarded not by blanket, lifetime job security, as is now
the case, but by contracts for relatively short periods—say, five
years. If performance remains good, the contracts might, of course,
be renewed any number of times, a feature that would provide an
incentive to employees who want to make a career of the civil service.
Additional tax auditors should be hired, since they can often bring in
$10 or $15 in additional, previously uncollected, tax revenues for
every dollar of their salaries. Ombudsmen can also increase government productivity, on occasion. Finally, incentives, probably of a
monetary sort, should be given to all employees whose performance
or suggestions help local government attain nongrowth objectives.
Such incentives will help employees incorporate nongrowth perspectives into their day-to-day work.

It should be noted that evaluating local bureaucracies closely
and trying to improve productivity within them will inevitably constrict some job possibilities. For example, when local budgets are
tight, when school enrollments are dipping, when schools are performing poorly, and when no one knows how to make them perform
better, it may not make any sense to indiscriminately hire new
teachers. A few existing jobs may even be threatened. However,
they are not likely to be the sort of jobs union leaders will wish to
defend. The overall outcome of the attempts to improve productivity
will be one that most union members can support. Peters shows
why:

What are the jobs that count? Like firemen and air
traffic controllers. What are the phony jobs, where

vague titles like planning analyst conceal hours of newspaper reading? Exposure of the phony jobs could do much
to eliminate the fat in the economy. And even the jobs
that count can stand a hard look. How can they be made
to count more? For example, police could be taken off
victimless crimes so that they could concentrate on
effective action against crimes of violence. One result
of job evaluation could be a reversal of present compensation patterns in which the action jobs are paid lower
salaries and given less respect than the planning analyst.
Washington is full of planning analysts making $36,000 a
year while the average air traffic controller receives
only $12,000. We could pay these controllers more and
fire the analysts.[47]

Or we could at least redesign the analysts' jobs, transferring some
of them to the few departments that can really use them or employing
their skills in the many departments in need of internal evaluation or
productivity improvement.

Using the Private Sector

There are a striking number of functional areas where the
private sector can outperform the public sector. Not all local services need be undergirded by an expensive public bureaucracy of questionable usefulness. Many services can frequently be delivered more
cheaply, more efficiently, and more satisfactorily by private contractors. In a number of cities and counties around the country, contractors are running schools, fire departments, hospitals, buses, police
departments, park systems, ambulance services, and building inspec-
tions. Work in America's comparison of New York and San Francisco
garbage men suggests some of the advantages of private enterprise:

In New York, where garbage men work for the city, and
receive decent wages, they often go on strike, the service
they deliver is generally regarded as poor, and the status
of their job is low. In San Francisco, where the garbage
men have formed private co-operatives and have high
incomes, they never go on strike, the service they deliver
is generally regarded as both cheap and excellent, and the
status of their job is surprisingly high. It is not because
they are involved in a private enterprise that the garbage

man's lot in San Francisco is better than his peer's in
New York, but the private sector employment allows for
two things: greater participation in the management of
the operation and participation in profits. Although one
cannot draw strong conclusions from one example, the
greater possibility of designing rewarding work in the
private sector probably should not be discounted when
choosing between direct government provision of services and buying such services from the private sector.[48]

Another way to use the private sector is to encourage individual
citizens to take simple self-interested preventive actions that would
also reduce public costs and attain nongrowth objectives. The performance of the fire department would be less expensive and more
effective if people fireproofed their buildings better. So would the
performance of the police department if people installed more and
better burglar alarms or hired private guards. The work of the sanitation department would improve if more citizens wrapped their
garbage themselves and put it in front of their homes. Car pools
would reduce the cost of street maintenance and the cost of traffic
control. And school vandalism would nearly disappear if a small
number of people were permitted to move their mobile homes onto
school grounds.[49] All such actions serve desirable public and private
ends, while forestalling the growth of public bureaucracy. All should
be fostered by local government.

The private sector can also be tapped by persuading citizens
to give local governments free services. Many civic-minded residents
would probably be happy to do so, and the results can often be surprisingly impressive. For example, in Riverside, California, a group
of volunteers recently produced city and neighborhood plans as good
as those that have been produced by high-priced planners, consultants,
and other bureaucratic experts. And, of course, the volunteer plans
have citizen participation built in rather than added on.[50] Sometimes,
too, the experts will donate their services. For example, Pacifica,
California, has a quite effective hillsides-preservation review board
that rules on all applications to build on the city's many slopes. The
board's work is highly technical, and its membership consists primarily of engineers, architects, geologists, and biologists. All of
them no doubt charge heavy fees for their services in their San
Francisco offices. But for the city they live in, they will do the work
for no fee.[51] Alert local governments can, if they try, find large
numbers of helpful citizens (for example, retirees), community
groups, and educational institutions that will willingly do fine, non-
bureaucratic work for them at little or no cost. All they have to do
is ask.

Enlisting the Support of Municipal Unions

Many of the suggested measures appear to threaten municipal unions, but on examination, they turn out not to do so. Where they present possibilities to humanize work, to increase the status of city employees, to raise their pay, to reduce antiunion sentiment, or to create more responsive and effective local bureaucracies, they, in fact, strengthen the unions. Although some workers will have their jobs considerably restructured and others will be transferred, very few actual dismissals are likely to occur. Nonetheless, nongrowth advocates will have to work carefully and hard to overcome suspicion and to get their message across. They should be able to get valuable union support, but only if they take pains to explain their proposals and the justifications for them.

The task may be easier than they think. Thoughtful union leaders in the private sector are beginning to move beyond the pork-chop politics of the past, are starting to realize that they owe their members more than annual pay increases. Ralph Helstein, president emeritus of the United Packinghouse Workers of America, has said:

> Learning is work. Caring for children is work. Community
> action is work. Once we accept the concept of work as
> something meaningful—not just as the source of a buck—
> you don't have to worry about finding enough jobs. There's
> no excuse for mules any more. Society does not need them.
> There's no question about our ability to feed and clothe
> and house everybody. The problem is going to come in
> finding enough ways for man to keep occupied, so he's in
> touch with reality.[52]

Progressive unionists in the public sector will eventually begin to understand that nongrowth does not threaten them. Organizational nongrowth in local bureaucracies will not harm municipal unions, just as nongrowth land use and economic terms will not harm construction unions. But, as with the construction unions, a great deal of argument and persuasion by nongrowth proponents will be necessary to obtain their support. That support is often likely to be absolutely vital.

And then there is the question of federal grants. The issues of bureaucratic nongrowth that these grants pose for local governments are sufficiently complex to require a separate chapter, which follows.

NOTES

1. Robert A. Dahl, "The City in the Future of Democracy,"
American Political Science Review 61 (December 1967), p. 969. The
paper was originally delivered as the presidential address at the
63rd Annual Meeting of the American Political Science Association,
Chicago, 1967.

2. For an insightful economic analysis of why such leaders
may often have a vested interest in growth, bureaucratic and otherwise, see David W. Rasmussen, Urban Economics (New York: Harper
and Row, 1973), pp. 166-67.

3. For examples, see Peter F. Drucker, Management: Tasks,
Responsibilities, Practices, 2 vols. (New York: Harper and Row,
1974); Bertram M. Gross, The Managing of Organizations, 2 vols.
(New York: The Free Press of Glencoe, 1964); James G. March and
Herbert A. Simon, Organizations (New York: Wiley, 1958); and
James Q. Wilson, Political Organizations (New York: Basic Books,
1974). For proof that prominent theorists of organization need not
be biased in favor of growth, see Warren G. Bennis and Philip E.
Slater, The Temporary Society (New York: Harper and Row, 1969),
pp. 53-76.

4. Werner Z. Hirsch, Urban Economic Analysis (New York:
McGraw-Hill, 1973), p. 433. For an examination of this growth by a
conservative, see Roger A. Freeman, The Growth of American Government: A Morphology of the Welfare State (Stanford, Calif.: Hoover
Institution Press, 1975).

5. Hirsch, op. cit., p. 433.

6. 1972 Census of Governments, Topical Studies, vol. 6,
Historical Statistics on Governmental Finances and Employment,
Number 4 (Washington, D.C.: Government Printing Office, December
1974), pp. 28, 32, 34, 44, 46, 124, 126.

7. Hirsch, op. cit., pp. 433-34.

8. Jon Margolis, "Fun City May Be First No-Fund City,"
Chicago Tribune, May 18, 1975, p. 1.

9. Donald H. Haider, When Governments Come to Washington
(New York: The Free Press, 1974), p. 95.

10. Ibid., p. 94.

11. The account here is drawn from Luther J. Carter, "Land
Use Law (I): Congress on the Verge of a Modest Beginning," Science
182 (November 16, 1973), pp. 691-97; Louis K. Loewenstein and
Dorn C. McGrath, Jr., "The Planning Imperative in America's
Future," The Annals of the American Academy of Political and Social
Science 405 (January 1973), pp. 15-24; and Francine F. Rabinowitz,
City Politics and Planning (New York: Atherton, 1969), pp. 3-4.

12. On this general subject, see David Stockman, "Social Pork Barrel," The Public Interest, no. 39 (Spring 1975), pp. 3-30.

13. For further discussion of these characteristics, see John Kenneth Galbraith, Economics and the Public Purpose (Boston: Houghton Mifflin, 1974); Richard N. Goodwin, The American Condition (New York: Doubleday, 1974); Jane Jacobs, The Economy of Cities (New York: Random House, 1969); and Theodore J. Lowi, The End of Liberalism (New York: Norton, 1969). Any report sponsored by Ralph Nader is also likely to deal with these points.

14. Elliott A. Medrich, "Innovation Under Conditions of Slow Growth" (Paper prepared for the Organization for Economic Cooperation and Development, June 1974), pp. 6, 7. See, also, Floyd L. Fowler, Attitudes Toward Local Government, Services, and Taxes (Cambridge, Mass.: Ballinger, 1974), pp. 199-221.

15. On education, see James S. Coleman et al., Equality of Educational Opportunity (Washington, D.C.: Government Printing Office, 1967); and Christopher Jencks et al., Inequality: A Reassessment of the Effect of Family and Schooling in America (New York: Harper and Row, 1973). On police work, see Police Foundation, Experiments in Police Improvement (Washington, D.C.: Police Foundation, 1972). On housing, see Bernard J. Frieden and Marshall Kaplan, The Politics of Neglect: Urban Aid From Model Cities to Revenue-Sharing (Cambridge, Mass.: MIT Press, 1975). On antipoverty programs, see Lowi, op. cit., pp. 214-49; and Daniel P. Moynihan, Maximum Feasible Misunderstanding (New York: The Free Press, 1969).

16. Allen E. Pritchard, "State of the Cities" (Paper delivered at the Annual Meeting of the National League of Cities, Puerto Rico, 1973), quoted in Ernest Holsendolph, "Urban Crisis of the 1960's Is Over, Ford Aides Say," New York Times, March 23, 1975, p. 23.

17. One exception is Elinor Ostrom et al., Community Organization and the Provision of Police Services (Beverly Hills, Calif.: Sage Publications, 1973). This study compared closely matched neighborhoods, some of them served by police departments of small communities and others by big city police departments. The small departments generally provided better service. The large departments invested in management services and detectives to solve crimes, while the small ones went in for patrol services to prevent them. There is an extensive empirical literature on economies and diseconomies of scale in the provision of local public services. Unfortunately, the results of this research are, in the words of the Advisory Commission on Intergovernmental Relations, "either incomplete, inconsistent, or inconclusive." For discussion and references, see Advisory Commission on Intergovernmental Relations, Substate Regionalism and the Federal System, vol. 4, Governmental Functions

and Processes: Local and Areawide (Washington, D.C.: Government Printing Office, 1974), pp. 82-87, 126-28, 136 (the quote above is from p. 128); Dahl, op. cit., pp. 965-67; and Hirsch, op. cit., pp. 331-34, 348-95.

18. David Rogers, 110 Livingston Street (New York: Random House, 1968), pp. 10-11.

19. Ibid., pp. 13-14.

20. Ibid., pp. 211, 222-23, 266-323, 342, 499-521.

21. Diana Gordon, City Limits: Barriers to Change in Urban Government (New York: Charterhouse, 1973), pp. 274-78. For a similar study of the bureaucracies of Oakland, see Frank Levy, Arnold Metsner, and Aaron Wildavsky, Urban Outcomes: Schools, Streets and Libraries (Berkeley: University of California Press, 1974).

22. Gordon, op. cit., pp. 34-36.

23. Robert C. Fellmeth (Project Director), Politics of Land (New York: Grossman, 1973), pp. 351-405.

24. William C. Wheaton, quoted in Norton C. Long, "Have Cities a Future?," Texas Town and City, April 1974, p. 12. For an argument explaining why Houston's lack of zoning is an advantage for the city, see Bernard H. Siegan, Land Use Without Zoning (Lexington, Mass.: Lexington Publishers, 1972).

25. See Lowi, op. cit., pp. 214-49, and Moynihan, op. cit., pp. 128-66.

26. Jane Jacobs, The Death and Life of Great American Cities (New York: Random House, 1961), especially pp. 291-317.

27. Work in America, prepared under the auspices of the W. E. Upjohn Institute for Employment Research (Cambridge, Mass.: MIT Press, 1973), pp. xv-xvi.

28. Ibid., pp. 15-16.

29. Ibid. The study cited is Robert L. Kahn's, "The Meaning of Work: Interpretations and Proposals for Measurement," in The Human Meaning of Social Change, ed. Angus A. Campbell and Phillip E. Converse (New York: Basic Books, 1972).

30. Work in America, op. cit., pp. 21-22. For an insightful fictional treatment of this general syndrome, see Joseph Heller, Something Happened (New York: Knopf, 1974).

31. Work in America, op. cit., p. 41.

32. Ibid.

33. Ibid. The poll cited is described in George Gallup, "Productivity Seen on Downswing," Washington Post, April 10, 1972.

34. Studs Terkel, Working: People Talk About What They Do All Day and How They Feel About What They Do (New York: Random House, 1974; Avon paperback edition, 1975, used here).

35. Ibid., pp. 739-62.

36. Ibid., pp. 688-704.

37. Ibid., pp. 448-49. For similar examples among planners, see Martin and Carolyn Needleman, Guerrillas in the Bureaucracy (New York: John Wiley & Sons, 1974).

38. Terkel, op. cit., p. 454.

39. Paul Goodman, Like a Conquered Province (New York: Random House, 1967), pp. 116-17.

40. For evidence that they do not, see Michael E. Gleeson et al., Urban Growth Management Systems: An Evaluation of Policy Related Research, Planning Advisory Service Report nos. 309, 310 (Chicago: American Society of Planning Officials, 1975), pp. 55-56.

41. For a discussion of this and other bureaucratic "population control" measures, see James D. Barber, "Some Consequences of Pluralization in Government," in The Future of the United States Government, ed. Harvey S. Perloff (New York: Braziller, 1973), p. 258; and Lowi, op. cit., pp. 309-10.

42. For further discussion and specific examples of work redesign, see Work in America, op. cit., pp. 93-105, 111-20.

43. See Howard W. Hallman, Government by Neighborhoods (Washington, D.C.: Center for Governmental Studies, 1973).

44. Charles Peters, "Putting Yourself on the Line," The Washington Monthly 6 (October 1974), pp. 26-27.

45. Sources of numerous excellent publications on how to conduct evaluation efforts of all kinds are the Council on Municipal Performance (84 Fifth Avenue, New York, New York 10011) and The Urban Institute (2100 M Street, N.W., Washington, D.C. 20037).

46. See John M. Greiner, Tying City Pay to Performance: Early Reports on Orange, California and Flint, Michigan (Washington, D.C.: Labor-Management Relations Service, 1975).

47. Peters, op. cit., p. 28.

48. Work in America, op. cit., pp. 163-64.

49. For an account of vandal-watching trailers in cities in California, Florida, Arizona, and Oregon, see Casey Banas, "Live-In Guards Curb Vandals at Schools," Chicago Tribune, December 26, 1975, p. 3. The next day, the Tribune reported that the Chicago Board of Education had decided to try to reduce its annual loss from vandalism, about $3.5 million, by installing modern lighting systems around each of the city's 660 school buildings. No costs for the lighting systems were given, but they were obviously high, as are the present costs of investigating 2,000 vandalism incidents a year and arresting 300 to 400 offenders. See Chris Agrella, "Board Will Shed Light on City's School Vandals," Chicago Tribune, December 27, 1975, p. 1. If the previous day's story was correct, the vandalism losses, the

lighting expenses, and the police costs are almost entirely unnecessary.

50. See Dan Stone and Merle Gardner, "Citizen Consultants for Riverside Plan," Western City 51 (September 1975), p. 31.

51. See Charles Thurow, William Toner, and Duncan Erley, Environmentally Sensitive Lands: A Practical Guide for Local Administrators (Chicago: American Society of Planning Officials, Planning Advisory Service, 1975), p. 140.

52. Quoted in Terkel, op. cit., p. xxviii.

ORGANIZATIONAL NONGROWTH:
LOCAL GOVERNMENTS AND
FEDERAL GRANTS

As a society, we must cut back, reduce the scale of our
aspirations, and brake the infinity of our desires. We
have joined our fate to vast Babel-like structures, and
like the ill-fated tower, the structures are about to be
scattered abroad "upon the face of all the earth." Perhaps then we shall see better than the men of Shinar who
built the great tower; perhaps see that the task is not
to construct ever-larger structures but to decompose
the organizations that overwhelm us, and to seek less
abstract and remote dependencies. After all, this is
what the revolt of two hundred years ago, the revolt
against a vast, impersonal and distant imperial structure, was originally about.[1]

As shown in Chapter 1, local governments are—despite all their
evident deficiencies—widely regarded as more responsive and
accountable to the public than higher-level governments. On the other
hand, as shown in Chapter 6, local governments are growing rapidly,
and many of the results of this growth are objectionable. A key factor
in this bureaucratic growth is the proliferation of grants to local
governments from federal and (to a much lesser extent) state agencies.
Although the grants of the 1972 federal revenue-sharing legislation
are an important exception, the grants typically are for specific
purposes, involve some degree of supervision by higher levels of
government, and require some local matching funds.

These grants have become a prime source of income for local
governments. They have also become a key determinant of their
discretionary expenditures. In addition, they are the major mechanism through which different levels of government relate to each

other. Finally, and most important, they are the primary means
through which federal domestic legislation is carried out.

Since World War II, this federal legislation has not, in the main,
consisted of specific instructions to the citizenry at large. The most
important pieces of legislation in a variety of fields have stated a
broad national purpose, assigned a federal agency to pursue it, and
told the agency to do so by giving grants to local and state governments. Even the revenue-sharing legislation fits this description,
since its basic purpose, carried out by the Treasury Department, is
to help finance local and state government functions by means of
grants.

Federal grants have profoundly altered the role of local and
state governments in the American system. The grants are the
agents of what University of Wisconsin political scientist Matthew
Holden calls a "most revolutionary political theory—that local
government is an instrument for national objectives."[2] But as seen
in the previous chapter, these grants have helped create immobile,
stifling local bureaucracies. Our concern in this chapter is to show
that these grants have also made local governments highly dependent—
too dependent—on the federal government for their financing and
operation. The grants erode local control and local government.
They make mayors (and, at the state level, governors) little more
than branch managers for the federal government.

All of this is plainly undesirable. It is bad enough that the
grants are making particular local governments grow in a rapid and
uncontrolled way. But it is far worse that the grants are in the
process of binding the constitutionally separate levels of government
into something not much different from one gigantic federal-state-
local entity. This situation plainly calls for the perspectives of
organizational nongrowth. This chapter outlines the recent history
of the federal grant system, shows what some of its political and
administrative effects have been, and suggests what nongrowth approaches can do about its more undesirable effects.

THE GRANTS EXPLOSION

Federal grants go back a long way—to the Highway Act of 1916,
which first authorized federal assistance for road construction; to
the Smith-Lever Act of 1914, which provided grants for state agricultural extension services; and to the Morrill Act of 1862, which
gave land grants to the new state colleges.[3] But the explosive growth
of federal grants, and their emergence as the prime mechanism the

federal government uses to deal with urban problems, is distinctly a phenomenon of the last 30 years, and especially the last 10.

According to one estimate, during the period 1946-71, the gross national product (GNP) multiplied by 4 times, federal spending by 5 times, state and local expenditures by 12 to 13 times—and federal grants to states and localities by approximately 30 times.[4] A great deal of this growth has occurred in the last decade. Total federal grants to state and local governments rose from $10.9 billion in 1965 to $48.2 billion in 1974. During this period, environmental grants rose from $.3 billion to $2.7 billion, housing grants from $.6 billion to $3.9 billion, education and manpower grants from $.9 billion to $6.8 billion, and health grants from $.6 billion to $7.5 billion.[5] And as the federal budget continues to rise, so do the amounts of its grants.

The amounts, however, do not tell the whole story, for the sheer number of different grant programs—and, therefore, the number of bureaucratic units administering them—has risen even faster than the dollar figures. It is now difficult to get even a rough idea of how many grant programs there actually are at any one time, but whatever the figures, the proliferation is impressive. According to Suzanne Farkas, for example, the number of federal programs giving grants to local governments rose from 28 to 435 during the 1960s.[6]

By 1972, the ramifications of these programs had become so complex that the New York Times was putting out a Guide to Federal Aid for Cities and Towns, which described 656 programs in 1,300 pages.[7] The book's advertising described it as intended

> for city officials who could make history with just a fair
> share of the federal funds now available . . . if they could
> fight their way through the jungle of federal requirements,
> limitations, allocation formulas, timetables, guidelines,
> eligibility factors, application procedures, critical
> abstracts, and the idiosyncracies of the thousands of
> separate federal departments, agencies, commissions,
> institutes, and foundations offering $40 billion in urban
> aid for 1973.[8]

By 1975, the Guide found that the number of programs was nearing a thousand. It had become an annual subscription publication, in two volumes, which had looseleaf binders for new programs that subscribers could add monthly.[9] And the official federal catalog of these programs consisted of 800 closely printed pages, also in looseleaf.[10]

The federal agencies disbursing these grants have, of course, grown rapidly too. The grants are the major reasons why relatively new agencies, such as the Department of Health, Education and Welfare, the Department of Housing and Urban Development (HUD), the Environmental Protection Agency (EPA), and the Department of Transportation are among the most rapidly expanding units of the federal government. At a further remove, the rapid expansion of these departments has helped make the Washington metropolitan area one of the fastest-growing regions in the country, certainly the fastest-growing one in the Northeast.

But the most important effects have naturally been on the local (and state) governments receiving the funds. In the previous chapter, the reader was asked to look up a city government in the telephone book in order to appreciate the growth of local bureaucracies. But such a demonstration is not really possible in the case of federal grants; nearly all departments in any city of any size are receiving substantial grants in one form or another. (A common hidden form consists of federal grants to states, which the states then pass on to localities, after taking off a percentage for themselves.) Planning, housing, urban renewal, and environmental departments are often receiving as much as one-half their total funding from such grants. Police, school, health, road, sanitation, library, and park departments are not far behind.

In recent years, the percentage contribution of federal grants to local governments, which had been rising rapidly, has leveled off somewhat. It is now a little above 20 percent—a very high percentage. In 1930, federal grants to states and localities totaled $200 million. This figure represented about 6 percent of federal domestic spending and about 3 percent of total state-local expenditures. In 1965, the grants totaled $11 billion, that is, 18 percent of federal domestic spending and 15 percent of state-local expenditures. By 1974, the grants had risen to at least $45 billion (estimates vary). This figure represented 25 percent of federal domestic spending and 21 percent of state-local expenditures. The state-local percentage had been nearly 24 percent the previous year.[11] It is clear that a large number of the budget decisions of local governments—especially those concerning discretionary expenditures rather than already committed costs—are, in effect, made for local governments by the federal government.

The federal influence here is not just financial, it is professional, as well. As emphasized in the previous chapter, a large number of occupations that are primarily practiced at the local level are, in fact, creations of the federal grant system. City planning is a good example of such a field. As Louis Loewenstein and Dorn

McGrath point out, the increasing number and (on occasion) influence of planners are primarily the result of federal grant legislation. They cite the Housing Act of 1954 (which created the 701 program), the Housing Act of 1961, the Highway Act of 1962, the Mass Transportation Act of 1964, the Housing Act of 1965, the Model Cities Act of 1966, the Housing Act of 1968, the the Intergovernmental Cooperation Act of 1968 as examples of grant legislation that strengthened the planning profession and planning considerations by requiring the preparation of local plans as a condition for the award of funds.[12]

Had they been writing even a few years later, they might also have cited such new federal grant legislation as the Clean Air Act Amendments of 1970, the Water Pollution Control Act Amendments of 1972, the Coastal Zone Management Act of 1972, the Noise Control Act of 1972, the Urban Mass Transportation Act Amendments of 1974, and the Housing and Community Development Act of 1974. All created more jobs for planners. In fiscal year 1974, when there were approximately 20,000 planners in the country, the 701 program alone financed 4,450 staff positions and an undetermined, but undoubtedly substantial, number of consultants.[13]

THE POLITICAL EFFECTS:
DEPENDENCY

What has come of all this legislation? There is no question that many of the effects of federal grant legislation on local governments have been desirable. The grants have frequently raised the level of services provided by their recipients.[14] They have made these services more equitable, for example, by often making aid conditional on a reduction of racial or sexual discrimination or on an increase in citizen participation on the part of local governments. By means of other conditions, they have often made these governments more aware of important budgetary, administrative, planning, regional, environmental, and, now, energy issues the governments might otherwise have neglected. They have substantially professionalized the personnel and improved the operating efficiency of these governments. They have encouraged some experimentation. They have promoted contact between officials of different levels of government and made them more sensitive to each other's concerns. And they have provided jobs.

Yet, despite these undoubted benefits, federal grants have generally had, in political terms, a preponderantly negative effect on the local governments that receive them. The problem is simply that the grants have made local governments rely far too much on the federal government for their choice, financing, operation, and evaluation of programs. In many instances, they have become part of, indeed satellites of, the federal government. They are politically dependent on it. In these cases, they are in the process of forming one big bureaucratic organism that is almost totally beyond accountability to citizens at the local level. It may often be beyond accountability to anyone at the federal level, as well.

The political dependency takes a variety of forms.[15] In its most obvious manifestation at the local level, the federal government comes to seem to be little more than a pile of cash. The cash is invariably accompanied by incomprehensible directives and impractical guidelines. Any sensible local official will take the money, obey what instructions he can, and finesse the rest. The transaction is primarily economic. No moral element whatever is involved. Nor is there any serious discussion at the local level as to whether the program is needed or is likely to accomplish its goals. Nor is there any suggestion that the city government would undertake the program were it not for the availability of federal funds.

Local government becomes simply one more competitor, one more claimant, for federal funds. It becomes just another self-serving interest group, another client looking for free money in the pork barrel, rather than an independent source of self-government. Needless to say, this posture does little for the stature of local government in the eyes of either its citizens or federal officials. And it does not do much for the stature of the federal government in the eyes of the citizens, either.

The local government listens to Washington at least as much as it listens to local residents. Local governments go to great lengths to develop or hire "grantspeople"—specialists in obtaining federal aid. The bureaucrat or consultant with a reputation for writing or overseeing successful grant applications, or for being aware of obscure sources of federal money, is a highly desirable person in local government. Many localities, even medium-sized ones, have established special offices of federal aid coordination, which are in charge of focusing the city's grant activities, that is, grabbing off as much grant money as they can. Some large cities and counties station full-time lobbyists in Washington. Other hire part-time ones. Most will readily tap their congressional delegations for spot lobbying duty; the senators and representatives will happily accept the assignment for the sake of the publicity they will get and the credit they will take if the grant goes through. And all local governments lobby for more funds though professional associations that represent particular levels of government or professional specialists, for example,

the National League of Cities, the International City Management
Association, and the American Institute of Planners.[16]
   Mayors are perfectly willing to admit this dependence on the
federal government, particularly when doing so is likely to yield
more grant money. Mayors such as Richard Daley in Chicago,
Joseph Alioto in San Francisco, Richard Hatcher in Gary, and Richard
Lee in New Haven have deliberately—and successfully—campaigned
on the promise that they could obtain more grants for their cities
than their opponents. Although Mayors Fred Hofheinz of Houston and
Richard Carver of Peoria disagreed somewhat, four mayors—Alioto,
Wes Uhlman of Seattle, Kevin White of Boston, and Coleman Young
of Detroit—recently stated on "Meet the Press" that "the seeds of
New York" (Carver's phrase) threatened their cities if new federal
antirecessionary aid was not forthcoming. And Hofheinz admitted
that Houston is relatively prosperous mainly because of its special
powers under Texas law to tax and annex surrounding suburbs.[17]
   A few weeks earlier, Mayor Lew Murphy of Tucson had
described the federal-local relationship with a clarity that was
almost embarrassing. He supported turning a nondescript road into
a freeway, thus qualifying it for federal aid, because "it is an opportunity to capture federal dollars. While I agree that federal dollars
may have made prostitutes of us all, it is a fact of life and I intend
to make the most of it."[18]
   In effect, then, the relationship of political dependency repeatedly
forces local governments to devote as much effort to hustling the
federal government for money as to governing their own populations.
Mayor Alioto has said that "no mayor can really do his job unless
he spends at least one day per month in Washington."[19] The initiative,
therefore, passes to the federal level. Local governments become
unwilling to make new departures or to undertake new programs on
their own initiative. They need not undertake these painful, risky
courses of action because they are unnecessary. They can always
rely on the likelihood that a new federal grant program of some kind
will come along to take them off the political, administrative, and
financial hook.
   The dependency relationship is comfortable. The only problem
is that it does not really produce very much for the people of the
city. The deficiencies of the services provided by local governments
have been discussed at length in the previous chapter; here, it remains only to suggest the ways in which federal grants contribute to
these deficiencies.[20] As argued in the previous chapter, federal
grants are a prime force in the creation of overgrown, ineffectual
local bureaucracies. In addition, the paperwork requirements of
federal programs are such as to keep large portions of these

bureaucracies busy producing the desired applications, plans, progress reports, final reports, and certifications rather than actually administering the programs in order to help local residents. These requirements create a situation where huge numbers of bureaucrats deal only with each other, and then in highly abstract terms. They hardly ever have to deal with genuine citizens or their real problems, and so they tend to neglect them.

Once one looks at the federal paperwork requirements, it is easy to see why. Highly specialized federal "categorical grant" programs, which tightly specify (indeed, dictate) the permitted uses of their funds, are notorious for the pickiness and pointlessness of their paperwork. But even generalist "bloc grant" programs, which are supposed to simplify the requirements for grantees and largely let them design their own programs, demand horrendous amounts of irrelevant documentation. For example, to receive funds under the Housing and Community Development Act of 1974, administered by HUD, a local government must submit the following paperwork.

1. There should be a three-year summary of the community's development plan that identifies local housing needs, outlines a strategy for meeting them, and specifies short- and long-term goals which accord with (unspecified) regional and national growth policies.

2. There should be a description of activities for the first year of the program.

3. There should be a housing assistance plan covering each year of the program. The plan should survey the community's housing stock and estimate the housing assistance needs of low-income persons—including the elderly, the handicapped, large families, and persons who will be displaced, each considered as a separate category. The plan should also specify a realistic yearly goal of the number of persons or dwelling units to be assisted—with new, rehabilitated, and existing units; different sizes and types of housing projects; different kinds of low-income persons; and varying forms of assistance for these persons, again each treated as separate categories. Finally, to allow for drawings instead of just charts, the plan should indicate the general location of proposed low-income housing, along with justifications of why these locations promote greater choice of housing opportunities and avoid undue economic or racial segregation. There should also be a map showing concentrations of minority groups in the census tracts or enumeration districts of the community.

4. There should be a detailed budget broken down by most of the categories already described. (Mercifully, HUD supplies the budget forms.)

5. There should be certifications of compliance with federal civil rights, equal employment opportunity, relocation, financial

management, citizen participation, and environmental requirements.

6. There should be annual progress reports covering all the above matters.

This is actually a somewhat compressed description of what this single, supposedly comparatively simple grant program requires.[21] Another HUD program once prompted then HUD Secretary George Romney to show a congressional committee the paper needed for one community to get a single grant—all three feet of it.[22] The head of an Atlanta antipoverty agency estimates that 20 percent of his staff's time is devoted to meeting federal reporting requirements.[23] All this is costly for local governments to produce and to follow up. If the task is contracted out to consultants, for whom the paperwork for grant programs represents a major source of income, the paper often becomes even more costly.

Moreover, there is little evidence that anyone in Washington reads all this paper, much less pays any serious attention to it. Local officials know this. The usual result is that the paper which comes in from Salt Lake City or Rockford contains a great deal of dull, useless fiction. The local residents—especially the deprived ones—receive very little help. The local bureaucracy does not accomplish anything of substance. And the local bureaucrats, stuck with the tasks of figuring out what the opaque federal requirements can possibly mean and how they can be met with a minimum of inconvenience, become that much more alienated by their work conditions.

Paperwork aside, the conduct of the federal bureaucracy does little to encourage local accomplishment. This level of bureaucracy is famously unpredictable, arrogant, aloof, and enigmatic in its relations with local government. It can afford to be; it controls the funds. And in any case, it usually encounters a great deal of obsequiousness at the local level. The federal bureaucracy, from time to time, talks about the need for understanding local conditions or tolerating special variations. But this talk usually produces nothing but a lot of guidelines and directives that do not bear on any community's specific problems. The federal bureaucracy rarely makes any serious attempt to inform itself about them.

In addition, the time the bureaucracy takes to process local applications is usually excessive. The general problem of communication between the federal level and the neighborhood one is such that the federal level is often about to give up on a particular grant program just as the neighborhood groups the program was intended to help are first beginning to hear about it.[24] The frequent reorganizations and rearrangements characteristic of the federal bureaucracy only confuse matters further.[25]

The overall result is programs of wax: futile efforts that no one—either at the federal, local, or neighborhood levels—really

believes in. They are usually undertaken by local governments for
no other reason than that federal money is available. Local governments unthinkingly believe they have to have it. Sometimes, too, the
grant laws contain sanctions against local governments that do not
participate in the programs; they may, for example, be made
ineligible to participate in other grant programs. In no sense are
the grant programs entirely voluntary. In no way do they originate
from local initiative. Thus, the programs inevitably perform at a
low level. And they repeatedly preempt the possibilities for locally
initiated programs that might have a better chance of working.

The dependency produced by the grant system has some even
more undesirable political effects. It promotes disrespect for government. Neither the federal government nor the local ones appear to be
able to do anything for local residents. Each level of government
appears to spend a great deal of time trying to con the other. And
both levels are continually telling citizens the superficial bureaucratic details of what they are doing for them. Yet, little action that
benefits the public ever seems to come of these efforts. Naturally,
the citizens get disenchanted, both with the programs themselves
and with the attempts to delude them about the program's results.
The inevitable outcome is a lack of respect for governments.

In addition, and most poignantly, there are a depressing
number of instances where federal funds intended to help deprived
portions of the local population have been used to strengthen the
locally powerful elements—political machines, real estate companies,
financial interests, local bureaucracies, and racists—that have created
or profited from the deprivation in the first place. Of course,
strengthening these elements by means of federal grants simply gives
them greater legitimacy to continue their activities, weakens and
sometimes divides the intended beneficiaries of the programs,
diminishes the possibilities of popular control of local government,
further decreases public respect for government—and continues the
dependence of local government on federal grants. Thus, for example,
Theodore Lowi, discussing the role of federal housing grants in
subsidizing local efforts at "Negro removal," writes that

> a close look at the actual impact of these Federal urban
> policies makes one wonder how there is any Federal
> political legitimacy left. Washington is over one hundred
> years away from apartheid policy, but after twenty years
> of serious Federal involvement, the social state of Ameri-
> can cities could only be a little worse if all the Federal
> agencies had been staffed all those years with white secret
> agents from South Africa.[26]

Similarly, Samuel Beer writes that

the immense funds of Title I of the Elementary and Secondary Education Act of 1965 have commonly been dis-
bursed simply as additional funds for local school boards
instead of reaching the disadvantaged children they were
intended to benefit. Salaries have eaten up inordinately
large portions of the money appropriated for antipoverty and model cities programs. Manpower training
has probably not increased the number of persons
employed. Speculators have profited handsomely from
recent housing acts.[27]

None of these undesired effects are likely to prevent their own
recurrence. All benefit conservative forces powerful in local government. All perpetuate the political dependence of local government on
federal grants.

THE ADMINISTRATIVE EFFECTS:
MORE DEPENDENCY

The administrative, procedural effects of federal grants on
local governments are, in some ways, even more destructive than
their more purely political effects. They are less visible to the
public, and no doubt less interesting to it. They are harder to undo
through the normal public processes of local government; they
originate at points in the huge federal bureaucracy that, from a local
perspective, are exceedingly hard to find, much less influence. The
administrative aspects of the grant system thus produce at least as
much dependency and ineffectuality as the system's political aspects.[28]
As discussed earlier, the paperwork requirements of federal
programs put local governments in thrall to an unpredictable, enigmatic, and decidedly nonlocal bureaucracy. But the administrative
effects of federal grants extend far beyond paperwork. The grants
complicate local administration, making it much more confusing and
complex than it need be.[29] They turn the local civil service inward,
forcing it to be more attentive to its counterpart at the federal level
than to local politicians or citizens. They make the local civil service
almost as unpredictable and enigmatic as the federal counterpart
and add to the pervasive lack of job satisfaction produced by working
in large public bureaucracies, local or federal. And they contribute
to the rigidity, slowness, and lack of sensitivity of local government.[30]

Donald Haider outlines the administrative dilemmas the grants
pose for local chief executives, such as mayors:

> Most observers agree that grants contribute to the frag-
> mentation of participating governments, undermine what
> executive controls exist, and dilute chief executives'
> policy, coordination, and budgetary roles. The financial
> and administrative problems that accompany most grants,
> for some, may far outweigh whatever fiscal, political,
> and programmatic advantages they intrinsically have.[31]

These "financial and administrative problems" can be quite
burdensome. And they become greater as more and larger bureaucracies are brought into play. In terms of administration, York Willbern
argues that

> where two (or, in many instances, three) levels of govern-
> ment are involved in a public service program, there
> appear often to be tremendous costs in communication,
> negotiation, application, approval, supervision, and re-
> porting. These costs, where each level of government
> has its own political and administrative structures, seem
> to be much higher than is the case when only one bu-
> reaucracy is involved.[32]

And in terms of finances, Haider found that, over time, governments receiving grants had to put up matching funds of roughly $1
for every $2.50 coming from the federal government. These matching
funds comprised approximately 10 percent of the total expenditures
of state and local governments. So as federal aid rose from $13
billion in 1966 to $24 billion in 1970, the costs to state and local
governments climbed from $5.5 billion to about $12.5 billion (these
costs have since gone even higher). Haider concludes that when one
also adds in "increased public employment, administrative costs,
and indirect expenditures, many states and localities paid, on the
average, more to obtain federal monies than they in return received."[33] Despite appearances, federal grants are in no way free
money.

Moreover, the federal grants restrict the administrative actions
of local governments. They deform local planning, budgeting, implementation, and evaluation activities by making them depend on whatever grants happen to be available from the federal government.
Local governments become increasingly unable to conceptualize,
much less resolve, their own problems in the absence of federal aid.

The notion, often associated with Justice Oliver Wendell Holmes, that localities and states are the laboratories of federalism, the places where government can experiment with a range of potentially fruitful approaches, dissipates. Bureaucratic standardization sets in; localities and states, in effect, abdicate much of their initiative and responsibility. Local capability declines. The federal level comes more and more to seem the sole source for the conception and resolution of public problems. Local administrative dependence on the federal level becomes nearly total.

Examples of this constrictive administrative dependence are quite common. In Hartford, for instance, James Sundquist found that $1.5 million was being spent for little-used streets, while heavily traveled arteries were being disregarded because no one could find a grant for them.[34] Loewenstein and McGrath write that "no master plan prepared in the sixties for any major American city dealt with any aspect of air, water, or noise pollution. Similarly, interest in the disposal of liquid and solid waste matter was equally non-existent."[35] The reason for these omissions was simple: the federal government did not then require such provisions as a condition for federal aid. Now that it does, local governments show a great deal of interest in these matters. Some of the interest is genuine, but much of it is no more than a reflection of federal grant requirements. There are a lot of paper plans, but little evidence that the requirements have actually produced better environmental conditions for city residents.

In some cases, the grants may actually worsen local environmental conditions. For example, a recently released study of EPA grants to 52 localities to build sewage treatment plants and interceptors, conducted by Urban Systems Research and Engineering, a Boston-area environmental consulting firm, found that grantees were being encouraged to build sewer systems of a capacity far greater than they needed. This excess capacity relieved current pressures on the systems, but also ensured that the localities would attract a great deal of growth. The grants, intended for environmental purposes by the nation's chief clean-air-and-water agency, were in fact encouraging sprawl, leapfrog development, out-migration from central city areas that already had some excess sewer capacity, and all the other environmental evils and wastes of rapid, badly planned urban growth. When localities paid their 25 percent of the costs of the sewer systems, they were literally buying trouble.[36]

Another way that the grants constrict local freedom of administrative action is by tying local governments to federal objectives and devices of a sort that can only be called faddish. The fads sometimes turn out to be worthwhile innovations, but more often, they are phony

or foolish. And in any case, being fads, they rarely last long enough
to accomplish anything. The multitude of "general," "comprehensive," or "long-range" plans different federal programs require of
any local government is an obvious example. The fact that all the
plans a local government has to produce are likely to seriously contra-
dict each other is largely mitigated by their fictional quality.[37]

In another area, a few years ago, the Justice Department's
Law Enforcement Assistance Administration (LEAA) was heavily
committed to the idea that corrections facilities—prisons, reform
schools, and various minimum-security installations—should have
close ties to local communities, so that offenders could be rehabilitated
in settings with which they were familiar. Plenty of grants were
available to develop these community-based corrections facilities.
But now, LEAA, for no apparent reason, has lost interest in the idea;
funds are distinctly less abundant, and large numbers of localities
are stuck with facilities and programs they would never have undertaken without federal support. Some communities have abandoned
the undertakings altogether, while others have tried to support them
themselves. All have been taken for a ride. "The feds tell us that
we must have day-care, senior-citizen, and legal-aid programs,"
says Pennsylvania Governor Milton Shapp. "Then they cut back on
the money and we're forced to choose between the young, the old,
and those in trouble."[38]

In the field of housing, new, and supposedly revolutionary,
approaches seem to issue from HUD almost yearly. Section 202
begat Section 312, which begat Section 115, which begat Section 236,
which begat Section 235, which begat the current descendant, Section 8,
whose life expectancy is anybody's guess. In housing and other fields,
a wide variety of federal "model" or "demonstration" programs
have produced little, if anything, of lasting value. The present authors
do not know of any case where a local project funded by such a program ever inspired another locality to undertake and pay for a similar
project on its own initiative. There are, however, countless cases
where such projects convinced other localities to apply for federal
funds. The "demonstration" for localities was not that they could
perform substantial projects on their own but that they could get the
federal government to finance projects where accomplishment would
never become an issue.

Moreover, a host of federal programs—the prototype is, perhaps, the War on Poverty—provide examples of innovations that,
from a local perspective, seem to appear triumphantly but without
warning, are pursued frantically, and then disappear for reasons
that have little or nothing to do with local conditions. These bureaucratic shooting stars are nothing to which local governments should

hitch their wagons. But, unthinkingly, they nearly always do. They are left with practically nothing to show for it. And the continual availability of federal funds usually keeps them from drawing the obvious lessons from the experience.

So, the federal grants consistently weaken local planning, distort local priorities, sap local initiative, and diminish local capability. The problem extends to evaluation, too. Federal agencies repeatedly evaluate the local programs they fund by means of criteria that are locally inapplicable, meaningless, or largely beyond the control of local governments under any circumstances. Average reading scores for school children are used to assess the quality of schools. Numbers of people below the poverty line are used to evaluate local antipoverty programs. Numbers of manpower trainees who succeed in finding jobs are used to measure the effects of employment programs. It makes no difference if the local population is changing, if the regional economy is declining, or if the local government's services have for decades been sapped by inadequate taxing powers. The same obtuse federal yardsticks get applied, regardless of local conditions. In response, local governments contort themselves and suffer.

Even in cases where the federal government seems to realize that it is suffocating local government and hindering local experimentation, it appears unable to let go. Efforts such as HUD's Planned Variations Program, for example, allow HUD, rather than localities, to largely determine the permissible range of variations. HUD ends up doing the most essential part of the planning, local governments tag along, and local initiatives are further obstructed.

This smothering sort of behavior is destructive enough in even the most affluent suburbs, but impoverished Indian tribes, many of which are incorporated as local governments, are particularly vulnerable to it. At the tribal level, the obstruction and smothering become exploitation and corruption. In 1971-72 one of the present authors was working for a Chicago consulting firm that had a contract with the Bureau of Indian Affairs (BIA) to provide management services to an extremely poor Chippewa tribe in North Dakota. The contract was an offshoot of a grant from the BIA to the tribe. The author twice visited the reservation and found that the BIA's conditions for the grant had produced a situation where the white management consultants from New York and Pennsylvania were teaching a time-consuming course on public administration to a busy tribal council. They were using a textbook suitable for advanced college students, but most of the council members could not read at the eighth-grade level. The council responded with yawns, Uncle Tomahawk mannerisms, and large, intimidating shotgun shells left around the classroom.

On one occasion, the consulting firm's office manager had to
fly up from Chicago to put the tribe's files in order according to
BIA standards. On another occasion, a white Yale Law School gradu-
ate from Ohio wrote the basic (and final) draft of the tribe's constitution without, to the author's knowledge, every leaving Chicago, and
mailed it to North Dakota to be translated into Chippewa by those
whom it would govern. It was eventually defeated in a very violent
election.

The tribe put up with all this abuse and waste, of course,
because it had no choice. It needed the money. The BIA grant, no
matter how much it propped up (more accurately, created) a brutal
and dishonest tribal government, at least showed that the BIA cared
in its own inept way. Other federal agencies were not even that
raggedly benevolent in their grants. There was no operational alcohol-
ism program, although roughly one-quarter of the tribe suffered from
it. There was no juvenile delinquency or probation program, although
one-half the tribe's adolescents got in trouble with the law. (The
author was there to write an application for an LEAA grant for a
probation-and-parole program—a community-based correction
facility, in fact—which the tribe got.) There was no serious manpower or economic development program, although tribal unemployment often approached the figure of 70 percent. There was one odd
bright spot: the day-care and Head Start facilities were superior to
those in a moderately affluent Chicago neighborhood at the time.

It was clear that the tribe, in its poverty and desperation, was
devoting most of its efforts to getting grants, however bogus or
ineffectual, from the BIA and other federal agencies. No other sources
of jobs or income were available. The tribe was fast becoming a
pitiful arm of the federal government. This situation is extreme in
both its hopelessness and its degree of federal dominance, but similar
ones are not unknown in urban ghettos or other poor areas.[39]

Finally, federal grants also distort the priorities of local government by strengthening particular local functional departments or
specialists at the expense of multipurpose agencies and their generalist executives. Many local highway departments, heavily financed by
federal grants, have historically operated as if they were independent
of the rest of local government. But they merely offer an especially
sharp case of a widely prevalent relationship. For example, when
Cincinnati's police department receives a grant from LEAA, it is not
the bond between the city of Cincinnati and the federal government
that is strengthened most. Nor is it the connection between Cincinnati's
mayor or police chief and the attorney general or the president.
Instead, what is most strengthened is the alliance between the particular civil service specialists in the Cincinnati police department who

applied for the grant and their opposite numbers in LEAA who approved it. They become the clients of each other. They help each other build anonymous empires. The other figures—the political figures who are not functionaries—are virtually irrelevant.

This pattern of alliance is quite common. It reduces office-holders, such as mayors, to surprising powerlessness. Haider writes that mayors testifying at Senate hearings on the federal role in urban affairs "could not render an accounting of the magnitude and scope of federal activities in their cities nor any specification of how much federal money was spent annually in their jurisdictions."[40] A HUD survey of Oakland found that the city's mayor controlled less than 15 percent of the federal grant money coming into the city government.[41] The Office of Management and Budget expanded and replicated the Oakland study in several other cities, coming to the same conclusions.[42] Haider thus writes that federal aid programs "increasingly insulated chief executives from budgetary and organizational influence, and frequently thwarted efforts at reorganization."[43]

Because the federal grant programs foster such deep and permanent alliances between specialists, they often become entrenched nearly to the point of immovability. Their clientele is too strong. The invisible empires are secure. Willbern perceptively describes the entrenchment process, when he writes that the specialists

> try to secure an institutionalized arrangement for program support which, to the greatest extent possible, can escape the necessity of recurring competition with other program areas. When a categorical grant authorization gets well established, vested interests which become very powerful form around it. . . .
>
> The advocates for funds at the national appropriating level get political support from lower levels, which would rather secure grants than take the political costs of raising money locally. And the specialist grant recipient at the state or local level, claiming much of his sustenance from "outside," is probably in a stronger position vis-a-vis the local budget officer or politician than are other specialists without outside connections. The alliance between governmental levels forged by the grant program may thus provide peculiar political strength for the specialist at each level.[44]

This strengthening of civil service functional specialists means, of course, that it is foolish to even hope to coordinate the federal grant programs affecting a particular locality. Real coordination is impossible at both the local and federal levels. Mayors and other local officials cannot have any serious influence over what federal agencies are doing in—and to—their communities. Neither can anyone else, including the multitude of federal officials who are unable to mesh their respective programs. The system seems to be out of popular or government control. Bureaucratic growth seems to have become unstoppable.

PROMOTING NONGROWTH IN FEDERAL GRANTS

Despite appearances, the situation is not hopeless. Federal grants to local governments need not keep growing endlessly. The grants need not be the bureaucratic equivalent of a heroin habit. Local governments need not have their independence inexorably eroded by grants that do them and their citizens no good. Organizational nongrowth approaches described previously can be used to combat the expansion of worthless or destructive federal grants.

To successfully resist the objectionable effects of federal grants, nongrowth proponents must take to heart several of the realizations discussed in the previous chapter. They must realize that reform will not occur naturally. The local and federal bureaucracies in question will not cease growing of their own accord. Nor will any reduced expansion produced by the constraints of a recessionary or inflationary economy necessarily serve desirable nongrowth ends. What is needed is a deliberate, controlled policy of nongrowth in federal grants to local governments.

This policy must, as emphasized earlier, spring from direct acts of political will on the part of citizens and their elected representatives. These acts must be animated by a profound distrust of bureaucratic functioning of all kinds. In particular, nongrowth proponents must distrust federal agencies; from a local perspective, they are remote, abstract, and nearly impervious to citizen control. Large local bureaucracies are bad enough. Large state bureaucracies are worse. Large federal bureaucracies are virtually impossible. Citizen advocates of nongrowth can, with some effort, achieve a substantial degree of influence over local and, perhaps, even state bureaucracies. The same effort, applied at the federal level, is likely to yield much less—perhaps, nothing at all. For proponents of nongrowth in federal grants, the solutions lie primarily at the local level. Only over the very long run can they expect to have any influence at the federal level.

What, therefore, should nongrowth advocates be trying to do at the local level? How can they use their approach to prevent the undesirable effects of federal grants in their communities? The previous chapter suggested one good general principle: Oppose any scheme that is presented primarily with bureaucratic initials or acronyms. Another is to oppose any proposal or procedure for which a consultant has to be hired. If a consultant is necessary, the idea is likely to be too complex, both administratively and intellectually, to succeed on any worthwhile terms. Some more specific suggestions, all of them adaptable to particular local conditions, appear below.

Distrust of All Expansions of Grants

Local nongrowth proponents should oppose enlargements of federal and state grants to their communities unless these enlargements appear necessary. Whether the expansions consist of new grants, additions, or extensions to existing grants, they should be resisted unless there is some overriding—that is, local—reason to accept them. They should not be accepted simply because they are available, because other communities are obtaining them, or because the local grantspeople are optimistic about the community's chances to get money. Some substantive local accomplishment ought to be realistically possible. Genuine local need should be the main criterion for deciding whether to apply for federal or state funds. If the need should dissipate during the period while the application is being processed, the funds should not be accepted.

These suggestions are not as extreme as they may sound. For years, a number of maverick communities around the country—for example, Indianapolis and LaPorte, Indiana—refused to accept federal funds or did so only grudgingly precisely because they did not want to compromise their independence. In recent years, largely because of the federal revenue-sharing program, which has relatively few conditions attached, many of these communities have reconsidered their stand.[45] But they had the kernel of a very good idea. Communities should not take federal or state money unless it is for projects that they would want to undertake, even if outside funds are not available. Before submitting their applications, they should carefully consider the possibility that accepting the money may lead to unexpected costs—new personnel, administrative costs, or indirect costs, perhaps in other program areas—that will leave the community, on balance, worse off. Fremont, Nebraska, whose population is 22,000, recently turned back a grant of $800 because, as the town's administrator said, "It would have cost us more than that to justify it."[46] This is the kind of thinking larger localities should be doing about larger amounts.

If localities do decide to accept outside money, they should, in polite administrative terms, "take it and run." (This is easy in the case of the revenue-sharing program but somewhat harder in the case of other federal programs.) Communities should, in general, prefer to use federal money to pay for one-shot capital construction projects (for example, school buildings) rather than continuing operating expenses (for example, teacher salaries). Communities should have a financial contingency plan for what they will do if, as happens so often, federal or state support disappears. All these policies are likely to produce local savings if only because they mean that local grantspeople can be shifted to other duties and that application-writing consultants need not be hired. And as an adjunct to their efforts to divest themselves of dependence on federal grants, individual communities should at least consider whether they wish to continue competing to become the site of proposed federal facilities, such as office complexes, research establishments, highways, energy extraction sites, or military bases. Such facilities can weaken local government, deform local public finance, and destroy distinctive local amenities at least as decisively as federal grants.

Establishment of Local Financial Self-Sufficiency

Local governments should reduce their present reliance on federal and state funds. These funds should not be the basis of local public finance, the key determinant of local discretionary expenditures. Local governments should not just be wary of expanding their dependence on grants; they should also actively strive to stand on their own financially. Whenever possible, projects that are entirely local should get their financing from sources that are entirely local.

If they must apply for federal or state funds, localities should not insist, as they do now, that their own share or percentage of matching funds—that is, their own stake in the project—be as small as they can make it. Instead, they should insist that their shares be as large as possible, both in existing programs and in new ones. Local governments do not really get away with anything by diminishing their proportions of these investments. In the end, they only increase their dependence, irresponsibility, and lack of public credibility.

Establishing local financial self-sufficiency also means reinvigorating local public finance. Localities will need to raise funds on their own, probably, in part, from new sources, in order to replace at least some of the federal and state funds they will be forgoing. Communities should seek revisions of state law so that they can use local corporate and personal income taxes rather than the property tax as the basis of local finance. They should also work for statewide uniformity in local property, corporate, and income taxes so as to increase collections and prevent possible abuses by taxpayers (particularly corporations) and local governments.

They may wish to increase other existing local taxes, for example, on cigarettes, liquor, automobiles, or business licenses. Or they may wish to introduce new ones, for example, on commuters, chain stores, luxury items of food or clothing, or activities that consume large amounts of energy. They may want to consider holding lotteries. They may wish to impose new user fees on such public facilities as water supplies, sewage systems, solid waste disposal systems, roads, parks, beaches, libraries, and city universities. Hiring additional tax auditors should also be worthwhile, since, as mentioned in the previous chapter, such employees can often produce an additional $10 or $15 in tax revenues for every dollar of their salaries. And localities with substantial private nonprofit institutions—schools, hospitals, foundations, libraries, religious organizations, and charitable or professional associations—may wish to gently persuade them to make voluntary contributions to the locality in recognition of the public services rendered them free as tax-exempt property owners.[47]

These measures plainly involve political risks. They will impose new costs, some of them heavy, on local residents. And localities will have to work hard to make sure that the new impositions do not fall disproportionately on deprived portions of the community or on ones that are already carrying especially heavy tax burdens. But, if executed adeptly, fairly, and effectively, the impositions will free the locality from financial and administrative dependence on outside sources. They will allow the locality, in some fields for the first time in many years, to control its own activities for the benefit of its own citizens.

Evaluation of Programs and Improvement of Their Productivity

Nongrowth advocates should support all attempts to assess and raise the level of performance of local projects that are funded by federal grants. These efforts are most likely, as discussed in the previous chapter, to come from journalists, citizen groups, and Nader-like organizations. They are likely to focus on such questions as necessity of performance, output, quality of working life, decentrali-

zation, determination of compensation, private versus public performance of tasks, and future hiring and assignment practices.

In the case of federal programs giving grants to localities,
evaluation and productivity efforts need to devote special attention to
two additional issues. The first is a matter of social equity. Federal
grant programs seem to have a peculiar tendency to be used by local
governments to help local elites and to harm local deprived populations. They often benefit precisely the wrong people or become primarily a source of pork barrel. Do federally supported local housing
programs enrich local building companies, while only providing
housing for the wealthy or without providing worthwhile housing for
anyone? Do revenue-sharing funds pay for tennis courts or bridle
paths in rich neighborhoods rather than basketball courts or swimming
pools in poor ones? If so, local nongrowth advocates should publicize
and fight such tendencies.

The second issue is the matter of administrative freedom. Federal grant requirements often inhibit local flexibility (or encourage
the wrong kind) by forcing local governments to pay more attention
to Washington than to the needs of local residents. Are the programs
of the local government that are in question tied up in federal paperwork, pursuing money rather than accomplishment, neglecting local
priorities, out of touch with local people who need them, and too close
to local people who do not? If so, nongrowth proponents should again
investigate and combat such tendencies.

Redirecting Local Lobbying Efforts

The national lobbying activities of local governments and their
professional associations have heretofore been directed primarily at
the federal level of government. They have been aimed largely at
obtaining new legislation that would increase federal grants or
securing various complex administrative alterations in existing legislation, again to increase grants.[48] The state lobbying activities of
local governments and their associations have been similarly directed.

These efforts are somewhat misplaced. Local governments and
their representatives should be lobbying, themselves, for many of the
measures recommended previously. For instance, they should be
lobbying, themselves, for having genuine local need used as the prime
criterion for deciding whether to apply for a grant, for having a
financial contingency plan in case outside funds dissipate, for increasing the share of local matching funds, for restructuring local tax
systems, and for undertaking evaluation and productivity efforts. In

some cases, local government professional associations might conduct research or give particular local governments technical assistance on how to avoid destructive dependence on outside grants.

Local governments and their professional associations should confine their federal and state lobbying to efforts to reduce their dependence on outside funds and to gain greater control over the funds they do obtain. They should lobby for fewer and more unified federal grant programs. Bloc grant programs and the revenue-sharing program, both of which allow communities to use funds for a comparatively wide range of purposes, should become the preferred forms of grant programs, at the expense of the more common categorical grant programs, which tightly—often rigidly—specify the permitted uses. The categorical programs should, if possible, be phased out, perhaps by consolidating them into the bloc grant or revenue-sharing programs. The administrative arrangements in some programs that allow state governments to skim off a percentage before passing on federal funds primarily intended for local governments should be abolished. The occasional sanctions against local nonparticipation should be dropped. And ideally, the overall level of federal grants should fall. At the very least, the rate of growth of both their sizes and numbers should slack off from the explosive pace of recent years.

In addition, local governments and their associations should lobby for reductions in the required federal paperwork and for abatements in the strangling quality of many federal guidelines and directives. For example, the elephantine Housing and Community Development Act paperwork requirements, described earlier in this chapter, could, with no loss, easily be reduced to three simple elements: (a) a description (including a budget) of planned first-year activities, (b) subsequent annual progress reports (with a budget and a description of any changes planned or undertaken after the first year); and (c) certifications of compliance with relevant federal laws. The guidelines by which the federal government will evaluate specific local programs should be agreed on in advance, with the local government as an equal party to the agreement. Local consent should be understood to mean that the locality explicitly agrees that the guidelines have local relevance. If a local government feels that the guidelines are not relevant to its case, it should be free to suggest new ones. Local governments should be free to ignore federal directives if they can demonstrate local inapplicability or overriding local need.

Lead times for the federal processing of local applications should be cut. Every federal agency should standardize its application procedures, program requirements, and reporting mechanisms across all its grant programs. Ideally, all federal agencies should standardize their grants-management activities to produce simple, uniform routes that any local government can follow to secure and maintain any grant from any federal agency. Local governments should be allowed to combine into one program funds received from different sources within a federal agency, or from more than one federal agency, without having to seek the permission of anyone at the federal level.

Evaluation and productivity efforts should be undertaken at the federal and state levels, as well as at the local one. And, to develop humility and perspective, federal bureaucrats administering grants should be encouraged to periodically visit—or better live—in the areas for whose affairs they are responsible, for example, neighborhoods, schools, or housing projects. For the same reasons, there should be institutionalized mechanisms by which federal bureaucrats can at regular intervals work in local governments so they may grasp the actual local effects of federal grant programs.

Enlistment of the Support of the Municipal Unions

One of the best alliances for nongrowth advocates and local government people to cultivate is with municipal unions. A number of the measures proposed above, like those in the previous chapter, appear to threaten municipal unions—mainly by eliminating jobs. But in fact, as argued there, the measures do not do so. Indeed, since they give local government more to do, they may well create more jobs. And since they assert the independence and vitality of local government, making employment there more interesting, responsible, and prestigious, they may well strengthen the position of the unions. All the same, nongrowth advocates and their associates will, to say the least, not have an easy time disarming union suspicion. They will have to do a great deal of work to overcome it. However, if the work is done well, if it gets its message across, it can often be invaluable. Nongrowth proponents and their allies should not neglect this potentially fertile ground.

NOTES

1. Sheldon S. Wolin, "Looking for 'Reality'," New York Review of Books 21 (February 6, 1975), p. 17.

2. Transcript of a discussion on "Local and Metropolitan Government," in The Future of the United States Government, ed. Harvey Perloff (New York: Braziller, 1973), p. 349.

3. On the early history of federal grants, see W. Brooke Graves, American Intergovernmental Relations (New York: Scribners, 1964); Morton Grodzins, The American System (Chicago: Rand McNally, 1966); and Donald G. Haider, When Governments Come to Washington: Governors, Mayors, and Intergovernmental Lobbying (New York: The Free Press, 1974), pp. 46-52.

4. York Willbern, "Current Problems in American Federalism," in John C. Lincoln Institute and National Academy of Public Administration, Problems and Response in the Federalism Crisis: A Seminar (Washington, D.C.: National Academy of Public Administration, 1971).

5. U.S., Department of Commerce, Bureau of the Census, Statistical Abstract of the United States: 1974 (Washington, D.C.: Government Printing Office, 1974), p. 249.

6. Suzanne Farkas, Urban Lobbying (New York: New York University Press, 1971), p. 69. See, also, Haider, op. cit., pp. 52-83.

7. New York Times Guide to Federal Aid for Cities and Towns (New York: World, 1972).

8. New York Times Book Review, April 23, 1972, p. 37.

9. New York Times Guide to Federal Aid for Cities and Towns (New York: Rowland Federal Aid Service, 1975).

10. See Executive Office of the President, Office of Management and Budget, 1975 Catalog of Federal Domestic Assistance (Washington, D.C.: Government Printing Office, 1975).

11. Haider, op. cit., p. 92.

12. Louis K. Loewenstein and Dorn C. McGrath, Jr., "The Planning Imperative in America's Future," The Annals of the American Academy of Political and Social Science 405 (January 1973), pp. 15-24. For similar examples in other fields, see David Stockman, "Social Pork Barrel," The Public Interest, no. 39 (Spring 1975), pp. 3-30.

13. Bernard Cohen, "701: Stung and Shaken . . . But Surviving," Planning 41 (June 1975), p. 8.

14. Many of the effects mentioned in this paragraph are also suggested and demonstrated in Martha Derthick, The Influence of Federal Grants: Public Assistance in Massachusetts (Cambridge, Mass.: Harvard University Press, 1970), pp. 43-189.

15. For other discussions of this dependency, in more theoretical terms or focused on specific fields, see Stephen K. Bailey and Edith K. Mosher, ESEA: The Office of Education Administers a Law (Syracuse, N.Y.: Syracuse University Press, 1968); James David Barber, "Some Consequences of Pluralization in Government," in Perloff, ed., op. cit., pp. 242-66; Robert A. Dahl and Charles E. Lindblom, Politics, Economics, and Welfare (New York: Harper and Row, 1953); Derthick, op. cit.; and Daniel J. Elazar, "Cursed by Bigness, or Toward a Post-Technocratic Federalism," in Toward

'76: The Federal Polity, ed. Daniel J. Elazar (a special issue of
Publius, Fall 1973), pp. 239-98.

16. For studies of this lobbying, see Farkas, op. cit., and
Haider, op. cit.

17. Peter Negronida, "2 Mayors Deny Need for More Aid,"
Chicago Tribune, July 7, 1975, pp. 1-7.

18. Bob Svejcara, "City Council Backs I-710 as Freeway,"
Arizona Daily Star, May 20, 1975, p. 1.

19. Joseph Alioto, quoted in Haider, op. cit., p. 98, quoting
National Journal 4 (December 16, 1972), p. 1924. Haider then adds
that "commenting on the demise of its city's four-term Mayor Arthur
Naftalin, the Minneapolis Star editorialized in 1968, 'The mayor lost
press support because he spent too much time away from the city on
his missions seeking federal aid.'"

20. For an excellent case study of how federal grants harm
local governments and cities—specifically, a study of the Economic
Development Administration's activities in Oakland—see Jeffrey
Pressman and Aaron Wildavsky, Implementation: How Great Expecta-
tions in Washington Are Dashed in Oakland, or Why It's Amazing That
Federal Programs Work at All (Berkeley: University of California
Press, 1973).

21. For a more complete and complex description, see Daniel
Lauber, "HCDA: Some Tips on the New Housing Act," Planning 41
(November 1974), pp. 21-23.

22. Dan W. Lufkin, Many Sovereign States (New York: McKay,
1975), p. 134. Not that the situation is any better in other fields or at
the state level. Lufkin, former Connecticut Commissioner of Environmental Protection, has written that one of his section heads estimated
that the paperwork demanded by EPA's water-quality compliance
requirements:

> would literally reach the ceiling of our State Office Building
> if piled in one stack. (Our offices at the State Office
> Building had monumentally high ceilings.) More impor-
> tant, these federal requirements were taking an estimated
> one third of his time, and contributing nothing to getting
> his job done.
>
> Indeed, I estimate that at least 50 percent of the
> time of the staff of our Water Compliance Unit was spent
> answering questions from EPA, both regional and Washing-
> ton based, about our program, rather than achieving the
> reductions in pollution the overall program was supposed
> to bring about (idem., p. 132).

23. David Alpern et al., "Big Government," Newsweek 86 (December 15, 1975), pp. 34-41.

24. For examples of this problem in the War on Poverty, see Daniel P. Moynihan, Maximum Feasible Misunderstanding (New York: The Free Press, 1969), pp. 128-66.

25. For an example in housing, see Robert Cassidy, "And Now, Section 8," Planning 41 (June 1975), pp. 10-11.

26. Theodore J. Lowi, The End of Liberalism (New York: Norton, 1969), p. 251, as well as pp. 250-56 generally. For an analysis of how War on Poverty grants pitted different poor groups against each other in such a way as to confirm the local power structure, see idem., op. cit., pp. 239-48.

27. Samuel H. Beer, "The Modernization of American Federalism," in Elazar, ed., op. cit., pp. 53-95. On the specific case of manpower programs, see Leonard Goodwin, Can Social Science Help Resolve National Problems? Welfare, Case in Point (New York: The Free Press, 1975). For an indication that the revenue-sharing grants are having similar effects, see David Caputo and Richard Cole, "Major Trends in the Spending of Revenue Sharing Funds Cited," Planning 40 (March 1974), pp. 5-7. And for a similar indication concerning Housing and Community Development Act funds, see Bernard Cohen, "Does HUD Ignore Low-Income Areas?," Planning 41 (November 1975), pp. 6-7.

28. For other discussions of this administrative dependency, see Bailey and Mosher, op. cit.; Barber, op. cit.; Dahl and Lindblom, op. cit.; Derthick, op. cit.; and Elazar, op. cit.

29. For an example from the field of housing, see Lauber, op. cit.

30. For an example from the field of economic development, see Pressman and Wildavsky, op. cit. For examples in housing, see Bernard J. Frieden and Marshall Kaplan, The Politics of Neglect: Urban Aid from Model Cities to Revenue-Sharing (Cambridge, Mass.: MIT Press, 1975).

31. Haider, op. cit., p. 97.

32. Willbern, op. cit., p. 21.

33. Haider, op. cit., p. 81.

34. James L. Sundquist, "Revenue Sharing and Its Alternatives: A Report from the Hartford Seminar," in John C. Lincoln Institute and National Academy of Public Administration, op. cit.

35. Loewenstein and McGrath, op. cit., p. 23.

36. See "EPA Sewer Grants May Foster Urban Sprawl," Planning 41 (November 1974), p. 2. No bibliography on the study was given.

37. For a discussion of these problems in the 701 program, see Bernard Cohen, "701: Stung and Shaken . . . But Surviving," Planning 41 (June 1975), pp. 8-11.

38. Quoted in Michael Kramer, "Northeast Presage: Regional Depression," New York, December 15, 1975, p. 11.

39. For a discussion of such situations in low-income areas of San Francisco, see Tom Wolfe, Radical Chic & Mau-Mauing the Flak Catchers (New York: Farrar, Straus and Giroux, 1970; Bantam paperback edition, 1971, used here), pp. 115-84.

40. Haider, op. cit., p. 87, citing Hearings on the Federal Role in Urban Affairs, 89th Cong., 2nd sess., Senate Government Operations Committee, Subcommittee on Executive Reorganization (Washington, D.C.: Government Printing Office, 1966).

41. See Oakland Task Force, San Francisco Executive Board, Federal Decision-Making and Impact in Urban Areas: A Study of Oakland (New York: Praeger Publishers, 1970).

42. Haider, op. cit., pp. 87-88.

43. Ibid., p. 87.

44. Willbern, op. cit., p. 22. See, also, Beer, op. cit., pp. 76-80; Haider, op. cit., pp. 83-88; and Stockman, op. cit., pp. 3-30.

45. See, for example, Sondra Thorson, "Revenue Sharing: In LaPorte, Folks Find Big Brother's Not So Bad," Planning 40 (December 1974), pp. 8-9.

46. Alpern et al., op. cit., p. 41.

47. For a discussion of such contributions to New York City by one such institution, see the Twentieth Century Fund's Annual Report 1975 (New York: Twentieth Century Fund, 1975), p. 32. Between 1967 and the end of 1975, the fund, a medium-sized foundation (23 full-time employees in mid-1975) contributed $116,500 to the city as an expression of its civic interest and concern. Of its 22 trustees, only 4 are residents of New York City; the chairman and the treasurer are from Washington, and the vice-chairman from Boston. Even before New York's fiscal crisis, a number of the city's other foundations were beginning, on a modest scale, to emulate the fund's example. Harvard University makes comparable payments to Cambridge, Massachusetts.

48. For an example of the maneuvering surrounding such alterations, see Paul O'Mara, "The Senate Wants Strings on BCA Funds," Planning 40 (March 1974), p. 5.

8

CONCLUSION:
PLANNING AS IF
PEOPLE MATTERED

The whole point of the nongrowth movement is to put people in control again in the place where it will do them the most good, namely, at the community level, where they live and work. The community is the place where people really have the chance to influence matters that immediately affect their own lives. At the local level, their voice and their vote count, visibly and tangibly.

Nongrowth is important because the way that a community grows affects virtually every aspect of the lives of its residents. It is difficult to overstate how varied, how individual, and how pervasive the impacts are. When we say that growth influences the local environment, we really mean that it makes the air easier or harder to breathe, that it makes the local lake suitable for swimming or sewage, or that it wipes out the beauty of the local hillside or enhances it. When we say that growth determines the economy of the community, we really mean that it puts some people to work and cuts others out, that it produces a good income for some and a poor one for others, and that it gives some people jobs through rough economic times and makes others join the unemployment lines. In terms of public services, growth patterns can determine whether the garbage will be picked up, how well the schools will educate the children, what the crime and fire damage rates will be, and whether people will be able to get around the community easily. Growth affects local people, individuals in the community, all day and throughout their lives.

Since local growth is so important to the average person, it is vitally important for the community to be in control of it. Previously, most communities assumed that growth, as well as its consequences, were inevitable, that growth was a process beyond community control. They believed that, as a result, the quality of community life was also beyond its control. But the nongrowth movement is beginning to change

these attitudes. It is changing the way people think about growth.
Nongrowth is a new, and still somewhat tentative, state of mind. The
basic questions that nongrowth poses are simple. What can growth
do for people? Does the community need every increment of growth
that is proposed for it? What will be the impacts, individual and
cumulative, environmental and economic, social and bureaucratic, of
the increments? Who will benefit from the increments? Who will
not? The basic ethical principle of the nongrowth movement is that
growth should benefit the people who must experience it. Not the
narrow, powerful circle of the growth winners, but larger segments
of the community: average workers, low-income people, ordinary
families, and minorities.

Nongrowth really argues for a return to smallness. The country
cannot escape to the rural or small-town past of the 1830s or the
1920s. But nongrowth approaches can allow it to recapture some of
the virtues—self-sufficiency, for example—that are associated,
accurately or not, with these periods. Nongrowth pushes communities
to depend upon themselves—not the federal government, not the
national economy, but themselves. It argues that communities should
actively strive to determine their own fate, not passively accept
whatever schemes outside forces offer them. It maintains that communities that rely primarily on themselves will be better communities.

Self-sufficiency also has implications for community responsibility. Being self-sufficient means taking care of oneself. Communities are, above all, responsible for their own people. If communities
are unable to take care of their own, then they certainly cannot do
anything for anyone else. Thus, problems of unemployment, crime,
pollution, and the like are, from a local perspective, primarily local
problems, not regional or national ones. Communities, the nongrowth
movement suggests, can have surprising success in solving their own
problems. All they have to do is control new growth.

Self-sufficiency also demands a responsible and accessible
local government. Nongrowth promotes responsibility and accessibility by relieving local government of the duty of "accommodating"—
more accurately, contorting itself to—new growth. Many local governments around the country seem to have a single function: encouraging
new growth. But by regarding growth as what it should be, as a community priority that is secondary at best, local governments can concentrate on their real responsibility: improving the daily lives of their
citizens. When they make the growth that does occur work for all
their citizens, local governments show that they are responsive to
genuine community needs.

Nongrowth also increases personal and communal freedom. A
self-sufficient person or community is one that is free from dependence on the good wishes, dollars, or commands of others. Growth

used to mean—in most places, it still does mean—an erosion of
personal and community freedom (the causes range from the constrictive effects of new federal programs to increased reliance on
uncontrollable, practically random regional or national economic
swings). But when nongrowth approaches are applied, when growth
is controlled so as to reduce dependency, to solve local problems,
to increase economic opportunities, or to improve local environmental quality, then freedom is increased. When local governments
restrain supergrowth, they are plainly pursuing worthwhile public
and private values.

Nongrowth means that all new growth becomes a legitimate
question for public choice. It becomes an explicit, conscious community decision. The community can make the growth work for whatever ends it wishes. It can opt for greater social equity, a stronger
local economy, a better local environment, a more responsive local
government, or a combination of these goals. Local nongrowth objectives will be as varied as the communities themselves. This is as it
should be. Local problems demand local solutions. Nongrowth offers
localities the opportunity to find these solutions.

Until recently, the benefits of growth were exclusively for the
select few: the large landowners, real estate and development companies, big banks, newspaper publishers, utilities, union chiefs,
bureaucratic managers, and the like. Dollars and power were the
incentives for the growth winners. More growth meant more dollars
and more power. But only for the growth winners. Everyone else was
on the long list of growth losers. The costs of growth fell onto ordinary
citizens throughout the community. It was the average citizen who
paid the highest price for the supposed benefits of growth. The costs
were being exacted through explosive tax rates; bloated, remote
bureaucracies; poor public services; traffic congestion; crowded,
bad schools; environmental deterioration; decreased incomes; and
increased unemployment. At first, the dollar costs to the average
citizen were not as direct or as large as the dollar gains to the growth
winners. But the costs mounted. People began to discover that their
communities were changing in undesirable ways. They were no longer
the places they once were.

As citizens began discovering the costs of growth, they set out
to influence growth decisions. At first, the movement was a matter
of isolated opposition to a new freeway, housing development, or city
hall. But then it began to take on a clearer focus, one that involved
more than simply opposition to new growth. It began to emphasize
selective choice, that is, specific decisions on community growth
goals. Some forms of growth might be desirable; these should be
encouraged. A few years ago, the nongrowth movement could rightly

be accused of being essentially negative, but not any more. Now,
nongrowth means more than anything else that communities have
the right and obligation to choose among new possibilities for growth
and development, that is, to make an explicit choice (at the local level)
of what they want and what they do not want. And many communities
are beginning to make these choices.

It is no accident that the first communities to adopt nongrowth
approaches were suffering from severe rates of population and economic growth. Communities in high-growth states, like California,
Florida, Colorado, and Oregon, or in areas like the Virginia and
Maryland suburbs of Washington, D.C., were among the first to raise
questions about the real costs and benefits of growth. They devised
new controls to make growth work for them instead of against them.
In examining their growth patterns, they had discovered that the conventional wisdom was wrong. Population, construction, or economic
growth, for example, rarely paid its own way. Taxes increased
dramatically in precisely the places where economic and population
growth were the highest, where building rates were greatest. The
local bureaucracy became larger and more remote. Many local
politicians became, essentially, representatives of growth interests.
Citizens had trouble finding them, much less talking to them. The
crime rate went up. The schools got worse and went on shifts. Housing, new as well as old, became very expensive. Lower- and even
middle-income families were often driven out of the new housing
market. Mobile homes began to appear. New housing was primarily
for the rich and the near-rich. Growth did not bring more housing
that was less expensive. It brought less housing that was more expensive. It brought fewer units for more people; naturally, most of the
people could not afford the high price. The overall costs of growth
fell squarely on the lower- and middle-income members of the community.

But the last, most prevalent, and best defense of growth was
that it brought economic benefits to the middle class. New growth,
it was said again and again, would add jobs, income, and opportunities.
It would lower unemployment and increase average family income.
But even here, the conventional wisdom broke down. Economic growth
did add to the total number of jobs and the total size of income, but
it also added to the total number of people who wanted both. The
added jobs and income had to be shared by a much larger population.
When the pie was finally divided, too many people had less of it.
Incomes leveled off or decreased; unemployment increased or stayed
about the same. The benefits of growth were elusive, indeed.

Thus, in the private market as well as in the public one, the
benefits of growth proved a sham. There were no real benefits

except for that short, powerful list of growth winners. Beyond them,
it was a game of chance—nearly always a losing one. For every
growth winner, there were dozens, even hundreds, sometimes thousands
of growth losers. And so, by late 1975, literally hundreds of nongrowth communities around the country had adopted nongrowth policies.

In its brief life, the nongrowth movement has gone through four
distinct phases. First, as mentioned, citizens and the elected officials
who represented them (rather than special interests) began discovering that growth was not all it was supposed to be. This was a phase
of acquiring knowledge, of asking the kinds of questions that precede
any public action. The second phase was direct action. Citizens and
elected officials began to question the merits of individual developments: the new freeway, the new airport, the regional shopping
center, the new industry. Opposition would focus on specific proposals
where the impact of the new development was clear. The freeway, for
example, would destroy neighborhoods; the shopping center would
destroy a major wetland or prime agricultural area.

But it became obvious that such isolated opposition came at a
high cost. The development in question might be stopped, but nothing
was accomplished for the larger community. Other developments
were proceeding, developments that were often worse. But one could
not oppose everything. So, the strategy shifted to communitywide
controls over new development. The objective of this third phase was
to institutionalize nongrowth into the overall development patterns of
the community. Nongrowth plans and land-use controls were developed
with the specific intent of controlling new growth. New concepts
emerged—timed growth, phased growth, urban limit lines, development districts, conservation districts. Communities began attempting
to influence overall community growth, to control the rate of population growth.

Yet, the potential of nongrowth was just beginning to be tapped.
If communities could minimize the costs of growth, they could also
maximize its benefits. The concept of using nongrowth to capture
benefits for the community is the fourth, current phase of the nongrowth movement. It is the one that seems likely to last, whatever
national economic or energy conditions obtain. Nongrowth has become
a wholly positive movement. It has come a long way from simple
opposition to new development or support for strong land-use controls.
Nongrowth has come to mean that new growth, if it is to be permitted,
must work for the people of the community. As argued in this book,
nongrowth approaches can be used to increase the supply of local
housing, to make that supply less exclusionary, to make the local
economy stronger and more equitable, and to create a more effective,
more accessible local government that is less dependent on the

vagaries of remote federal bureaucracies. Nongrowth encourages community control that is exercised for the benefit of all local residents. The nongrowth concept, now being pursued in communities across the country, is simple, attractive, and plausible. Would it work in your community?

DEMOGRAPHIC ASPECTS

Morrison, Peter A. The Current Demographic Context of National
Growth and Development. The Rand Paper Series. Santa
Monica, Calif.: Rand Corporation, 1975.

U.S. Department of Commerce, Bureau of the Census. Population of
the United States, Trends and Prospects 1950-1990. Current
Population Reports, Series P-23, no. 49. Washington, D.C.:
U.S. Government Printing Office, 1974.

Westoff, Charles F., and Robert Parke, Jr. Demographic and Social
Aspects of Population Growth. Commission on Population Growth
and the American Future. Washington, D.C.: U.S. Government
Printing Office, 1972.

ATTITUDES

City of Tucson Planning Department. Community Response, A Report
for Community Information. Tucson, Ariz.: 1974.

Watts, William, and Lloyd A. Free. The State of the Nation, 1974.
Washington, D.C.: Potomac Associates, 1974.

SOCIAL EQUITY AND NONGROWTH

Agelasto, Michael. "No-Growth and the Poor: Equity Considerations
in Controlled Growth Policies." Planning Comment 9, nos. 1
and 2 (Spring 1973): 2-11.

Finkler, Earl. "Strategies to Expand Equal Access to Housing."
Mimeographed. Paper presented at the Midwest Regional
Housing Conference of the National Committee Against Dis-
crimination in Housing in Chicago, Ill., September 17, 1973.

Finkler, Earl. "Equity in the Steady State—Lessons and Directions from Local Communities." In Alternatives to Growth, eds. Robert E. Sweeney and Dennis Meadows. Forthcoming.

Franklin, Herbert M., David Falk, and Arthur J. Levin. In-Zoning: A Guide for Policy-Makers on Inclusionary Land Use Programs. Washington, D.C.: The Potomac Institute, 1974.

Pope, Carl. "Growth and the Poor." Sierra Club Bulletin, April 1975.

Smith, James Noel, ed. Environmental Quality and Social Justice in Urban America. Washington, D.C.: The Conservation Foundation, 1974.

ECONOMICS AND NONGROWTH

Appelbaum, Richard et al. The Impacts of Growth: A Population Impact Analysis. New York: Praeger, 1976; forthcoming.

Conroy, Michael E. The Challenge of Urban Economic Development. Lexington, Mass.: D.C. Heath and Company, 1975.

Deknatel, Charles, and Susan Harris. Zoning to Preserve Agriculture. Columbia County, Wisconsin. Madison, Wisconsin: Department of Administration, State Planning Office, 1974.

Gilmore, John S., and Mary K. Duff. The Process for Policy and Objectives for Growth Management in Sweetwater County, Wyoming. Denver, Colo.: University of Denver Research Institute, 1974.

Gleeson, Michael et al. Urban Growth Management Systems: An Evaluation of Policy Related Research. Chicago: American Society of Planning Officials, 1975.

Hansen, Niles M., The Challenge of Urban Growth. Lexington, Mass.: D.C. Heath and Company, 1975.

Hudson, Bruce L. Local Impact and Requirements of Manufacturing Industries. Dover, Del.: Delaware State Planning Office, 1974.

Long, Norton E. The Unwalled City: Reconstituting the Urban Community. New York: Basic Books, 1972.

Schaenman, Philip S., and Thomas Muller. Measuring the Impacts
    of Land Development: An Initial Approach. Washington, D.C.:
    The Urban Institute, 1974.

Sundquist, James L. Dispersing Population: What America Can Learn
    from Europe. Washington, D.C.: The Brookings Institution, 1975.

ORGANIZATIONAL NONGROWTH

Barber, James David. "Some Consequences of Pluralization in
    Government." In The Future of the United States Government,
    ed. Harvey Perloff. New York: Braziller, 1973.

Gordon, Diana. City Limits: Barriers to Change in Urban Govern-
    ment. New York: Charterhouse, 1973.

Haider, Donald G. When Governments Come to Washington: Governors,
    Mayors, and Intergovernmental Lobbying. New York: The Free
    Press, 1974.

Loewenstein, Louis K., and Dorn C. McGrath. "The Planning Impera-
    tive in America's Future." The Annals of the American
    Academy of Political Science, January 1973, pp. 15-24.

The New York Times Guide to Federal Aid for Cities and Towns.
    New York: Rowland Federal Aid Service, 1975.

Peters, Charles. "Putting Yourself on the Line." The Washington
    Monthly, October 1974, pp. 19-28.

Pressman, Jeffrey, and Aaron Wildavsky. Implementation: How
    Great Expectations in Washington are Dashed in Oakland, or
    Why It's Amazing That Federal Programs Work at All.
    Berkeley, Calif.: University of California Press, 1973.

Rogers, David. 110 Livingston Street. New York: Random House,
    1968.

Special Task Force Report to the Secretary of Health, Education
    and Welfare. Work in America. Cambridge, Mass.: MIT Press,
    1973.

Stockman, David. "Social Pork Barrel." The Public Interest, Spring
    1975.

Terkel, Studs. Working: People Talk About What They Do All Day and How They Feel About What They Do. New York: Random House, 1974; and Avon paperback, 1975.

ABOUT THE AUTHORS

EARL FINKLER is a planner and a free-lance writer based in Tucson, Arizona. He was the co-author, with David Peterson, of Nongrowth Planning Strategies, a Praeger book published in 1974. In October 1975, he was one of 13 finalists in the Mitchell Prize competition based on implementation themes and ideas following the Club of Rome's 1972 report, The Limits to Growth. The competition attracted over 300 entries from 30 countries.

Mr. Finkler has worked for the American Society of Planning Officials in Chicago and has planning experience in Alaska, Canada, and Milwaukee, as well as in Tucson. He is a frequent conference speaker and has published articles on nongrowth in Landscape Architecture, the Chicago Tribune, Planning, and Equilibrium. He is a part-time instructor in planning at the University of Arizona and has an M.A. in urban affairs from the University of Wisconsin—Milwaukee and a B.A. in journalism from Marquette University.

WILLIAM J. TONER is a Senior Research Associate with the American Society of Planning Officials in Chicago. At ASPO he has co-authored or directed a series of reports on local land-use regulations as well as on state-level land-use planning. Among these are Performance Controls for Sensitive Lands and Critical Areas: A Guidebook for State Programs. Mr. Toner has published many articles in Planning and has given numerous speeches at local, state, and national conferences for citizen and professional groups. Mr. Toner recently established the Rural Planning Network for citizens, officials, and planners working in rural planning and is currently engaged in research on methods to preserve prime agricultural land. Previous to his position at ASPO he worked as a Growth Policy Analyst for the Orange County, California, Planning Department and co-authored People, Policy, and Growth: A New Direction.

Mr. Toner received a B.A. in economics and a M.P.A. in public administration from California State University at Fullerton.

FRANK J. POPPER is a Chicago-based planning and environmental consultant. He has worked at the Twentieth Century Fund, Public Administration Service, and the American Society of Planning Officials. Dr. Popper is the author of The President's Commissions (1970) as well as articles in planning, political science, and medical journals.

He is presently directing a project, sponsored by the Twentieth Century Fund, that will result in a book on the politics of state land-use planning.

Dr. Popper received a B.A. in psychology from Haverford College, and an M.P.A. in public administration and a Ph.D. in political science from Harvard University.

RELATED TITLES
Published by
Praeger Special Studies

BICYCLE TRANSIT: Its Planning and Design
                Bruce L. Balshone, Paul L. Deering
                and Brian D. McCarl

COORDINATING SOCIAL SERVICES: An Analysis of Community,
Organizational, and Staff Characteristics
                Neil Gilbert and Harry Specht

THE EFFECTS OF URBAN GROWTH: A Population Impact Analysis
                Richard P. Appelbaum, Jennifer Bigelow,
                Henry P. Kramer, Harvey L. Molotch
                and Paul M. Relis

INNOVATIONS FOR FUTURE CITIES
                edited by Gideon Golany

LAND USE, OPEN SPACE, AND THE GOVERNMENT PROCESS:
The San Francisco Bay Area Experience
                edited by Edward Ellis Smith and
                Durward S. Riggs

THE POLITICAL REALITIES OF URBAN PLANNING
                Don T. Allensworth

SYSTEMATIC URBAN PLANNING
                Darwin G. Stuart